D1506742

Second Stories

Property of Library
Cape Fear Community College
Wilmington, NC

GENDER & AMERICAN CULTURE

Coeditors

Linda K. Kerber

Nell Irvin Painter

Editorial Advisory Board

Nancy Cott   Mary Kelley

Cathy Davidson   Annette Kolodny

Thadious Davis   Wendy Martin

Jane DeHart-Mathews   Janice Radway

Sara Evans   Barbara Sicherman

SECOND STORIES

The Politics of Language,

Form, and Gender in

Early American Fictions

Cynthia S. Jordan

The University of North Carolina Press

Chapel Hill and London

© 1989 The University of North Carolina Press
All rights reserved

Library of Congress Cataloging-in-Publication Data

Jordan, Cynthia S.
    Second stories: the politics of language, form, and gender in
early American fictions / Cynthia S. Jordan.
        p. cm. — (Gender & American culture)
    Bibliography: p.
    Includes index.
    ISBN 0-8078-1839-9 (alk. paper)
    1. American fiction—19th century—History and criticism.
2. American fiction—18th century—History and criticism. 3. Sex
role in literature. 4. Patriarchy in literature. 5. Fathers in
literature. 6. Authority in literature. 7. Social structure in
literature. 8. Language and languages in literature. I. Title.
II. Series.
PS374.S46J67   1989   88-27661
813'.009'355—dc19   CIP

The paper in this book meets the guidelines for permanence and durability
of the Committee on Production Guidelines for Book Longevity of the
Council on Library Resources.

Printed in the United States of America

93 92 91 90 89   5 4 3 2 1

Portions of the introduction to Part I appeared as "'Old Words' in 'New
Circumstances': Language and Leadership in Post-Revolutionary America,"
in *American Quarterly* 40 (December 1988): 491–513. An early version of
Chapter 3, entitled "On Re-reading *Wieland*: 'The Folly of Precipitate Conclusions,'" appeared in *Early American Literature* 16 (1981): 154–74. A section
of Chapter 5 was published as "Poe's Re-Vision: The Recovery of the Second Story," in *American Literature* 59 (March 1987): 1–19 [copyright 1987 by
Duke University Press].

In loving memory
of my father,
Edward Haven Jordan

Contents

Preface

The last ten or fifteen years have seen two major changes in the way critics define American literature. Challenges to the notion of an exclusive literary canon have shown that there has always been more than one way to tell the American story; indeed, that there has been more than one story to tell—not just that of the American Adam, for instance, but also that of the American Eve; not just that of the American Scholar, but also that of the American Slave; and not just that of "Life in the Woods," but also that of "Life in the Iron Mills," "Life among the Lowly," and life in "The Wide, Wide World." We have also begun to revise, or at least to enlarge, our perceptions of the classic American "story" as told by our earliest major authors, Cooper, Emerson, Thoreau, Hawthorne, and Melville. Although that story might explore the possibilities of a world elsewhere or a pastoral world by itself, studies such as Richard Slotkin's *Regeneration through Violence* (1973), Annette Kolodny's *The Lay of the Land* (1975), Michael Paul Rogin's *Fathers and Children* (1975), Nina Baym's *The Shape of Hawthorne's Career* (1976), Eric Sundquist's *Home as Found* (1979), and Michael T. Gilmore's *American Romanticism and the Marketplace* (1985) are reminders that it is nevertheless securely grounded in and shaped by specific historical, cultural, political, economic, social, and psychosocial realities. Thus we have learned that the American classics, no less than their popular, contemporary rivals, allow us imaginative reentry into those realities.

This study is a product of both of these revisionary trends in American literary scholarship. Part I examines three early American fictions, Benjamin Franklin's *Autobiography*, Hugh Henry Brackenridge's *Modern Chivalry*, and Charles Brockden Brown's *Wieland*, which have traditionally been pigeonholed as historical oddities or failed literary experiments. Written in eighteenth-century prose styles and about subjects that to modern readers seem antiquated and overdetermined, these first attempts to tell the American story have seldom been viewed in relation to each other or to those later, romantic fictions that have so long been considered the first products of "serious" American literary endeavor. Franklin's *Autobiog-*

raphy has not generally been classified as fiction at all. Although I admit to stretching the term somewhat in applying it to this work, I do so on the grounds that its author not only fictionalized his self-image so as to present his readers with a model American hero but that he also conceived of his text as a fictional construct, a carefully shaped work of literature, rather than as a merely factual life history.

Part II examines classic nineteenth-century fictions that are much more familiar but that exhibit a new dimension when viewed as revisions of an American story that had already seen its first tellings. Twentieth-century criticism has traditionally regarded the writings of Cooper, Poe, Hawthorne, and Melville as being cast pretty much from the same mold. Their novels and tales have been read as escapist fantasies, the idealized products of "wish-fulfillment" (D. H. Lawrence, *Studies in Classic American Literature*, 1924); of "a willingness to abandon moral questions or to ignore the spectacle of man in society" (Richard Chase, *The American Novel and Its Tradition*, 1957); and of a desire to "sacrifice" the "relation between art and life, imagination and actuality" (Michael Davitt Bell, *The Development of American Romance*, 1980). They are reread here as astute and troubled commentaries on the problems of men, women, and artists ethically and psychologically burdened with the task of rejecting the sociopolitical views—and the false stories—bequeathed to them by their "fathers."

What links these seven authors together is, finally, a concern with the language of "fathers," and my general thesis is that their concern with the patriarchal politics of language in America informs both the thematic content and the overall shape of their fictions. More specifically, Franklin, Brackenridge, and Brown, writing in the wake of the Revolution, which granted authority to new Fathers, believed with varying degrees of optimism that language could be used to maintain a patriarchal social order in the new nation. The narrative fictions they wrote to promote such a belief, however, are curiously doubled: their promotional surface narratives are constantly threatened by evidence of opposing views, and that evidence constitutes a rival second story which the authors try to suppress or defuse but which they find increasingly difficult to hold in check. In the romantic period that followed, Cooper, Poe, Hawthorne, and Melville repeatedly criticized the patriarchal linguistic politics that tried to silence other views—"otherness" itself—in American culture, and their own experiments with narrative form reflect their attempts to unmask the fraud perpetrated by their cultural fathers and to recover the lost second story.

Some explanation is in order regarding my terminology, for although

my critical perspective has been influenced and no doubt shaped by current trends in literary, historical, psychoanalytic, and linguistic scholarship, I have allowed my choice of terms to be governed by the phenomena
I have found in the literary texts. By "patriarchal language," for example, I
refer primarily and literally to the politicized language which my authors
see originating with fathers or paternalistic authority figures and which
they associate, implicitly or explicitly, with a belief in a sociopolitical paradigm that privileges white males above all others, as heroes, leaders, preferred models of public and private behavior. Whether, like Franklin,
Brackenridge, and Brown, they promote that belief, or, like Cooper, Poe,
Hawthorne, and Melville, they censure it, the authors considered here all
view patriarchal language as a historically determined phenomenon, and
thus I use the term not as it is employed by, say, the French linguistic
theorists Luce Irigaray and Hélène Cixous, to describe language that is
inherently andro- or phallocentric, but rather as Dale Spender does, to
describe a "man-made" language that has become androcentric over time.

  In its most general sense, "second story" refers to a competing story
line within the narrative proper, or more specifically, an ordering of experience according to values and attitudes that run counter to, and are thus
perceived as posing a threat to, the dominant culture's patriarchal ideology. The term takes on additional referents over the course of this study,
however, for though each of the fictions treated here contains a second,
politically subversive story line, all of the authors after Franklin call attention to its presence by giving it distinct formal and/or metaphorical status.
Three brief examples should suffice as explanation. In the *Autobiography*,
Franklin merely and fleetingly suggests the existence of a rival version of
historical reality whenever he acknowledges the popular "Objections, and
Reluctances" to his paternalistic attempts at leadership; his narrative
strategies highlight instead his ability to defuse that marginal second story
and get on with the business of being a good Father. In marked contrast
to such artful authorial suppression, Cooper in *The Last of the Mohicans*
first alerts his readers to the presence of competing versions of American
history, in Natty Bumppo's early pronouncement that "there are two sides
to every story," and then gives both white (patriarchal) and Indian (matriarchal) "sides" equal representational space in a bifurcated narrative form
that develops one plot and then another. Finally, Hawthorne is only one
of the authors included here who calls attention to the presence of competing sociopolitical perspectives through the use of a conjoined archi-
tectural/narrative metaphor. Hawthorne announces in the autobiographi-

cal sketch that prefaces *The Scarlet Letter* that he found the materials for his romance in "the second story" of the Custom House and that to bring Hester Prynne's long-forgotten story before the public eye he had to remove himself from that symbolic bastion of patriarchal politics and androcentric thinking.

My choice of authors is admittedly selective, and for that reason I use the word early American *fictions* rather than *fiction* in my subtitle. Certainly there are other eighteenth-century narratives that highlight the new American family's need for effective patriarchal guardianship—William Hill Brown's *The Power of Sympathy* (1789), Susanna Rowson's *Charlotte Temple* (1794), and Hannah Foster's *The Coquette* (1797) come immediately to mind. Similarly, the nineteenth-century authors discussed here were not alone in their criticisms of a system of sociopolitical governance which they felt had dangerously divided the American family against itself, or even in their use of a second or two-sided story metaphor as a way of imaging such a critique. Though she did not write fiction herself, Margaret Fuller employed such a metaphor in *Woman in the Nineteenth Century* (1845) when she warned her readers that American "men do *not* look at both sides" of social and political issues and that American women must look elsewhere—at the plight of "the Red Man, the Black Man," and their sisters in all walks of life—if they wished to know the whole story of their country's history and moral degeneration. In *Ruth Hall* (1855), Fanny Fern [Sara Payson Willis] stressed the hypocrisy and moral blindness of one of her most evil father figures by having him repeatedly, smugly, and ever mistakenly insist that he knew "the whole story" regarding his long-suffering daughter-in-law, all the while revealing in her own two-sided narrative that he most emphatically did not. And in *Hitherto: A Story of Yesterdays* (1869), A. D. T. Whitney would continue to remind her American audience that "stories in this world tell themselves by halves. There is always a silent side; many silent sides, perhaps."

I have chosen the seven male authors included in this study because their works have silent sides that have not previously been explored. Franklin's, Brackenridge's, and Brown's narratives have rarely been viewed in thematic relation to each other, and it is their similar emphasis on the sociopolitical function of stories and storytelling in the new nation, as well as their concern over the form that the "American" story should take, that is my main interest here. Cooper, Poe, Hawthorne, and Melville obviously fall into a different category, but I include them because, for all the extensive and excellent critical attention that has been paid them, I believe that their versions of the American story contain a political and a formal dimension that in its imaginative richness and complexity amply repays any attempt to recover it. I have finally to echo Leslie Fiedler's hope, in his Preface to the first edition of *Love and Death in the American Novel* (1960), that whether or not individuals in my audience ultimately accept my readings they will never again be able to "half-read" the curiously doubled narratives to which this study is devoted.

Acknowledgments

It is my great pleasure to acknowledge the many forms of help and support I have received in the course of writing this book. My special thanks go to Michael T. Gilmore, who has valiantly read the complete manuscript in its various drafts. His astute substantive and stylistic suggestions, his enthusiasm, and his friendship have been invaluable. Cecilia Tichi is another who, as friend and mentor, has given most generously of her time and assistance at every stage of the book's composition. I am also grateful to my friends and readers from Brandeis University—Philip Fisher, Karen Klein, Susan Staves, Claudia Yukman, and Ivy Schweitzer—for helping me through the arduous first stages of this project; to my colleagues from Indiana University—Terence Martin, James Justus, Raymond Hedin, Christoph Lohmann, David Nordloh, Paul John Eakin, and Mary Burgan —for helping me bring it to a timely end; and to my two readers for the University of North Carolina Press—Linda K. Kerber and Philip F. Gura, whose detailed critiques included many valuable suggestions for improvements. Different but no less heartfelt thanks are owed to Deborah Valenze, Mary Gay Daly, Deborah Hudson, Lisa Simon, Iwona Hedin, Cornelia Nixon, and Barbara Johnson, who generously took time out of their own busy work schedules to offer encouragement, to share writing and other survival strategies, and often just to listen. Finally, I want to thank Indiana University for research fellowships that allowed me to devote two summers to this project.

The New American Story

Introduction: A Revolutionized Language

Hannah Arendt has remarked how our modern concept of revolution, dating from "the two great revolutions at the end of the eighteenth century," is "inextricably bound up with the notion that the course of history suddenly begins anew, that an entirely new story, a story never known or told before, is about to unfold."[1] The three narratives treated in Part I, Benjamin Franklin's *Autobiography* (1771–90), Hugh Henry Brackenridge's *Modern Chivalry* (1792–1815), and Charles Brockden Brown's *Wieland; or, The Transformation* (1798), represent their authors' attempts to tell that "new story" to a newly constituted American audience. Each of these texts is self-consciously framed as an "American Tale" (Brown's subtitle), and each offers much needed, though still experimental, behavioral models to meet the unprecedented challenges to social stability and personal identity ushered in by the American Revolution. Essentially, these first national stories all tell the same "new" tale, that of a society that has to make itself up as it goes along and of representative Americans who have to name and rename reality as new circumstances continue to arise.

These first American stories are "new," at least to modern readers, in another way. The three eighteenth-century narratives treated here are informed by a very different ethos from the one we are used to finding in nineteenth-century American fictions. The heroes are different. Instead of those free-spirited sons and daughters who attain their heroic status by rejecting the false world view they have inherited from fathers and father figures (such as the young Natty Bumppo, Redburn, Hester Prynne, Ruth Hall, George Harris and George Shelby, Huckleberry Finn), the heroes of these earliest American fictions are in fact agents of patriarchal authority: in Franklin's and Brackenridge's narratives, father figures themselves; in Brown's, a dutiful daughter who triumphs by reenacting her father's mode of authority and authorship. These heroes' motives are different. Instead of the desire for greater personal autonomy, so characteristic of nineteenth-century heroic endeavor, we find in these first heroes the desire to repress self-serving, antisocial "passions" in themselves and in others and thus to provide models of socially and politically acceptable behavior. Finally, these heroes' methods are different. Instead of acquiring the firsthand knowledge of the world that will allow them to see and speak the truth—the true names of things—the heroes promoted by Franklin, Brackenridge, and Brown derive their understanding of the world from texts, and they have less interest in the truth value of language than in its political or rhetorical value. They suppress the truth more often than not, attempting to maintain order in their fictional worlds by glossing over conflicts and silencing dissident views. In other words, they use language artfully, as a means of social and psychological control.

Twentieth-century scholarship has been eager to piece together the story of this nation's founding, as told in the various political writings, memoirs, and letters left by the revolutionary generation. Scholars have not been as eager to decipher the more obviously fictional stories of the same period, although they have begun seriously to consider that "our first real decade of fiction-writing coincided with the first decade of our national life."[2] Close readings of the *Autobiography*, *Modern Chivalry*, and *Wieland* suggest that the coincidence was not gratuitous. Franklin, Brackenridge, and Brown set out to tell "an entirely new story, a story never known or told before," and to understand the content and the form of this new American story requires an understanding of how the experience of an unprecedented Revolution produced new ideas concerning the function of language and authority in the new republic.

In a letter to grammarian John Waldo, dated August 16, 1813, Thomas Jefferson stressed his ongoing belief that in the United States, "the new circumstances under which we are placed, call for new words, new phrases, and for the transfer of old words to new objects. . . . Necessity obliges us to neologize."[3] Nine years later he would reiterate this sentiment in a letter to one of the founders of the American Academy of Language and Belles Lettres (1820), William S. Cardell, a grammarian who hoped to improve the common language of America and England and, in particular, "to form and maintain, as far as practicable, an English standard of writing and pronunciation, correct, fixed, and uniform, throughout our extensive territory."[4] "There are so many differences between us and England," Jefferson had written to Cardell, "of soil, climate, culture, productions, laws, religion, and government, that we must be left far behind the march of circumstances, were we to hold ourselves rigorously to their standard. If, like the French Academicians, it were proposed *to fix* our language, it would be fortunate, that the step were not taken in the days of our Saxon ancestors whose vocabulary would illy express the science of this day. Judicious neology can alone give strength and copiousness to language, and enable it to be the vehicle of new ideas."[5]

Nationalistic fervor following the American Revolution occasioned prolonged and impassioned debates over whether to "fix" a distinctly "American" language.[6] What is unusual, however, and especially revealing of the volatile semantic environment during the early years of the republic is that even those thinkers who argued in favor of fixing (settling, determining, standardizing) the form of American English—its spelling, grammar, or vocabulary—tended often and purposefully to *un*fix the traditional meanings of the words they argued about; to engage, if not in "judicious neology," at least in judicious redefinition.

Noah Webster, for example, who opposed Jefferson's views on language (and on most other issues as well), began his long career as self-proclaimed arbiter of American English by lobbying for a uniformity of pronunciation and orthography in America, arguing that a "sameness of pronunciation is of considerable consequence in a political view; for provincial accents are disagreeable to strangers and sometimes have an unhappy effect upon the social affections. . . . Our political harmony is therefore concerned in a uniformity of language."[7] Although he disapproved of "neology"—"vulgarisms" and "Americanisms"—on similar political grounds, as being productive of confusion, dissension, and thus divisiveness, nevertheless he too would allow that the nation's "new circumstances" justified the coining of *some* new words and especially the transfer of "old words" to "new objects." "Some words are either new in the United States," he explained of his choices for inclusion in the *Compendious Dictionary* of 1806, "or what is more usual, English words have received a new sense. Words of these kinds, *when in general use in a state or number of states, or sanctioned by public authority* in laws and judicial proceedings, are admitted into this work" (my emphasis).[8]

In addition, as Richard M. Rollins has shown, when giving definitions, Webster intentionally manipulated the meanings of individual words throughout his career so as to instruct Americans in what he considered to be their duties and responsibilities as a nation. Immediately following the Revolution, he designed a series of school lessons that would simultaneously promote proper—American—spelling and revolutionary ideology, incorporating into his famous blue-backed speller (1783) a "Chronological Account of Remarkable Events in America" and instructional exercises, which he hoped would inspire young people with "a love of virtue, patriotism and religion."⁹ In 1790, describing his new schoolbook, *The Little Reader's Assistant*, he had written to a friend, "I have introduced into it some definitions, relative to the slave trade, calculated to impress upon young minds the detestableness of the trade." Webster also revised definitions as, in his opinion, changing political circumstances demanded. Rollins has found that such revolutionary bywords as *freedom, equality, liberty*, and *duty*, to name but a few, took on different meanings in Webster's later writings, reflecting the more authoritarian, Federalist cast to his thinking in the wake of the French Revolution and Jefferson's ascension to power in 1800.[10]

It would be difficult to find a contemporary historical analysis of America's revolutionary and postrevolutionary years that does not devote at least some space to discussion of how the meanings of specific words changed during that era. The definitions of key political terms such as *democracy, republic* and *republicanism, liberty*, and *virtue* underwent rapid change, we are told, and even seemingly common words like *candor, passion, greatness, experience*, or *happiness* took on new and unusual meanings.[11] One study shows, for example, that as used in the constitutional debates, the word *experience* referred both to political wisdom gained by participation in events, and wisdom gained by studying past events."[12] Another notes that although the *Federalist* is not very explicit in defining *happiness*, "there are firm indications that what it had in mind has little in common with traditional philosophical or theological understandings of the term."[13] Finally, a third, broader-based study explains that "in this first era of national life. . . . Americans were likely to use a word for any purpose it served."[14] This statement refers specifically to the new national tendency to turn nouns into verbs, adjectives into nouns, and so forth, but that tendency reinforces our sense of the general elasticity of language following the Revolution.

As John P. Diggins has pointed out, however, "a study of linguistic terms in a given historical situation can only tell us how language was used, not why," and the question that must now be asked is why the language of the revolutionary generation changed so dramatically; why, as another historian has phrased it, their words did not possess "a timeless application."[15] The above examples from the writings of Jefferson and Webster suggest an answer, for they reveal the extreme self-consciousness with which political thinkers of the Early National period monitored—and initiated—changes in their own language. More important, the terms

Jefferson and Webster use to discuss language reveal how the main political concerns of their day helped shape their own and their contemporaries' language practices. The texts of this period are informed by a heightened awareness of the newness of the United States's political, social, and cultural circumstances in the wake of its unprecedented Revolution and by an increasingly sophisticated understanding of the uses of "calculated" political psychology in bringing about the "political harmony" necessary to ensure the new nation's survival. In the specific area of language, such politicized thinking resulted in a sharper comprehension of how words might be unfixed from their traditional meanings so as to accommodate change and to influence popular opinion and behavior. These efforts left subsequent generations with a surface vocabulary of words that look familiar but whose meanings change from context to new context and thus necessitate frequent reinterpretation.

This latter point suggests the final key to any understanding of the language practices of the Early National period, for although the most prolific thinkers and writers of the revolutionary generation may have begun by redefining individual words to meet their needs, they ultimately produced a sophisticated system of public language in which meaning became virtually dependent on interpreters—specifically, on learned men, like Jefferson and Webster, who would know how to make a judicious transfer of old words to new objects, how to calculate definitions so as to ensure political harmony. In other words, the picture that finally emerges from the texts of the Early National period reveals how inextricably their authors' views on language were tied in with their views on sociopolitical leadership. It is the picture of a new nation conceived of in the literary-legal language of an educated, paternalistic elite heavily invested in valorizing the art of political interpretation.

Any explanation of the revolutionary generation's increasingly politicized use of language must start with their views on human nature and, subsequently, on the limitations of human language as a vehicle of absolute meaning, for those views begin to explain the extreme self-consciousness and judiciousness with which they came to choose their words. America's politicians and political writers of the late eighteenth century were well acquainted with Enlightenment thought, which saw human beings as infinitely fallible, self-interested creatures who, though believing themselves rational, were constantly swayed by nonrational motives; and, more specifically, in Lockean associationist psychology, which posited that though knowledge was based on sense impressions, those impressions might be unconsciously colored or distorted by ideational patterns associated with previous sensations (a psychological structuring similar to that addressed by Freud's free-association technique).[16] That they understood the implications of these theories in the area of language behavior is shown nowhere more clearly than in *Federalist* No. 37, in which James Madison delineates a communication model based so insistently on human fallibility that it might better be called a model of miscommunication.

Stressing the arduousness of the Constitutional Convention's task of marking the boundary between the federal and state jurisdictions, Madison moves to the difficulty of defining in general and cites "three sources of vague and incorrect definitions: indistinctness of the object" (here he emphasizes the difference between objects in the natural world, whose "delineations are perfectly accurate and appear to be otherwise only from the imperfection of the eye which surveys them," and the "institutions of man, in which the obscurity arises as well from the object itself"), "imperfection of the organ of conception, [and] inadequateness of the vehicle of ideas." By the last he means language, which he describes as adding "a fresh embarrassment" to "men" in their attempt at accuracy, for "no language is so copious as to supply words and phrases for every complex idea, or so correct as not to include many equivocally denoting different ideas. Hence it must happen that however accurately objects may be discriminated in themselves, and however accurately the discriminations may be considered, the definition of them may be rendered inaccurate by the inaccuracy of the terms in which it is delivered. And this unavoidable inaccuracy must be greater or less, according to the complexity and novelty of the objects defined."[17]

Given this picture of the communication process, in which there are three potential sources of error before any verbal expression even enters the world, it is small wonder that Alexander Hamilton would have opened the *Federalist* with the lengthy disclaimer that though "consciousness of good intentions disdains ambiguity," he would not "multiply professions on this head," for his "motives must remain in the depository of [his] own breast": "My arguments will be open to all and may be judged of by all. They shall at least be offered in a spirit which will not disgrace the cause of truth."[18] The last sentence in particular, in which "truth" is relegated to a subordinate phrase at the tail end of a subordinate clause, is virtually an epigrammatic version of Madison's implicit model, for both bespeak the sophisticated self-consciousness—and self-questioning—of the eighteenth-century rationalist frame of mind.

To say that the revolutionary generation's self-consciousness about language derived only from their essentially European intellectual background, however, is to leave out the novelty, the Americanness, of their situation; to ignore the effects of an accomplished revolution on language and attitudes toward language. Madison's theoretical model, for example, could conceivably have been constructed by any of his European contemporaries, but the fact that he begins and ends his discussion of the communication process by stressing as the controlling factor the degree of "complexity and novelty" of the "man"-made object suggests the central preoccupation of his compatriots: the unprecedented degree to which their revolutionary enterprise had been accomplished by collective human action. As Arendt has pointed out in her brilliant study of modern revolution, in which she sees the American as the first, it was "only in the course of the eighteenth-century revolutions that men began to be aware that a new beginning could be a political phenomenon, that it could be the result of what men had done and what they could consciously set out to do."[19]

If, according to Madison's model, a long-standing object (traditional secular government) could be willfully replaced, redesigned, by collective action, then language itself, another "man"-made object, could also be reformed, tailored to fit the new circumstances, and thus used as a powerful tool by the new political community to establish its new order. As a contemporary French commentator suggested, one of the most heated issues at the Constitutional Convention was over who would be "first in giving the denominations (a matter so important in a revolution!)."[20] His parenthetical stress of the principle involved perhaps testifies only to the redundancy of having to point out what the revolutionary generation had so obviously come to understand: the link between language and authority, language and power—specifically, the power of "men" to reshape reality according to ideology by renaming the world according to their own image of it. And Madison's conclusion to *Federalist* No. 37 reveals how this motivation came to dominate the Convention and to assimilate those "first" contending voices into "a unanimity almost as unprecedented as it must have been unexpected." He distinguishes the American endeavor from "the history of almost all the great councils and consultations held among mankind for reconciling their discordant opinions" for a number of reasons but most strikingly because even those "deputations" that had not been totally satisfied by the final act of the Convention "were induced to accede to it by a deep conviction of the necessity of sacrificing private opinions and partial interest to the public good."[21] Granted, Madison's description of the psychology of political compromise in this instance veers dangerously toward rhetorical backpatting. In *Federalist* No. 10, however, he describes the same group sanctioning process in more theoretical terms: "Communication is always checked by distrust in proportion to the number whose concurrence is necessary."[22]

Thus the sense of a new beginning effected a new awareness of the political power of collectively sanctioned naming; or to put it another way, the experience of the accomplished Revolution Americanized the basic Enlightenment communication model by adding the factor of effective political reform. Americans consciously set out to change their language to fit their changing goals, and the work—and words—of the Founders were in this sense in keeping with the revolutionary fervor that had led that patriotic dictionary maker, Noah Webster, to publish in 1783 his first blue-backed speller, which became one of the first national best-sellers (estimated to have run to around 404 editions by Webster's death in 1843) and which presented revolutionary ideology in the form of spelling instruction. That same fervor could be seen as late as 1813, when Jefferson insisted that the "new circumstances under which we are placed, call for new words . . . and for the transfer of old words to new objects."

Such late and continuing emphasis on new circumstances, however, points to another politically engendered factor that contributed to the Americans' enthusiasm for redefinition, one that seems at first glance irreconcilable with the former. Once awakened to the possibility of a new beginning, members of the revolutionary generation were reluctant to delimit that possibility too hastily by overly dogmatic definitions. If, for example, the power inherent in naming could be politically useful in establishing a new order and securing the public good, it could over time become politically oppressive. "Power" is the key word here: even the power of naming could become dangerous and restrictive if left unchecked. Thomas Paine's early outrage against Britain's claimed right to "BIND us in ALL CASES WHATSOEVER"—"and if being *bound in that manner* is not slavery, then is there not such a thing as slavery upon earth"— evolved during the course of the successful rebellion into a general distrust of any fixed, artificial forms that might bind mankind unnecessarily and unnaturally: "If we consider what the principles are that first condense men into society, and what the motives that regulate their mutual intercourse afterwards, we shall find, by the time we arrive at what is called government, that nearly the whole of the business is performed by the natural operation of the parts upon each other. . . . All the great laws of society are laws of nature . . . followed and obeyed, because it is the interest of the parties so to do, and not on account of any formal laws their governments may impose or interpose." Paine's phrasing, "what is called government," with its sense of how a word tainted by history could leave a bad taste in the mouth, reveals the extent to which such distrust of fixity had spread into the area of language. Even more revealing is his metaphorical praise of the now self-evident truth of human liberty, first brought to light, to the world's eye, by the American Revolution: "The sun needs no inscription to distinguish him from darkness."[23]

The formality and the unnatural stasis of "inscription," of fixed definitions of the world, were indeed perceived by many not just as an imposition but as a possible danger to a nation conceived in liberty and dedicated to realizing the untried potential of human nature. Jefferson, who ever considered himself a friend to "neology," occasionally railed against those who "look at constitutions with sanctimonious reverence, and deem them like the ark of the covenant, too sacred to be touched": "No society can make a perpetual constitution, or even a perpetual law. The earth belongs always to the living generation: they may manage it, then, and what proceeds from it, as they please, during their usufruct."[24] In characteristically didactic fashion, Franklin dramatized a slightly less secular version of this belief and this distrust of subscribing too literally to authoritative inscription in the *Autobiography*. After describing the public embarrassments of the Quakers, who, "having establish'd and published it as one of their Principles, that no kind of War was lawful, and which being once published, they could not afterwards, however they might change their Minds, easily get rid of," he was moved to remember another sect's "more prudent Conduct." He had apparently offered to publish the articles of belief of the Dunkers, a much maligned because much misunderstood group, to better their public image but had been rebuffed by one of their "Founders":

When we were first drawn together as a Society, . . . it had pleased God to inlighten our Minds so far, as to see that some Doctrines which we once esteemed Truths were Errors, and that others which we had esteemed Errors were real Truths. From time to time he has been pleased to afford us farther Light, and our Principles have been improving, and our Errors di-

minishing. Now we are not sure that we are arriv'd at the End of this Progression, . . . and we fear that if we should once print our Confession of
Faith, we should feel ourselves as if bound and confin'd by it, and perhaps
be unwilling to receive farther Improvement; and our Successors still more
so, as conceiving what we their Elders and Founders had done, to be
something sacred, never to be departed from.[25]

Written in 1788 by a specialist in public relations, this anecdote of the
prudent founders serves as virtual allegory of the larger founding experience in which Franklin had so recently participated. At the Convention,
for example, he had voiced his ambivalence to the Constitution in similar
terms: "I confess that there are several parts of this constitution which I
do not at present approve, but I am not sure I shall never approve them:
For having lived long, I have experienced many instances of being obliged
by better information or fuller considerations, to change opinions even on
important subjects, which I once thought right, but found to be otherwise. It is therefore that the older I grow, the more apt I am to doubt my
own judgment, and to pay more respect to the judgment of others."
Franklin's personal resolution of his ambivalence, which allowed him finally to call for unanimous approval of the document, was, he announced,
"to consent . . . to this Constitution because I expect no better, and because I am not sure, that it is not the best." More telling of his insistence
on the need for political—and textual—flexibility, however, was the belief
he later expressed to the Duc de la Rochefoucauld that the first and
subsequent congresses would be able to "mend" the errors of the Constitution as they saw fit.[26]

If the Founders were anxious to spell out the newly won national authority, they and their contemporaries were still wary of the power of
authority per se, having just worked so hard to overthrow so many exist-
ing forms, and were equally anxious lest they should entrap themselves or
their posterity in any shortsighted authoritarian literality. Their insistence
on open-endedness, on providing for continual improvement, further
modified the "revolutionized" communication model by adding an ad-
monishing element of futurity, by counterbalancing the exhilarating
awareness of "men's" power to rename the world with the sobering sense
of the need for periodic reassessment of those acts of renaming. In sum,
based on their Enlightenment view of the fallibility of human nature, the
leading thinkers and writers of the revolutionary generation had been
educated to the need for self-consciousness and circumspection in their
use of language, to expect "vague and incorrect" definitions. The experi-

ence of the Revolution, however, recast this attitude by imposing on the language of the new republic a politicized psychology of checks and balances: on one hand, a political impetus, a belief in and an enthusiasm for the political power of collectively sanctioned naming, redefining, improving what was "incorrect" in the past; and, on the other, a political restraint, concession to unforeseeable future developments that would necessitate periodic acts of renaming or redefining. The result was the peculiar elasticity of language that twentieth-century scholars find so bothersome. The words of the new republic were uncommonly used; they did not possess "a timeless application." Indeed, its words were timely in the extreme, burdened with the multiple task of breaking with the past, interpreting the present in the interests of the "public good," and remaining flexible enough to accommodate future reinterpretations. Thus in 1813, over thirty years after the close of the Revolution, new circumstances would still call for "new words . . . and for the transfer of old words to new objects."

The experience of the Revolution valorized the *act* of renaming while limiting the temporal power of the "names" themselves, and the prime example of this politically time-conscious language is the Constitution itself. That text illustrates both in form, conceptually, and in content, as a set of practical guidelines, its makers' newly politicized attitudes toward language.[27]

The Framers stressed, for example, that conceptually, the Constitution was a new articulation of governing authority: "The important distinction so well understood in America," wrote Madison in *Federalist* No. 53, "between a Constitution established by the people and unalterable by the government, and a law established by the government, seems to have been little understood and less observed in any other country." Written constitutions, as Bernard Bailyn has explained, "had existed, had been acted upon, had been assumed to be proper and necessary, for a century or more," but the American document reflected a native transformation in the concept—and definition—of constitutionalism that required a new political text, a new mode of political discourse authorized by universal principles of natural rights (as Alexander Hamilton had imaged, rather grandiosely, in 1775: "The sacred rights of mankind are not to be rummaged for among old parchments or musty records. They are written, as with a sunbeam, in the whole *volume* of human nature, by the hand of divinity itself, and can never be erased or obscured by mortal power"). Tracing this conceptual transformation, specifically between the years 1764 and 1776, Bailyn has shown how American discourse began "to distinguish fundamentals from institutions and from the actions of government so that they might serve as limits and controls." In 1764, for example, a pamphlet writer might still refer to "a legal constitution, that is, a legislature," conjoining the two concepts. By 1773, however, *constitution* was defined as "'the standard measure of the proceedings of government' of which rulers are 'by no means to attempt an alteration . . . without public consent.'" And by 1776 the definition emerged that would become "so well understood" by the later Convention. Not surprisingly, the author of *Four Letters on Important Subjects* self-consciously frames his argument as an attempt to rectify prior "vague and incorrect" definitions: "A constitution and a form of government are frequently confounded together and spoken of as synonymous things, whereas they are not only different but are established for different purposes." The purpose of a constitution was to delimit the actions of government. To do so, the constitution had to be grounded in some "higher authority than the giving out [of] temporary laws"—that is, in Madison's later words, it had to be "established by the people" as constituent power and expressive of fundamental principles "unalterable by government."[28]

The Constitution, then, differed from past texts because of its newly conceived authority. Conceptually, it was a text authorized by virtue of its articulation of and adherence to collectively sanctioned principles providing for the public good. It was also burdened with the unprecedented task of founding a practical system of government to enact that authority. Hamilton might taunt the crumbling authority of the past in 1775 with a vision of rightful principles that "can never be erased or obscured," but a pamphleteer of 1776 captured the awesome burden of responsibility entailed by such immutable inscription: "Men entrusted with the formation of civil constitutions should remember they are *painting for eternity*: that the smallest defect or redundancy in the system they frame may prove the destruction of millions."[29] Similarly, Hamilton, with an eye to the past, would disdain "old parchments or musty records," but the Framers of the Constitution, apprehending the eyes of the future, were compelled to scrutinize the practicality of their own work and to evaluate it in similar terms. The *Federalist* makes frequent reference to "how unequal parchment provisions are to a struggle with public necessity"; to "the insufficiency of a mere parchment delineation of the boundaries" between the departments of the government. Madison opens No. 48 with the question, "Will it be sufficient to mark, with precision, the boundaries of these departments in the constitution of the government, and to trust to these parchment barriers against the encroaching spirit of power?" He ends it with the answer: "The conclusion which I am warranted in drawing . . . is that a mere demarcation on parchment of the constitutional limits of the several departments is not a sufficient guard against those encroachments which lead to a tyrannical concentration of all the powers of government in the same hands." What Bailyn has described as the conceptual "process of disengaging principles from institutions and from the positive actions of government" resulted in a mode of discourse that delineated principles, not particulars; and "parchment" principles were not enough to restrain the encroaching spirit of power from usurping control over what must in time become a proliferation of significant particulars.[30]

The Founders' resolution of this textual dilemma was to separate the government into executive, legislative, and judicial branches, which would allow for the necessary checks and balances of power and, in particular, to reserve what Alexander Hamilton called "the majesty of national authority" for the judiciary, whose task would be to "ascertain [the Constitution's] meaning as well as the meaning of any particular act proceeding from the legislative body" as time went on. Robert A. Ferguson, for example, who has aptly described the Constitution as "a crayon sketch waiting to be filled up," "a shadow requiring constant recalculation," has pointed out that "modern preoccupation with the constitutionalism of checks and balances overlooks the fact that judicial review was designed primarily to catch the dangerous mistakes that [the Framers] feared and assumed within the accelerated lawmaking of the new republic": "Only the ongoing legal process could *define* [that] republic" (my emphasis). Arendt's description of the Framers' rationale is similarly suggestive of the language issue involved: "In the American republic the function of authority is legal, and it consists in interpretation. The Supreme Court derives its own authority from the Constitution as a written document," and "this authority is exerted in a kind of continuous constitution-making." In other words, the Founders located national authority in a text that authorized successive, specified representative bodies to reinterpret it, to remake its various particular meanings. "Thus," as one historian has described a specific instance, "we can ask what the Framers meant when they gave Congress the power to regulate interstate and foreign commerce, and we emerge, reluctantly perhaps, with the reply that . . . commerce was *commerce*, and if different interpretations of the word arose, later generations could worry about the problem of definition." In general terms, the right to periodic reinterpretation—and the need for it—are guaranteed by this supremely time-conscious text.[31]

The Constitution demonstrates how the psychological experience of an accomplished Revolution had valorized the *act* of renaming while denying any transcendent power to the names themselves. In theory, by creating this unique founding text, members of the revolutionary generation were acknowledging and establishing what Stanley Fish has called "the authority of interpretive communities": "It is interpretive communities [rather than a text itself] . . . that produce meanings and are responsible for the emergence of formal features. Interpretive communities are made up of those who share interpretive strategies not for reading but for writing texts [cf. Arendt's "continuous constitution-making"], for constituting their properties. In other words these strategies exist prior to the act of reading and therefore determine the shape of what is read rather than, as is usually assumed, the other way around."[32] In practice, the Founders displaced the production of meaning from the text to human agents authorized to interpret the popular will and ethos of future generations of Americans. Anxious to be the "first in giving denominations," to authorize the new nation, yet wary of the power that must accompany such authority, they aimed at the impossible compromise—and attained it, achieving in the Constitution the durability of inscription and the elasticity of definition needed to accommodate national growth, change, and improvement. And certainly, the elasticity of their language still fulfills its original function: our interpretive communities, judicial and lay, are still hard at work.

I have been trying here to delineate more fully the aftereffects of the American Revolution on language and on attitudes toward language; to suggest, in particular, the complex links between language and authority, and language and power, that came to exist in the minds of the men who first shaped this country and that led them so often to "unfix" the traditional meanings of the words they used in response to their new circumstances. Lynn Hunt has reached a similar conclusion regarding the language of the French revolutionary era. In France, her research shows, "revolutionary language did not simply reflect the realities of revolutionary changes and conflicts, but rather was itself transformed into an instrument of political and social change. . . . The language itself helped shape the perception of interests and hence the development of ideologies. In other words, revolutionary political discourse was rhetorical; it was a means of persuasion, a way of reconstituting the social and political world."[33]

According to Hunt, the question that remains to be asked is who, in a postrevolutionary environment in which language has become the vehicle of authority, "a replacement for the charisma of kingship," would be the new authority figures? who would "speak for the Nation"?[34] For America's Early National period, the question must be, who would be deemed capable of creating and interpreting the new mode of political discourse, which delineated principles but not particulars? The picture I have reconstructed, of a nation dedicated to providing for periodic reinterpretations of its founding text, reveals how inextricably its political writers' views on language were enmeshed with their views on leadership, for it is the picture of a nation conceived of in the literary-legal language of an educated, male elite heavily invested in valorizing the verbal proficiency needed to make astute and timely interpretations of American interests. It is the picture, finally, of a new variant of patriarchy.

It is well known, for example, that the Founders were a bookish group, that "they were, if anything, more learned in the ways of 'ancient and modern prudence' than their colleagues in the Old World, and more likely to consult books for guidance in action." Moreover, "they liked to display authorities for their arguments, citing and quoting from them freely; at times their writings become almost submerged in annotation." But, Bailyn found, such "elaborate display" of book-learning, and especially of classical authors, was somewhat "deceptive" and testified more to their highly selective interest in "authorities" who might be used to bolster their previously conceived arguments, than to their broad range of knowledge.[35] In other words, though they read much, they seem to have read always with a political purpose: to interpret texts in what they considered the best interests of the New World enterprise.

To call their artful reading deceptive is thus an accurate assessment, insofar as the word points to the duplicity of their authority in such instances, the double vision that allowed them to fix in their own readers' minds those political theories which temporarily served the collective purpose of leadership and to unfix—downplay or ignore—those which did not. Merely to call their reading deceptive, however, is to leave out of the picture the politicized sense of temporal urgency that motivated them to engage in such double vision and, in addition, the expectations of their contemporary audience. The Founders' artful reading—that is, their skill

at making educated *interpretations* of what constituted American interests—was precisely what qualified them, in the eyes of most of their countrymen, as authority figures. "Respect for the educated man," as a study of
revolutionary Virginia has revealed, "was not limited to the gentry":
"Philip Mazzei, friend and neighbor of Jefferson, when speaking of 'those
who work in the fields, or who practice some mechanical trade,' observed
that 'Those with only a limited education have great respect for persons
who have had more than they. They take it for granted, whenever in
doubt, *especially in matters pertaining to the public weal*, that they have a
right to consult a person with a better education'" (my emphasis).[36]

In the new republic, being educated was virtually equated with knowing how to interpret Americanness, how to secure one's rights as an
American. Thus in describing his plan "to diffuse knowledge more generally through the mass of the people," Jefferson would stress that among
the purposes of his proposed educational system, "none is more important, none more legitimate, than that of rendering the people the safe, as
they are the ultimate, guardians of their own liberty." "Every government
degenerates when trusted to the rulers of the people alone. The people
themselves therefore are its only safe depositories. And to render even
them safe, their minds must be improved to a certain degree." That he
equated such mental improvement with securing the stability of the new
nation is further demonstrated in his comment that the "first stage of this
education being the schools of the hundreds, wherein the great mass of
the people will receive their instruction, the principal foundations of future order will be laid here."[37]

Granted, Jefferson's proposed system was intended to "democratize"
education, to establish a "natural" aristocracy based on talent. This nation
involves two implications regarding language and leadership, however.
The first is that in the mental culture in which such an intentionally
politicized theory of education could germinate verbal proficiency was
already equated with sociopolitical authority, and that authority was
vested in those who, by virtue of their academic training, could now
interpret for those less educated what it meant to be an American. Brackenridge's *Incidents of the Insurrection in Western Pennsylvania in the Year of
1794*, a prose account of what is commonly known as the Whiskey Rebellion, provides strikingly literal examples of how necessary such interpreters were in implementing the new government's jurisdictions. Brackenridge, a college graduate and lawyer, whose reputation derived primarily
from his literary and journalistic productions, describes how the local

authorities, frantically trying to ward off the rebellion against new federal taxation laws, repeatedly sought his help in interpreting their own elective duties:

> John Wilkins, Jr., of Pittsburgh, brigadier general of the militia, . . .
> wished to have my opinion as to their authority to call [the militia out].
> Having given the question a short consideration, I thought they had not
> the power. The governor, under an article of the constitution, has con-
> structively the power. . . .
>
> General Wilkins returned to me a short time afterwards and . . . wished
> my opinion with respect to their power [to raise the posse of the county].
> Giving it a short consideration, I was of opinion that they had not the
> power.
>
> I was requested . . . to explain to the sheriff his authority. I did so, fully.
> The sheriff appeared alarmed at the talk of raising the posse and thought it
> not practicable. I was asked my opinion. . . . I gave it decidedly, that it was
> not practicable. All concurred.[38]

Such official acknowledgment of Brackenridge's qualifications as inter-preter of the "public weal" bespeaks the mental outlook of his age and of a nation predicated on the need of maintaining an educated elite.

The second implication arising from Jefferson's plan for a "natural" aristocracy is that there were and would continue to be popular revolts like the Whiskey Rebellion, and learned authority figures were needed not just to interpret and protect the people's interests but to shape them, to impose order in a society in which misconceived notions of freedom and equality could in the heat of any given moment turn "the people" into a disorderly "mob." Jefferson imaged his plan for maintaining an educated elite as raking "the best geniuses . . . from the rubbish annually," and his phrasing is telling of the hierarchical social order he and his colleagues deemed necessary for the continued success of their national experiment. "It is highly interesting to our country," Jefferson explained, "and it is the duty of its functionaries, to provide that every citizen in it should receive an education proportioned to the condition and pursuits of his life. The mass of our citizens may be divided into two classes—the laboring and the learned. The laboring will need the first grade of education to qualify them for their pursuits and duties; the learned will need it as a foundation for further acquirements." The use of the pronoun *his* is, of course, the most telling indicator of the sort of authority figures Jefferson and his compatriots had in mind. The sophisticated language education that would allow "learned" citizens of the new republic to engage in and con-trol public discourse, thereby providing for leadership, was virtually restricted to white males. Although Jefferson generalized about education for "the great mass of the people," when he specified his targeted group, the term he used was *boys*.[39] The most influential political thinkers and writers of the revolutionary generation, themselves white males, gave little thought to education for blacks or Native Americans, and even the most egalitarian of educational reformers, such as Benjamin Rush, who offered "Thoughts upon Female Education" (1787), proposed that women study subjects that would make them good wives and mothers, not authoritative interpreters of public texts. "That some well-known couples, like John and Abigail Adams, were equally facile with words," Linda Kerber suggests, "has perhaps camouflaged the extent to which they were exceptional in their generation. There was more likely to be severe disparity in the verbal fluency of husband and wife, brother and sister. . . . Even in bookish families the literacy gap was marked."[40]

Finally, in the early days of the republic, which Edmund S. Morgan has aptly depicted as "the union of three million cantankerous colonists into a new nation," there were bound to be those, even among the more privileged white male population, who resented being slotted as "rubbish." After decades of rebelling against established authorities, rank-and-file Americans had become understandably jealous of their new rights, and if they were quick to turn to educated interpreters for elucidation, they were equally quick to turn against such newly constituted authorities if an interpretation did not serve their immediate interests. Brackenridge's ultimate failure as an authority figure in the Whiskey Rebellion is a case in point. He had tried to act as mediator between the rebels and the government, working with middle-level, local officials to interpret each side's point of view to the other, but when the rebels refused to be pacified by his compromise tactics, President George Washington called out fifteen thousand militiamen to quell the insurrection. Brackenridge was vilified by each side for his verbal "duplicity," and he was later made to answer charges of treason for consorting with the locals.[41]

The problem confronting the founding generation, then, was how to devise a system of sociopolitical leadership capable of securing popular acceptance, and the solution they envisioned was the creation and maintenance of a male educated elite that could use language as a means of social and psychological control. What they created—although historians have been hesitant to call it such—was a new variant of patriarchy and patriarchal authority.

For most scholars, there no longer seems to be any question but that the founding generation came to conceive of the American Revolution as a revolt *against* patriarchal authority and that that revolt represented the culmination of a lengthy and complex historical process. Edwin G. Burrows and Michael Wallace's influential study, for example, has shown that in England, changing conceptions of social, economic, and religious bonds during the second half of the seventeenth century resulted in a steady deterioration of patriarchal authority within the family. In response to a declining belief in the biological father's absolute, arbitrary, and interminable authority over his children, political patriarchalism, as promoted by divine-rights theorists such as Sir Robert Filmer, "drifted slowly out of the mainstream of English natural law thinking," to be replaced with "a new, consensual definition of political obligation." "The chief credit for demolishing Filmerism and establishing a new conception of natural law on a new reading of parental authority," Burrows and Wallace argue, "belongs, of course, to John Locke," who articulated and popularized such ideas first in his *Two Treatises of Government* (1689–90) and later in *Thoughts Concerning Education* (1693), in which he more thoroughly explains the natural father's role as that of loving friend and respectful guardian of his children until such time as they can act responsibly for themselves. "The emergence of new attitudes toward childrearing practices in England during the eighteenth century thus went hand in hand with the acceptance of Lockean contractualism in English political theory, for as patriarchalism in the family lost its appeal so did the ideas of royal absolutism and passive obedience that it supported lose their credibility." Finally, the "same transformation of attitudes" toward family relations as a paradigm for political ones can also throw further light on the dramatic "reemergence of [such] analogical thinking during the American Revolution," for "what happened to parental control over children in England during the seventeenth and eighteenth centuries appears to have been closely paralleled in the American colonies, with similar consequences for the spread of contractualist ideology."[42]

This trend helps to explain why Thomas Paine, for example, seems to have been able to capture the imagination—and focus the anger—of his audience so forcefully in 1776 with his attacks on George III as a bad or unnatural father, a "wretch" who, under "the pretended title of FATHER OF HIS PEOPLE," had broken faith with his children and tried to usurp their inalienable rights; and why, more generally, American revolutionaries came to espouse an antipatriarchal ideology that allowed them to cast themselves as Sons of Liberty, struggling to assert and establish their rightful independence.[43] It does not, however, explain why, as Winthrop D. Jordan has pointed out, "the sons of the Revolution soon lapsed into acclaiming their staunchest leader as the Father of His Country." Washington was first referred to by that title in the *Lancaster Almanack* for 1778, and Michael T. Gilmore's research into the eulogies delivered for American revolutionary leaders during the first half-century of the republic's existence has revealed that a shift in rhetorical emphasis from "insurgent sons" to statesmenlike "fathers" began to appear by the middle 1780s. Yet another study has shown that by the mid-1820s the Founders were not only "collectively and possessively referred to as 'our fathers'" but that such rhetoric "commonly" described America's relatively short history as one unbroken line of paternalistic endeavor. For nineteenth-century Americans, George B. Forgie explains, "The phrase 'our fathers' commonly included all participants in the founding process since the first colonial settlements." "We look back to the earliest struggles of our fathers," wrote the proud author of "Thoughts upon the Character of the Age" in 1824; "we follow their records down to the establishment of our country, and see them brought out from bondage, and led through the desolations of famine, pestilence and war, to this, the promised land. We look around and find the nation which they planted, multiplied with unprecedented rapidity, and now enjoying an accumulation—we had almost said an intensity, of blessing, which no other nation has shown."[44]

How are we to account for this relatively rapid and seemingly contradictory turnabout from anti- to pro-"father" rhetoric and for the apparently changed attitudes toward patriarchal leadership implied by such terminology? Certainly, within the span of five decades, the laudatory application of the term *father* to authority figures seems to have been informed by different historical needs. Gilmore argues, for instance, that "the fateful question confronting the American leadership" in the wake of Shays's Rebellion (1786) and the Whiskey Rebellion (1794) was "How could the state erected by revolutionary sons command the permanent loyalty of future generations?" Patriotic eulogists responded, he explains, by creating "the mystique of the Founding Fathers," "holding up the revolutionary leaders to the youth of the country not as insurgent sons but rather as symbols of paternal authority." Forgie explains the early nineteenth-century "father" rhetoric primarily as a response to socioeconomic changes: "Postrevolutionary American society ceased to take it almost as a matter of course that a son would eventually step into the occupation of his father or that of a village neighbor, and that he would then spend the rest of his life residing near and attached to his parents. At a time when expanding economic opportunity meant that boys were beginning to need a wider range of models than their surroundings were likely to provide, history stepped in to supply them in the form of the founding heroes."[45] Neither of these contextual formulations, however, can explain why Washington was lauded as Father of His Country as early as 1778, or, more generally, why the revolutionary generation of self-proclaimed sons could accept that title—and thus a new father figure—so readily. Taken together, they suggest an answer that by now should sound familiar: the name of "father," as it was applied to sociopolitical authority figures in the pre- and postrevolutionary years, did not possess a timeless application. It was an old word upgraded to meet new circumstances, for as Jay Fliegelman has phrased it, one of the major revolutionary insights for Americans was that "the title of father was transferable."

Fliegelman is today one of the best-known proponents of the idea that the American Revolution was antipatriarchal in nature. Expanding on the work of Burrows and Wallace, he has shown how eighteenth-century literary treatments of Locke's ideas on family relations and childrearing, in novels, political treatises, theological exegeses, and philosophical discourses on childrearing, helped expedite the development of a revolutionary—antipatriarchal—ideology in America. For example, his remark about the title of father being transferable is used to support his argument that the "Christian doctrine, which required all children to look beyond their natural parents to their heavenly parent and insisted that all men be born again into a new family and to a new father for their own salvation," was reinforced by the Lockean "definition of a true parent as one who forms a child's mind rather than one who brings that child into the world." Together, these two strains of thought "permitted colonial Christians to consider abandoning one father without having to deny either their deep-seated desire for a father surrogate in general or their self-image as children." Fliegelman's acknowledgment of such a "desire for a father surrogate," however, like a number of his other phrasings, suggests what he never names as such, the revolutionary generation's gradual assumption of a new form of—a newly defined—patriarchy. Washington, he explains, became "the embodiment of the new understanding of paternity," an "adoptive" father for the "reconstituted" national "family." His examples of the ways Washington's paternal title itself came to be "expanded" and qualified provide more specific evidence of the cultural impetus to redefinition in this era. "In the references to Washington in the last quarter of the eighteenth century," for example, the famous phrase Father of His Country "is more often to be found in one of two expanded forms: 'Father and friend of his country,' or 'Father, friend and guardian of his country.'" "As we have seen," Fliegelman explains, "by the third quarter of the eighteenth century 'father' no longer had unequivocally positive connotations, so that these complementary terms make clear the specific, Lockean nature of Washington's paternity."[46]

Thus although Fliegelman is certainly right in claiming that, "far from betraying the Revolutionary ideology, the mythologization of Washington as founding father enthroned the antipatriarchal values that made up that ideology," his following remarks typically imply a newly conceived form of patriarchal leadership: "The point is not that [Washington] is described as America's father, but rather what kind of father he is described as being. He would at last be the parent who would provide the forming example Britain had failed to provide." The primary functions of this new father figure were to inspire popular confidence rather than to command it; to inculcate good "habits" in a society still in its "forming state" and thus, like a child, still unable to regulate its own behavior; and above all, to "properly form the American mind." The *Federalist*, of course, describes in similar terms the parental functions not of Washington per se but of a class of national leaders. The purpose of instituting a representative democracy, it explains, is to "refine and enlarge the public views by passing them through the medium of a chosen body of citizens, whose wisdom may best discern the true interest of their country and whose patriotism and love of justice will be least likely to sacrifice it to temporary or partial consideration." Those chosen men thus act as "confidential guardians of the rights and liberties of the people," for "there are particular moments in public affairs when the people, stimulated by some irregular passion, or some illicit advantage, or misled by the artful misrepresentations of [self-] interested men, may call for measures which they themselves will afterwards be the most ready to lament and condemn. In these critical moments, how salutary will be the interference of some temperate and respectable body of citizens, in order to check the misguided career and to suspend the blow meditated by the people against themselves, until reason, justice, and truth can regain their authority over the public mind?"[47]

The language practices of the revolutionary generation's leading political thinkers and writers—the frequent acts of redefinition and reinterpretation that modern readers find so bothersome—represent these men's attempts to maintain a newly conceived mode of patriarchal authority over a citizenry in need of timely instruction and regulation. The *Federalist* also insists, for example, that the people's "passions ought to be controlled and regulated" by representatives of the government and that "the *means* ought to be proportioned to the *end*; the persons from whose agency the attainment of any *end* is expected ought to possess the *means* by which it is to be attained."[48] Translated into the area of language, these political axioms allowed for words to be redefined, stretched, or juggled to re-channel misdirected popular energies and effect a greater common good. Thus Jefferson would envision a natural aristocracy of "boys" educated to be "fathers" capable of carrying out the judicious redefinition of old words as new circumstances demanded. Thus Webster would include in his nationalistic schoolbooks and dictionaries definitions "calculated to impress upon young minds" their proper duties and responsibilities as new citizens. And thus Franklin, Brackenridge, and Brown, translating political ideology into didactic fictions, would portray America's first liter-ary heroes as patriotic confidence artists who used verbal artifice to main-tain order in the new patriarchy and in the new American story.

The three literary works treated in Part I dramatize very clearly the interconnected functions of language and authority in postrevolutionary America. The first two, Franklin's *Autobiography* and Brackenridge's *Mod-ern Chivalry*, assert themselves as texts self-consciously representative of the revolutionary generation's values and attitudes and thus as instructive models of patriotic—and patriarchal—endeavor. "All that has happened to you," reads the well-known fan letter from Benjamin Vaughan, which Franklin so artfully chose to include in his own text, "is also connected with the detail of the manners and situation of *a rising* people. . . . Shew then, sir, how much is to be done, *both to sons and fathers*; and invite all wise men to become like yourself"[49]—which is the equivalent of saying, to become artful readers, writers, and interpreters of texts. Begun before the actual opening of the Revolution and continued after its close, the *Autobiography* tells the new American story from the standpoint of Frank-lin's personal transformations from boy to man, son to Father, and colo-nial entrepreneur to American hero. It thereby demonstrates the transfor-mative effects of the accomplished Revolution on a model American's use of language.

Brackenridge chose to use satire in telling the new American story, but his satiric novel is similarly instructive of the patriotic uses of language.

Early on he announces, tongue-in-cheek, that "this work is intended as a model or rule of good writing"; later, "I hope to see it made a school book." It soon becomes clear, however, that what he hopes to teach is not just "writing" but a variety of language "arts"—including "counterfeiting" and judicious prevaricating—which he archly presents as the necessary means for maintaining a patriarchal social order in the new nation. "There is nothing so difficult as to manage the public mind," readers are taught; thus they "deserve . . . praise, who by study and reflection, have rendered themselves capable of managing the minds of men."[50] Written during the trying first years of the American experiment, *Modern Chivalry* is virtually a training manual, aimed at producing an educated elite. It argues, with more urgency than the *Autobiography*, that language must be used artfully, as a system of psychological checks and balances, if the stability of the state is to be preserved.

Jacques Ehrmann has theorized that when "a revolution storms a country," "those who direct it must guide it through two successive stages: the first, political, must raise the level of instruction of the masses. . . . The second, literary, stage is the province of the artists of the new society, whose job it is to create a new art."[51] Charles Brockden Brown's novel *Wieland; or, The Transformation: An American Tale* is truly representative of such new art. Born in Philadelphia in 1771, the same year Franklin began his memoirs, and later to become an acquaintance and admirer of the aging patriot, Brown was in fact one of those "instructed" by the revolutionary generation during the first stage of postwar Americanization, and his Gothic version of the new American story shows the effects of that cultural indoctrination.[52] In *Wieland*, the fate of a family is metaphorically and didactically linked with the fate of the new nation, and the art of interpretation has become a necessity, indeed, a survival skill. The moment-to-moment survival of the narrator-daughter of this "American Tale"—and the survival, or continuity, of the tale itself—depends upon her ability to use language judiciously and artfully, as her father and the other male authority figures in her life have taught her.

The second major characteristic of these early American fictions is nowhere more obvious than in Brown's Gothic stress on the precarious nature of such verbal control strategies. Viewed in sequence, these three works reveal a growing sense of urgency, a growing need to maintain an enlightened, rational social order in a world increasingly threatened by counterproductive factions and passions, and the conflict is revealed not only in individual language transactions within the texts but finally within the narrative forms themselves. In each text, the surface narrative, the orderly rendering of what I have called the new American story, sets out to promote the revolutionary generation's patriarchal world view, but it is inevitably threatened by opposing views and by random unforeseen events, all of which constitute an inauspicious rival narrative, a second story, that must be suppressed or defused.

Franklin's *Autobiography* is essentially made up of a series of conflicts in which Franklin's personal and political success as a wise man is effected by his knowing how to subordinate the "Objections, and Reluctances" of those who oppose his ever well-intentioned projects.[53] Franklin's interpretation of any given incident, which is dictated by his conception of how the new American story should be told, necessarily takes precedence over any other, but the more important point is that he constructs a narrative paradigm in which narrative and political precedence are equated. Any second story, including those aspects of his personal life that do not square with the heroic persona he presents as a model to American sons and fathers, must fall by the wayside.

Brackenridge's novel follows the same basic political paradigm, but whereas Franklin's narrative strategy had been to elide the story of political deviance, Brackenridge chooses to delineate that second story in exaggerated, farcical detail, to satirize it and thus to instruct his readers in politically acceptable behavior. The problem with this strategy, and with Brackenridge's novel, is that over the course of the twenty-three years in which the various volumes of *Modern Chivalry* were written, the second story seems to have become increasingly resistant to such politicized control. *Modern Chivalry* is structured as a series of picaresque incidents in which a former revolutionary war hero, traveling the roads of the new nation, repeatedly tries to maintain the new sociopolitical order by artfully instructing his less-educated countrymen in their duties as proper citizens. Each farcical incident is followed by didactic authorial observations on the specific political issues involved. In the early sections of the novel, the authorial persona speaks confidently, in discrete, parenthetical "chapters." In the latter sections, however, in which the hero's language of social control repeatedly fails to perform that function, Brackenridge's authorial voice intrudes defensively and rapaciously to correct the folly of Americans who will not be counseled by wise leadership, and at times the novel's form degenerates to the point of having one paragraph of plot to six of ad hoc commentary and interpretation. The formal disintegration of *Modern Chivalry* thus speaks as loudly as its content of what the revolutionary generation perceived to be the ever-present threat of failed authority, and despite Brackenridge's best efforts to the contrary, the second story establishes itself in this early novel as an ever-present problem for the American author.

Brown's fiction takes up that problem where Brackenridge left off, and if he does not actually resolve the conflict between surface narrative and second story, he deftly maintains a precarious balance between them with an artistry that critics have yet to acknowledge fully. *Wieland*'s narrator, Clara, is beset by a series of unexpected and ghastly events, and her task is to maintain order in her mind, in her household, and in her narrative. To do so, she must negotiate between the many fictitious stories told by family, friends, and enemies, using the language skills she has learned from the various father figures in her life. In other words, she must learn to interpret those conflicting stories in her own best interests, an act that requires her to accept some versions of reality and suppress others, not according to any belief in literal "truth" but according to the survival requirements of any given moment. She does survive, with her sanity intact, to establish a happier household and to append a happier ending to a narrative that first appears to have ended in despair, and so her interpretive skills in this national allegory are promoted as those of the model American. Moreover, because we are made to witness the urgent and continuous reworking of her surface narrative, we are ever reminded of the need to defuse any second story that threatens the desired narrative—or sociopolitical—order.

ᚴ I

A Fatherly "Character": Franklin's *Autobiography*

There is certainly nothing out of the ordinary about an autobiographer beginning his work with a brief genealogy as a backdrop for the central identity about to emerge, rather like pulling out the family album to show which physical traits can be traced back through the generations. Indeed, at the beginning of his narrative Benjamin Franklin reinforces in his son-reader this tendency to seek out familial correspondences by reminding him, at the end of a short sketch of Franklin's Uncle Thomas, "The Account we receiv'd of his Life and Character from some old People at Ecton, I remember struck you, as something extraordinary from its Similarity to what you knew of mine. Had he died on the same Day, you said [referring to Thomas's death four years to the day before his famous nephew's birth], one might have suppos'd a Transmigration."[1]

What distinguishes the *Autobiography*, both as an artful self-portrait and as a literary work thematically structured according to pre- and post-revolutionary concerns with the language of fathers, is the extent to which Franklin characterizes his relatives not by physical or even personality traits so much as by verbal ones. Readers come to know the various generations of his family by their mastery of language skills and are made to witness how, in Franklin's view, their lesser or greater sociopolitical authority is determined by the way they use texts. In Part One, written on the eve of the Revolution (1771) and addressed to his natural son William, Franklin didactically portrays the youthful false starts and successes of an insurgent son trying to establish an autonomous identity, and this trial-and-error process of establishing independence serves as a consistent metaphor for a son's determination to acquire more and better language skills than his ancestors'. In the three sections written after the Revolution (in 1784, 1788, and 1789–90) and addressed, as the fan letters from Abel James and Benjamin Vaughan attest, to his nationalized family, *"both to sons and fathers"* (p. 136) of the new republic, Franklin characterizes himself as a new type of father figure, increasingly secure in his authority by virtue of his now artful reading, writing, and interpreting of texts.

To say that the *Autobiography* exhibits thematic continuity, however, is not to say that it achieves formal unity. The last distinguishing feature of this text is that it lacks wholeness: it does not tell the whole story, either of the man or of the times. In making his life history into a model for other American wise men to follow, Franklin repeatedly chooses to gloss over any counterevidence that would undermine his exemplary self-portrayal or his confident promotion of political ideology. In the process, his authentic self gets lost beneath a carefully fabricated public persona, and the views of any who oppose his political endeavors are expediently subordinated or suppressed so as to dramatize his politically astute use of language and texts. Thus the politics of language he promotes throughout results finally in a politics of form as well, for readers are left with a disturbing sense that Franklin's artfully contrived surface narrative has an underside, a second, more authentic story that has not been told.

A number of critics have pointed out that Franklin's emotional ambivalence toward his own father can be traced in the *Autobiography*, especially in his search for parental surrogates and role models after he left home.[2] But readers encounter three father figures before Josiah Franklin effectively enters the picture, each allotted a goodly amount of filial admiration and yet each, to judge by the details Franklin saw fit to include, displaying authorial limitations that he himself refused to inherit. The first two are Josiah's older brothers, Thomas and Benjamin.

"Thomas was bred a Smith under his Father, but being ingenious, and encourag'd in Learning . . . by an Esquire Palmer then the principal Gentleman in that Parish, he qualify'd for the Business of Scrivener, became a considerable Man in the County Affairs, was a chief Mover of all publick Spirited Undertakings, for the County, or Town of Northhampton and his own Village, of which many Instances were told us at Ecton and he was much taken Notice of and patroniz'd by the then Lord Halifax" (p. 47). Although his admirable (and apparently renowned) public role and his good fortune at being befriended by "principal" gentlemen serve to introduce thematic familial correspondences and seem to justify young William's witticism regarding a transmigration, Thomas's being a mere scrivener, a copier of others' writings, surely must have limited his stature in the eyes of a nephew intent on pointing out that, though he too had started out as a public-spirited printer, "Prose Writing . . . was a principal Means of my Advancement" (p. 60). Moreover, the inclusion of William's remark suggests that what the son knew of his father's political modus operandi, based heavily on invention or even paraphrase rather than mere imitation, was itself limited and in need of the fatherly instruction the *Autobiography* was intended to provide: "Imagining it may be . . . agreeable to you to know the Circumstances of *my* Life, many of which you are yet unacquainted with," Franklin had said in his opening paragraph, "I sit down to write them for you" (p. 43).[3]

A careful reader—and we can assume Franklin hoped his son would be one—can see that another of Franklin's uncles was a more likely candidate for the role of kindred spirit. The presence of the elder Benjamin, not Thomas, pervades the early pages of the *Autobiography* as an early version, perhaps an uncorrected first edition, of his more famous namesake. Uncle Benjamin was, like Thomas, "an ingenious Man" (p. 48) and "also much of a Politician." That he came to live with his Boston relations when Franklin was a boy and that he enjoyed "a particular Affection" (p. 49) from Josiah establishes him as the stronger and more immediate influence on his nephew. He "lived in the House with us some Years" (p. 48), Franklin states, and he fulfilled several paternal functions that are stressed as positive fatherly attributes throughout the book, but particularly in those sections, written after the Revolution, in which Franklin actively publicizes himself as a father figure.

Uncle Benjamin was, for example, a fairly prolific author, or at least producer, of texts (the qualification will become clear in a moment), compared to either Thomas or Josiah: "He left behind him two Quarto Volumes, M.S. of his own Poetry"; "many Volumes" of sermons which he had taken down in a shorthand of his own design; and "8 Vols. Folio, and 24 in 4to and 8vo" of "a Collection he had made of all the principal Pamphlets relating to Publick Affairs from 1641 to 1717" (pp. 48–49). Uncle Benjamin's persistence in writing poetry would likely have made him an attractive alternative authority figure to a young boy whose father had discouraged him from the same indulgence "by ridiculing my Performances, and telling me Verse-makers were generally Beggars" (p. 60) (although Franklin's maturing and ever more practical eye could not have escaped noticing that the poet-uncle had been reduced to living off his relatives). Regardless of the ambivalence that might have been generated by his verse-making, Uncle Benjamin is portrayed as a generous parental presence who perhaps gave better than he knew, for he "left behind" not only books but ways of thinking about books, ingenious models for the use of both texts and language in general.[4] For example, he showed his nephew that texts were to be used as guidance and even as a sort of practical insurance for future generations, as virtual models for future endeavors, as evidenced in Franklin's remark that, when his father had intended him for the ministry, "My Uncle Benjamin . . . propos'd to give me all his Shorthand Volumes of Sermons I suppose as a Stock to set up with, if I would learn his Character" (p. 53).

His "Character" refers to the older man's system of shorthand, but it is an intriguing phrase, considering how consistently Uncle Benjamin's actual character is portrayed in the *Autobiography* in relation to his interest in transforming or manipulating texts for some utilitarian purpose and considering how well Franklin would learn such verbal character traits. The inventive shorthand, which allowed the uncle to change the appearance, the literality, of a text and then to use the transformed version as he saw fit (in the one case we know of, as a model for future improvement), prefigures the many instances in which Franklin describes himself transforming a text for some "useful" purpose. The first instance occurs when the young Franklin sets out to better his writing style with paraphrasing exercises, initially trying to recreate *Spectator* articles from memory. "But I found I wanted a Stock of Words," he says, "which I thought I should have acquir'd before that time, if I had gone on making Verses"; the comment suggests Franklin's tendency to measure himself against his namesake. To improve his own "stock," he takes to more methodical and more artful transformations: "Therefore I took some . . . Tales and turn'd them into Verse: And after a time, when I had pretty well forgotten the Prose, turn'd them back again" (p. 62). His verbal ingenuity is not limited to paraphrasing, however, for thereafter we see him engaged in what can only be called pragmatic acts of forgery and counterfeiting: "Being still a Boy, and suspecting that my Brother would object to printing any Thing of mine in his Paper if he knew it to be mine, I contriv'd to disguise my Hand, and writing an anonymous Paper I put it in at Night under the Door of the Printing House. . . . I wrote and convey'd in the same Way to the Press several more Papers, which were equally approv'd" (pp. 67–68).[5] Later, he transcribes a piece written by his friend James Ralph, "that it might appear in my own hand" (p. 91) before their fellow club members, to test in similar fashion whether its literary effect would be more or less appreciated if its author remained unknown.

The most striking image of such artifice involving a text is that of

Franklin's ancestral Bible hidden under a stool. The placement of this image, in the early pages of the *Autobiography*, establishes yet another psychological link between the two Benjamins. "Dear Son," the narrative begins, "I have ever had a Pleasure in obtaining any little Anecdotes of my Ancestors" (p. 43). Within two pages we learn that the "Notes one of my Uncles (who had the same kind of Curiosity in collecting Family Anecdotes) once put into my Hands, furnish'd me with several Particulars relating to our Ancestors" (p. 45), and two paragraphs later, directly after the character sketch of Uncle Benjamin, Franklin tells the story of the ingenious concealment:

> This obscure Family of ours was early in the Reformation, and continu'd Protestants thro' the Reign of Queen Mary, when they were sometimes in Danger of Trouble on Account of their Zeal against Popery. They had got an English Bible, and to conceal and secure it, it was fastned open with Tapes under and within the Frame of a Joint Stool. When my Great Great Grandfather read in it to his Family, he turn'd up the Joint Stool upon his Knees, turning over the Leaves then under the Tapes. One of the Children stood at the Door to give Notice if he saw the Apparitor coming, who was an Officer of the Spiritual Court. In that Case the Stool was turn'd down again upon its feet, when the Bible remain'd conceal'd under it as before. This Anecdote I had from my Uncle Benjamin. [p. 50]

If this story reveals in uncle and nephew "the same kind of Curiosity" regarding family history, it likewise suggests a shared interest in how a text authorizing subversive or corrective principles of action might be concealed under a utilitarian facade.

In a variety of instances in the *Autobiography* Franklin shows himself manipulating texts—putting a new face on them, as it were—to subvert the governing authorities. His submitting articles in a disguised hand to his brother-guardian's newspaper loosely fits this pattern. Although we might reasonably expect to find such a stress on subversion in the prerevolutionary section of 1771, in which Franklin addresses his son (who would turn out to be a Loyalist) on the virtues of a son's rebelling against restrictive patriarchal authority, the most stress and the most detailed analysis of the continuing need for subversive texts appear in the sections written after the war's end. One might argue that since the chronology of events in the remaining sections had not progressed as far as the Revolution, the work breaking off around the year 1760, Franklin was still dwelling on the means by which the Revolution was brought about. But if we accept, as most contemporary readers do, the notion that the latter parts of the

Autobiography are intended as future-oriented exemplum rather than ret-
rospective private narrative,[6] that they provide, as in Vaughan's words, for
"the forming of future great men" in the newly constituted republic—"the
wisest man will receive lights and improve his progress, by seeing detailed
the conduct of another wise man" (p. 136)—then how are we to explain
why, in these sections, Franklin increasingly details his skill in manipulating texts, a skill apparently to be inculcated in "a *rising* people" (p. 135) and
yet one "learned" from his father's politically unregenerate generation?

One example from Part Three, which was begun only a month after the
Constitution was officially adopted, will suffice to show just how master-
ful he had become in his craft of concealment. In tricking his brother into
publishing his articles, he had merely contrived to change the surface
appearance of his writing. After the Revolution, he presents himself
artfully concealing the intended meaning of his text under cover of equivocal words carefully chosen from his greatly improved "stock." Reminisc-
ing about the opposition he had encountered from Quakers when, as a
member of the Philadelphia fire company, he had tried to raise defense
funds for buying guns, he sets the scene for his own heroic verbal ploy
with a chaffing anecdote about the Pennsylvania Assembly, "the Majority
of which were constantly Quakers" (p. 188). Whenever ordered by the
crown to help subsidize military expenses, they were "unwilling to offend
Government on the one hand, by a direct Refusal, and their Friends the
Body of Quakers on the other, by a Compliance contrary to their Principles. Hence a Variety of Evasions to avoid Complying, and Modes of
disguising the Compliance when it became unavoidable. The common
Mode at last was to grant Money under the Phrase of its being *for the
King's use*, and never to enquire how it was applied" (p. 189). Playing on
this theme of embarrassment to the Quakers and stressing his own skill at
one-upmanship, Franklin describes the verbal artifice he engineered to
subvert the Quaker antiweapon faction in the fire company: "Let us move
the Purchase of a Fire Engine," he persuaded a comrade; "the Quakers can
have no Objection to that: and then if you nominate me, and I you, as a
Committee for that purpose, we will buy a great Gun, which is certainly a
Fire-Engine." Characteristically, Franklin allows us to see his authority
admired by including his friend's response to the proposal: "I see, says he,
you have improv'd by being so long in the Assembly; your equivocal
Project would be just a Match" for the Quakers' own verbal machinations
(pp. 189–90).

Insofar as Franklin has contextualized his trick as a didactic anecdote and was unquestionably proficient in acquiring the tricks of his political trade, the man's remark has merit—and indeed is exemplary of the desired audience suggestibility. Nevertheless, readers of the earlier pages of the *Autobiography* can see in this act of concealing a "great Gun" under a "Fire-Engine" the instructive influence of Uncle Benjamin and ironic evidence that that influence was double-edged. The various images of textual transformation and concealment throughout the book, coupled with the suggestive details used to sketch his artful "Character," bespeak Uncle Benjamin's status as a positive fatherly role model by virtue of his authorial aspirations and inclinations. However inspirational, though, his literary authority was also perceived by his nephew to be limited, for the early character sketch is riddled with diminutives, images of substantive lack, and—if we have learned to read Franklin's own "Character"—a sense of his uncle's marginal effectiveness in the sociopolitical realm. We are told, for example, that Uncle Benjamin's poetry consisted of "*little* occasional Pieces address'd to his Friends" (my emphasis). He was more often, like Thomas, a mere copyist and a collector of others' writings, ultimately leaving a less than substantial bequest to his posterity, for in the collection of pamphlets that fell into Franklin's hands, many of "the Volumes are wanting, as appears by the Numbering." The last we hear of Uncle Benjamin's literary output is of "his Notes in the Margins" of other authors' works (pp. 48–50). If Franklin's fire-engine ruse "improv'd" on the assembly's stylistic model, it improved no less on his uncle's, for it demonstrates for the large readership Franklin would rightly envision how he effected his own transmigration from merely literary to sociopolitical authority by his artful use of texts.

The theme of authority, the dual issue of how to articulate it and how to secure it, appears more explicitly foregrounded in the portrait of the third paternal figure encountered in the opening pages. That portrait begins: "My Mother [Josiah's] 2d Wife was Abiah Folger, a Daughter of Peter Folger, one of the first Settlers of New England, of whom honourable mention is made by Cotton Mather, in his Church History of that Country, (entitled Magnalia Christi Americana) as a *godly learned Englishman*, if I remember the words rightly" (p. 51). The subordination and qualification in this sentence suggest Franklin's psychological placement, or displacement, of his grandfather in relation to himself, and the sense of an Oedipally tinged authorial displacement is reinforced by his appropriation of Mather's authority, ostensibly in praise of Folger. That is, if we accept Edward Said's definition that "quotation is a constant reminder that writing is a form of displacement," that "always, even when in the form of a passing allusion, it is a reminder that other writing serves to displace present writing, to a greater or lesser extent, from its absolute, central, proper place";[7] and if we note Franklin's substitution of "manly" for Mather's *"godly"* in praising Folger's qualities, a few sentences later, we can more readily see how the 1771 section of the *Autobiography* is informed by the struggle to establish a new literary authority and by a determination to usurp—to improve upon—the paternal power of naming.

The act of naming and the limited temporal effect of his act are what characterize Peter Folger. Franklin's description of him contains the same strains of praise and diminution seen previously: he was another public-spirited poet, turning out "homespun Verse" condemning government excesses and "written with a good deal of Decent Plainness and manly Freedom." But "he wrote sundry small occasional Pieces, [and] only one of them was printed." More important to our understanding of his unique thematic significance is the included sample of his work (limping lines, to be sure), and Franklin's introductory comment:

> The six last concluding Lines I remember, tho' I have forgotten the two first of the Stanza, but the Purport of them was that his Censures proceeded from *Goodwill*, and therefore he would be known to be the Author,
>> because to be a Libeller, (says he)
>>> I hate it with my Heart.
>> From Sherburne Town where now I dwell,
>>> My Name I do put here,
>> Without Offence, your real Friend,
>>> It is Peter Folgier. [pp. 51–52]

Thereafter throughout Part One Franklin presents his own experiments with naming and its figurative link with his inquiry into the various effects of literary authority.[8]

On one hand, as we have seen, his youthful acts of forgery and counterfeiting, pragmatic tests of whether a text might produce a more favorable effect on its audience if the name of the author were suppressed, both meet with resounding success and thus serve to rebuff his grandfather's old-fashioned sense of obligatory self-assertion. On the other hand, however, there are instances when Franklin's name is either given or taken away, and with it, his "manly Freedom." During his apprenticeship to his brother, for example, James's outspokenness evokes the assembly's censure and the order *"that James Franklin should no longer print the Paper called the New England Courant."* Although James, his friends, and his brother originally decide to "evade the Order by changing the Name of the Paper," they finally conclude, "as a better Way, to let it be printed for the future under the Name of *Benjamin Franklin"* (p. 69), contriving to make the apprentice-brother appear as a free agent. The anecdote demonstrates the unsatisfactory contrast between sociopolitical and mere literary authority. Franklin obediently trades one for the other, signing new indentures, "which were to be kept private," but eventually learns his lesson: "At length . . . I took upon me to assert my Freedom" (p. 70). Later in Part One, during his stay in England, James Ralph also takes his name, which apparently leaves Franklin with no "manly" authority whatsoever. Ralph solicits but refuses Franklin's aesthetic and practical advice regarding his poetic endeavors; a very bad epic poem comes into the world, weakly authored by an untalented "Benjamin Franklin"; and when Franklin, thinking to assume Ralph's identity in repayment for his own, attempts "Familiarities" with the man's mistress, his overtures are "repuls'd with a proper Resentment" (pp. 98–99).

If one of the thematic frames for the 1771 section is Franklin's search for the knowledge of when and how to use his name and, by extension, for a personal literary authority—an art of naming—that would have more practical and lasting effect in the sociopolitical realm, the postrevolutionary sections reveal the successful culmination of that search. Peter Folger's power of naming was hardly effective and, as Franklin twice suggests, barely memorable, despite his cameo appearance in another man's book. In contrast, in the 1784 section of the *Autobiography* Franklin shows how he established the first of many lasting monuments to his own ingenuity and how much he had improved on his grandfather's model for securing the public good by knowing when *not* to use his name. Although he mentions his "first Project of a public Nature" (p. 130) at the end of Part One, Franklin fittingly begins Part Two, which marks the change from private narrative to exemplum, by didactically stressing "the means [he] used to establish the Philadelphia publick Library" (p. 141):

> The Objections, and Reluctances I met with in Soliciting the Subscriptions, made me soon feel the Impropriety of presenting one's self as the Proposer of any useful Project that might be suppos'd to raise one's Reputation in the smallest degree above that of one's Neighbours, when one has need of their Assistance to accomplish that Project. I therefore put my self as much as I could out of sight, and stated it as a Scheme of a *Number*

of Friends, who had requested me to go about and propose it. . . . In this way my Affair went on more smoothly, and I ever after practis'd it on such Occasions; and from my frequent Successes, can heartily recommend it. [p. 143]

The moral is drawn in pragmatic terms: "The present little Sacrifice of your Vanity will afterwards be amply repaid" (p. 143). But the larger lesson here concerns the need for a revised rhetoric in a newly democratized society. Franklin's anecdote illustrates the postrevolutionary response to language discussed previously: a heightened awareness of the benefits derived from defining a situation loosely, with an eye to the future and to the public good; of the power inherent in collectively sanctioned naming; and of the need for authority figures to guide and instruct people in the ad hoc language of democratic community and cooperation. The verbal model Franklin provides for his readers is a far cry from that of his grandfather, who "would be known" for his good intentions, and it bespeaks a revolutionized sense of the new role to be enacted by learned authority figures. By 1788 Franklin tells us it had become his "usual Rule" to "[avoid] as much as I could . . . the presenting myself to the Publick as the Author of any Scheme for their Benefit" (p. 193).

The preliminary genealogy of fatherly relations and the catalog of their limited authorial successes thus introduce the theme of "manly" verbal improvement which informs Part One of the *Autobiography* and which takes on a more heavily national significance in the later sections. The three character sketches also set the scene for Franklin's presentation of his natural father, Josiah, and they suggest the criteria by which the father's relationship to his son may be judged. Josiah provides the most important model against which Franklin shows himself measuring his own accomplishments, and although the elder Franklin's limited and limiting vision comes across as a thematic foil to his son's inventive and pragmatic bent, nevertheless the man's virtues are precisely those assumed by Franklin in the postrevolutionary sections of his text.[9]

Apparently, like everyone else in the family, Josiah was "ingenious," but "his great Excellence lay in a sound Understanding, and solid Judgment in prudential Matters, both in private and publick Affairs," and in particular, in "his being frequently visited by leading People, who consulted him for his Opinion in Affairs of the Town or of the Church he belong'd to and show'd a good deal of Respect for his Judgment and Advice. He was also much consulted by private Persons about their Affairs when any Difficulty occur'd, and frequently chosen an Arbitrator between contending Parties" (pp. 54–55). Franklin's real-life successes as advice giver and mediator are, of course, legendary and need no enumeration. What is significant is his artful choice to exemplify those talents, in his postwar self-presentation, in terms that recall Josiah's "great Excellence" and thus establish Franklin's public role as a fatherly one. He depicts himself, like Josiah, as "being frequently visited by leading People"—of the church, in the person of the Rev. Gilbert Tennent, who ironically asks his advice on matters not ecclesiastical but financial (pp. 201–2); of the colonial government (e.g., Governor Morris, pp. 230–31); and even of the international political community (e.g., Lord Mansfield, p. 266). Lest any sluggish readers have missed his point, he communicates it vicariously yet explicitly in the remark of another of the colonial governors that Franklin was "one who was capable of giving him the best Advice" (p. 246). Franklin does for a rising people what Josiah had done so admirably within his own comparatively limited sphere, only better, on a grander scale. And not the least part of Josiah's paternal excellence consisted of his ability to give his son the sound literary advice that would lead to self-improvement.

Early in Part One, Franklin tells how his father had read some of his letters to a friend with whom he was engaged in a literary debating exercise and how Josiah, without entering into the "Discussion" (i.e., the content), had cautioned his son about the "Manner" of his writing, pointing out places in which Franklin "fell far short in elegance of Expression, in Method and in Perspicuity." "I saw the Justice of his Remarks," Franklin explains, "and thence grew more attentive to the *Manner* in Writing, and determin'd to endeavour at Improvement" (p. 61). Immediately follow his attempts at paraphrasing *Spectator* articles and transforming verse into prose and back. He learns the value of having a variety of "Words of the same Import but of different Length . . . or of different Sound" to reinterpret a fixed content, the mastery of which renders him "lucky enough to improve the Method or the Language" without changing the purpose of the original text (p. 62). Next, still "intent on improving [his] Language," he meets with the book that will instruct him in the Socratic method that will be of such "great Advantage" to him throughout his career. Although he first uses it to become "very artful and expert in drawing People even of superior Knowledge into Concessions the Consequences of which they did not foresee," he claims that he eventually left off the sheer ego satisfaction of the method, as he would later leave off his name, "retaining only the Habit of expressing my self in Terms of modest Diffidence, never using when I advance any thing that may possibly be disputed, the Words, *Certainly, undoubtedly*, or any others that give the Air of Positiveness to an Opinion; but rather say, I conceive, or I apprehend a Thing to be so or so, It appears to me, or I should think it so or so for such and such Reasons, or I imagine it to be so, or it is so if I am not mistaken" (pp. 64–65). After mentioning his numerous subsequent successes in group persuasion, he finally passes on to his son-reader stylistic advice similar to that his father had given him: "If you would *inform*, a positive dogmatical Manner in advancing your Sentiments, may provoke Contradiction and prevent a candid Attention. If you wish Information and Improvement from the Knowledge of others and yet at the same time express your self as firmly fix'd in your present Opinions, modest sensible Men, who do·not love Disputation, will probably leave you undisturb'd in the Possession of your Error; and by such a Manner you can seldom hope to recommend your self . . . or to persuade those whose Concurrence you desire" (p. 65).

Franklin's reenactment, and thus validation, of Josiah's father authority in Part One is closely paralleled in the later sections by his continued stylistic advice-giving to the "future great men" of the new republic. In the former pages, careful attention to style makes the man; in the latter, it makes the "wise man," the model American. Franklin urges the same attention, not to the "so and so" of content but to the mode of verbal expression when, at the end of Part Two, he again describes himself avoiding the "Use of every Word or Expression . . . that imported a fix'd Opinion; such as *certainly, undoubtedly*, &c." and adopting, "instead of them, *I conceive, I apprehend*, or *I imagine* a thing to be so or so" (p. 159). He attributes to his development of "this Mode" the fact that "I had early so much Weight with my Fellow Citizens . . . and so much Influence in public Councils"—and here the artfully "humble . . . Doubter" of Part One resurfaces (p. 64)—"for I was but a bad Speaker, never eloquent, subject to much Hesitation in my choice of Words, hardly correct in Language, and yet I generally carried my Points" (p. 160).

Twentieth-century scholarship may well continue to be frustrated by its ability to find "fix'd Opinions" and precise definitions in texts of the postrevolutionary era, but it should scarcely be surprised by the dilemma, considering the representative "Character" of this Founding Father, who generously admits to being "hardly correct" in his language and as generously advises his contemporary readers on how they might become hardly correct in their own. In 1784, estranged from the Loyalist William and reportedly esteeming Thomas Paine as "his adopted political son,"[10] Franklin had begun his new section of the *Autobiography* by stressing for his many son-readers the "means" by which he established the Philadelphia Public Library, achieving a fixed, publicly beneficial goal by submerging his "correct" name beneath the more politically acceptable guise of "a *Number of Friends*." He thus appropriates and enlarges upon Josiah's paternal role as provider of proper education and transforms his personal success story into a primer of politicized discourse for other "wise men" to follow.

Josiah's role in the *Autobiography* is linked even more specifically to the theme of literary authority, for although he had personally advised Franklin on the virtues of improved verbal expression, Josiah had also instructed his son from a text on style intended to articulate and inculcate binding communal values. His paternal function in this capacity is brought to our attention, appropriately, near the beginning of Part Two, where Franklin recalls his father's having, "among his Instructions to me when a Boy, frequently repeated a Proverb of Solomon, '*Seest thou a Man diligent in his Calling, he shall stand before Kings, he shall not stand before mean Men* [22:29]'" (p. 144). The father's choice of text and the son's authorial decision to recall it are, as ever in the *Autobiography*, multiply useful for promoting Franklin's vision of transformed authority.

Josiah's link with the wise Solomon's Book of Proverbs suggests, first, Franklin's revised—improved—opinion of his father's instructive role and, by extension, of the value of paternal role-modeling in the postrevolutionary era. In Part One, for example, Josiah had been cast more as a David, "the sweet psalmist of Israel" (2 Samuel 23:1), beloved servant of God but father of a much wiser son, for Franklin characterizes his deeply religious father as having had "a clear pleasing Voice, so that when he play'd Psalm Tunes . . . and sung withal . . . it was extreamly agreable to hear" (p. 54). If at times in that section Franklin seems more figuratively to be playing the fugitive Absalom than the wiser son Solomon to his father's David, nevertheless the Oedipal ambivalence is significantly lessened in Parts Two and Three, where Franklin historically upgrades Josiah's role to that of the giver of proverbial wisdom and then reenacts that role himself. In Part Two, directly after recalling Josiah's proverbial advice, Franklin validates that mode of instruction by giving "an English Proverb"—"He that would thrive / Must ask his Wife"—to introduce the virtues of having a wife "dispos'd to Industry and Frugality" (pp. 144–45). And early in Part Three the new Founding Father describes the genesis of his own Americanized book of proverbs, *Poor Richard's Almanack*, as "a proper Vehicle for conveying Instruction among the common People, who bought scarce any other Books" (p. 164).

The *Almanack* stands as an overt parallel to Josiah's earlier guidebook, but readers aware of the many submerged texts in the *Autobiography* may suspect that just as Franklin has assumed his father's mode of advice-giving, so has he modeled the present work on his father's chosen text. Solomon's section of the Book of Proverbs is framed as advice to his sons from a man carrying on a tradition of patriarchal instruction: "Hear, ye children, the instruction of a father, and attend to know understand-ing. . . . I give you good doctrine . . . for I was my father's son. . . . He taught me also, and said unto me, Let thine heart retain my words" (4:1–4). Solomon's text, like Franklin's, is intended to "give subtlety to the simple, to the young man knowledge and discretion": "A wise man will hear, and will increase learning; and a man of understanding shall attain unto wise counsels" (1:4–5).

There are many ironic parallels between the two texts, as when, in the biblical version, "wisdom" is said to "dwell with prudence, and [to] find out witty inventions" (8:12). But the most significant similarity is the stress, in both, on knowing the value of "a word fitly spoken" (25:11) and the proper mode of verbal self-presentation. "Put away from thee a fro-ward mouth, and perverse lips put far from thee" (4:24); "Let another man praise thee, and not thine own mouth" (27:2); "A fool uttereth all his mind; but a wise man keepeth it in till afterwards" (29:11). Parallels in the *Autobiography* are by now self-evident. Solomon's Proverbs and Franklin's *Autobiography*, like his *Almanack*, are primers of communal style, intended to perfect and preserve a chosen people: "For the upright shall dwell in the land, and the perfect shall remain in it" (2:21).

There is substantial ironic distance, of course, between the two authors' understanding of "uprightness," an irony that is nowhere more evident than in Franklin's description of the intended use of his own "Proverbial Sentences, chiefly such as inculcated Industry and Frugality, as the Means of procuring Wealth and thereby securing Virtue, it being more difficult for a Man in Want to act always honestly, as (to use here one of those Proverbs) *it is hard for an empty Sack to stand upright*" (p. 164). "The common people," as Franklin describes *Poor Richard*'s intended reader-ship, long accustomed to biblical rhetoric, might too often have missed such ironic transformations and taken "Richard Saunders's" advice as a fairly literal translation of Solomon's biblical exhortation; for example,

Franklin satirized such common readers in "The Way to Wealth," in the character of the backward-looking and ineffectual Father Abraham.[11] But the postrevolutionary sections of the *Autobiography* are addressed to the "wise men" of the new republic, those more attuned to a future-oriented rhetoric of ideology defined by one critic as "a structuring of the present according to 'ideas' that represented a distant future goal."[12] Although the duplicity of Franklin's "Character" would still enable him to reach both audiences, we may assume that he intended the more literate to see that he had transformed his father's chosen text into a distinctly American guidebook just as he had previously Americanized "the Wisdom of many Ages and Nations" (p. 164) in his almanacs.

One important clue to such readers would have been Franklin's obvious improvement upon his father's literary and sociopolitical authority, specifying what had only been generalized guidelines when Josiah had advised him to be "*a Man diligent in his Calling*," that such a man "*shall stand before Kings*." "I did not think that I should ever literally stand before Kings," Franklin diligently records, "which however has since happened.—for I have stood before five, and even had the honour of sitting down with one, the King of Denmark, to Dinner" (p. 144). Franklin's wit does not obscure his meaning; if anything, it highlights it. Placed in the opening pages of the 1784 section, this statement shows "*both to sons and fathers*," as Benjamin Vaughan had hoped, "how much is to be done" (p. 136), personally and nationally, to secure a prosperous future.

It suggests, on one hand, the revolutionary principle that had become so important to the young nation, that successive generations of sons have the right to reinterpret the authority—and the texts—of their fathers in their own interests and, as in Franklin's dealings with kings, in the interest of national prosperity. On the other, it demonstrates that wise fathers are capable of giving better than they can possibly know. The function of the father is to give texts, establish formalized guidelines, and authorize the means for improvement. The son's role is to recreate those texts by reinterpreting and improving them to meet the exigencies of a future the father could never have foreseen.[13] Three years after writing this passage Franklin would be one of that famous group of Fathers who would formalize these attitudes toward ongoing authority, in behalf of future generations, in the text of the Constitution. His stress in 1784 on his improved use of Josiah's text suggests a small-scale promotion of the later document's conceptual framework, for as Arendt has reminded us, "in the American republic the function of authority . . . consists in interpretation." "The very authority of the American Constitution resides in its inherent capacity to be amended and augmented."[14]

That "inherent capacity" could have been conceived and created only by minds that were highly skilled in the art of interpretation and conceived of that art as a means of establishing an unprecedented and enduring system of government, one stabilized by the priority of a controlling text, energized by the adaptability of that text's open-ended significations, and administered, guided into the future, by an educated elite. Franklin's "Character" in the *Autobiography*, his stylized self-presentation, is throughout representative of that revolutionary generation of thinkers and its growing investment, especially between 1771 and 1790, in the language skills needed to establish and maintain a new mode of sociopolitical authority. His successful reinterpretation of his father's chosen text functions merely as a symbolic turning point in a book largely devoted to promoting the development of such verbal proficiency, for Parts One through Four are linked by a thematic progression of verbal skills which structures the multiple transformations of Franklin's personae—from boy to man, son to Father, colonial entrepreneur to American hero—and effects an enlarged scope of authority in each new role.[15] This structural progression also suggests that although, as the well-known marginal note indicates, the "Affairs of the Revolution occasion'd the Interruption" of the *Autobiography*'s composition (p. 133), those affairs had only heightened Franklin's already keen sense of the "politics of literacy."[16] When he took up his pen in 1784, the experience of the accomplished Revolution seems to have focused his attention more specifically on the ultimate goal of educating wise men in the Americanized art of interpretation.

We have seen Franklin acting very much like his father, assuming in Parts Two and Three those beneficial functions Josiah had performed for him, giving model texts and useful advice on style in general. But we have also seen how much he improves on those functions, and his more far-reaching authority in these instances is portrayed as a direct result of his having acquired more and better language skills than his father and his father's generation. Reading is the first of these skills, and in Part One, where Franklin is intent on showing how he differed from his father, reading is consistently metaphorized as a means to enlarged personal and political self-sufficiency and advancement.

Early on, he writes that "From a Child I was fond of Reading, and all the little Money that came into my Hands was ever laid out in Books" (p. 57). Thereafter he proves the benefits accruing from such sound investments. His reading results twice in improved health, once when he meets with a book "recommending a Vegetable Diet," and trying it, finds that he not only saves food money (which he invests in more books) and eating time (which he invests in more study), but he also acquires "that greater Clearness of Head and quicker Apprehension which usually attend Temperance in Eating and Drinking" (p. 63). The second instance is more closely linked with his growing ability to outrun his father's authority. On the boat taking him from Boston, he had become "very feverish," but, he recalls, "having read somewhere that cold Water drank plentifully was good for a Fever, I follow'd the Prescription" (p. 73), quickly revived, and was able to continue his flight to Philadelphia. Reading is also connected with self-defense, as when, during his flight, he is saved from being arrested as a suspected runaway servant by an innkeeper, a retired doctor, who, "finding I had read a little, became very sociable and friendly" (pp. 73–74); and with the sociopolitical preferment that would so frequently further Franklin's career: "The then Governor of N[ew] York . . . hearing from the Captain that a young Man . . . had a great many Books, desired he would bring me to see him. . . . The Governor treated me with great Civility, show'd me his Library, which was a very large one, and we had a good deal of Conversation about Books and Authors" (p. 85).

If the largeness of the library and the gracious and respectful treatment from a great man mark the worldly advancement of the dedicated little reader who had spent all his pennies on books, they also are reminiscent of the Oedipal wellspring of Franklin's boyish motivation to improve his own stock of reading material. A son so "fond of Reading" must surely have felt oppressed by a father who denied him a college education and who had only a "little Library" to offer in its stead. In addition to his telling use of this diminutive, Franklin comments that he "often regretted, that at a time when I had such a Thirst for Knowledge, more proper Books had not fallen in my Way" (p. 58). The Josiah of Part One is hardly the model text-giver that he will be portrayed as in 1784. The few volumes he is said to own, consisting "chiefly of Books in polemic Divinity" (p. 58), exert a harmful influence, giving Franklin a "disputacious Turn," "a very bad Habit . . . productive of Disgusts and perhaps Enmities": "I had caught it by reading my Father's Books of Dispute about Religion" (p. 60). Franklin's career flourishes and his influence as a public speaker broadens in scope when he improves his verbal strategies, and late in the

Autobiography he expresses his rationale for verbal improvement most clearly: "Disputing, contradicting and confuting People are generally unfortunate in their Affairs" (p. 213).

Finally, the distance between Josiah's and Franklin's abilities to provide for their respective sons is masterfully delineated by the image that rounds off Part One, Franklin's "first Project of a public Nature." The "little Library" of the opening pages must be measured against "the Mother of all the N[orth] American Subscription Libraries," which are "now so numerous." And just as reading had enabled Franklin to surpass his father's authority, so has it empowered Americans to achieve their greater independence. "These Libraries," we are told, "perhaps have contributed in some degree [the lack of disputatiousness is noteworthy] to the Stand so generally made throughout the Colonies in Defence of their Privileges" (pp. 130–31).

Reading, then, functions as a metaphor for a much needed break with the past; it is the first step toward self-sufficiency, manly freedom. Writing is the next step toward a brighter future, for it is portrayed as a means of securing and improving the quality of that freedom. In Franklin's literary "shorthand," reading builds self-confidence, but writing affords the audience necessary for more active self-promotion and thus a larger influence in matters of public welfare. Franklin's famous statement that "Prose Writing has been of great Use to me in the Course of my Life, and was a principal Means of my Advancement" (p. 60) appears early in the *Autobiography* and introduces the didactic link between writing and worldly success that recurs throughout, but especially in Parts Two and Three, where the writer's intended audience becomes "*a rising* people" and success accrues to author and nation alike.

Initially, the statement serves to set Franklin apart from the paternal figures in his family and their limited literary authority. Throughout Part One Franklin experiments with his audience's response to his various acts of "naming," trying to establish a personal literary authority that will have broader sociopolitical impact. Near the end of that section, he begins to acquire the influential—and materially rewarding—literary voice that would raise him above what he had described in his opening as "the Poverty and Obscurity in which I was born and bred" (p. 43). "One of the first good Effects of [his] having learnt a little to scribble" is that because of his "spirited" articles, the *Pennsylvania Gazette*, his first bona fide newspaper, becomes a rapid success, and "leading Men, seeing a News Paper

now in the hands of one who could also handle a Pen, thought it convenient to oblige and encourage" him in his chosen career (p. 121).

The thematic movement that structures Franklin's break with his personal past in Part One, a movement from avid, acquisitive reading to his
own little experiments with verbal artifice, to the "first good Effects" of
his having learned so well how to write, is transformed in Part Two into a
program of conduct designed by a master craftsman and humbly yet stra-
tegically submitted to the fathers and sons of the new nation. Written with
a heightened postwar consciousness of the need for sociopolitical restruc-
turing and reform, Part Two equates Franklin's stature as a model American with his ability to *re*read and *re*write essential texts of the past. Beginning this section with a discussion of his founding of the public library, in
which he shows himself "rereading" the hidden springs of human motivation and thus rewriting his own script for soliciting donations, Franklin
moves to his very literal rereading of his father's religious guidebook as a
means of insinuating his international prominence as a representative
American, standing before kings; and then to an anecdote about a Presby-
terian preacher who had habitually interpreted his chosen text too nar-
rowly so as to make his listeners good Presbyterians rather than "good
Citizens." That characteristic of institutionalized religion, Franklin tells us,
had prompted him in 1728 to write his own nonsectarian "Liturgy, or form
of prayer," entitled *Articles of Belief and Acts of Religion*, and this first
example of formal and conceptual revision, of writing a new text to address the ethical duties of good citizens, leads finally to the main topic of
discussion in the 1784 section, Franklin's "bold and arduous Project of
arriving at moral Perfection" (p. 148).

Franklin stresses that his intentions in writing "The Art of Virtue" were
to provide himself and eventually his countrymen with an improved
model for ethical conduct: "Contrary Habits must be broken and good
ones acquired and established, before we can have any Dependance on a
steady uniform Rectitude of Conduct" (p. 148). Although he never completed his original plan of publishing it, his choice to give both a detailed
physical description of his own copy and an explanation of his rationale in
composing and following his new ethical code provides readers with the
original textual model and with a much larger conceptual one: "The Art
of Virtue" is a self-improvement program in which reformation of "Character" is equated with reformation of language and texts.

The first step in Franklin's program to guard "against the unremitting

Attraction of ancient Habits" (p. 150), for example, is to reinterpret ethical categories inherited from the past, specifically, to rename and redefine them: "In the various Enumerations of the moral Virtues I had met with in my Reading, I found the Catalogue more or less numerous, as different Writers included more or fewer Ideas under the same Name. . . . I pro-pos'd to myself, for the sake of Clearness, to use rather more Names with fewer Ideas annex'd to each, than a few Names with more Ideas; and I included under Thirteen Names of Virtues all that at that time occurr'd to me as necessary or desirable, and annex'd to each a short Precept, which fully express'd the Extent I gave to its Meaning" (p. 149). His emphasis on "Clearness" and on "fully express'd" meanings may seem ironic to modern readers, considering such morally ambiguous precepts as "RESOLUTION: Resolve to perform what you ought" or "SINCERITY: Use no .hurtful Deceit" (pp. 149–50). Nevertheless, the rationale for such relativistic defi-nitions is implicit in his temporal qualification, "all that at that time occurr'd to me as necessary or desirable." In other words, Franklin's method here exemplifies the time-conscious quality of postrevolutionary thinking and semantics that we have observed elsewhere: he renames a behavioral goal so as to break with past modes of thought and then gives "an extensive Meaning to the Word" (p. 159) so as to allow for a broad range of future applications. The purpose of such renaming is not to prescribe moral absolutes but to promote behavior that will facilitate so-ciopolitical harmony. We get a better sense of why he would define "sin-cerity" as the use of no "hurtful" deceit when he explains that if he did not have much success in acquiring the "*Reality*" of humility, he "had a good deal with regard to the *Appearance* of it," denying himself the "Pleasure" of egotistical and moralistic dispute, consciously modifying his language so as to avoid "every Word or Expression . . . that imported a fix'd Opin-ion" and thus smooth the way for cooperative ventures (p. 159).

Finally, the overall form of "The Art of Virtue" is as elastic as its defini-tions: it undergoes constant transformations, all in the interest of control-ling, or at least channeling, the endeavors of a flawed human nature. Franklin explains how he had first copied his precepts and tables for self-examination onto paper but eventually, to ensure durability, had inscribed them on "the Ivory Leaves of a memorandum Book," where defects, once noted, could be more "easily wipe[d] out with a wet Sponge" (p. 155). The transformation of the artifact is merely the outward manifestation of this text's inherent changeability, for the notation on any given page varies as, in the cyclical course of weekly and yearly self-evaluation, old patterns of faults are replaced by new ones. Designed to accommodate behavioral change and improvement, Franklin's "little Book" (p. 155) does so by allowing for infinite revisions, and consequently, Franklin's authority is shown to consist of his ability to rectify defects accumulated over time by renaming, rereading, and rewriting.

"The Art of Virtue" might be more accurately called "The Art of Interpreting 'Virtue,'" and that such an art and such a cavalier attitude toward literality are seen to be necessary in 1784 is evidenced in Part Two in the composite image of this project that ever remains "unfinish'd" (p. 158). "The Art of Virtue" is a future-oriented text with no foreseeable ending that allows for and encourages infinite new beginnings and new interpretations.[17] Three years later, at the Constitutional Convention, Franklin would participate with like-minded Fathers in creating a conceptually similar founding text, one that would provide, in Madison's words, "a convenient mode of rectifying [its makers'] own errors, as future experience may unfold them"[18] and that would thus be administered, in Arendt's apt phrasing, "in a kind of continuous constitution-making," that is, continuous acts of remaking and reinterpreting. And in the following year, a month after the official announcement of the Constitution's adoption, Franklin would begin the third section of his *Autobiography*, dramatizing the political usefulness of being able to interpret texts for "the people."

Part Three is framed as a series of lessons in the art of interpretation, and it becomes increasingly clear that such verbal art is synonymous with effective leadership. In 1788 the function of leadership is to instruct people, with "Discourse . . . well adapted to their Capacities" (p. 237), in the duties—and the opportunities for betterment—that befall them as "good Citizens." Franklin begins this section with the theme of writing-as-rewriting that informed Part Two, discussing a creed he had once written so as to contain "the Essentials of every known Religion" yet to exclude any sectarian trademark and stressing that his intent had been to form "a great Number of good Citizens" (pp. 162–63). He quickly moves on, however, to less spiritual, more mundane, and more practical means of educating a popular audience. He describes his almanac, which he considered a "proper Vehicle for conveying Instruction among the common People, who bought scarce any other Books" (p. 164), and next his newspaper, "another Means of Communicating Instruction" (p. 165). His reference to the untutored common people establishes his authorial role not only as an educator but as a model administrator concerned with developing strategies for administering education on a large scale. He goes on, for example, to show himself dispersing the *means* of lettered instruction, furnishing one of his journeymen with "a Press and Letters" and sending him off to a distant community "where a Printer was wanting" (p. 166). Next, he recommends an improved "Education for our young Females" (p. 166)[19] and soon after, encourages "those who superintend the Educating of our Youth" to improve "our common Mode of Teaching Languages." They must start their students off with modern tongues rather than ancient ones so that if "they should quit the Study of Languages, and never arrive at the Latin, they would however have acquir'd another Tongue or two that being in modern Use might be serviceable to them in common Life" (p. 169).

Making modern languages serviceable for the improvement of "common Life" is the lesson of this section. All of these suggestions for improving the education of the common people prepare the way for Franklin's promotion of the art of interpretation, of choosing the right language to channel popular energies into publicly beneficial projects. "My usual Custom in such Cases," he reveals, in describing his support of a scheme for procuring subscriptions to build a hospital, was "to prepare the Minds of the People by writing on the Subject in the Newspapers" (p. 200). He repeatedly uses such phrasing, apparently to instruct those would-be dogooders among his learned readership in the necessity of priming a potentially uncooperative audience, rendering it receptive to the subsequent request for its cooperation. Occasionally he gives step-by-step instruction, as in his depiction of his successful campaign for "establishing an Academy": "The first Step I took was to associate in the Design a Number of active Friends . . . : the next was to write and publish a Pamphlet intitled, *Proposals relating to the Education of Youth in Pennsylvania*. This I distributed among the principal Inhabitants gratis; and as soon as I could suppose their Minds a little prepared by the Perusal of it, I set on foot a Subscription for Opening and Supporting an Academy" (pp. 192–93). In this, as in his earlier scheme for founding the public library, he artfully creates the necessary context for cooperation, concealing his proper name as the author and presenting the proposal "not as an Act of mine, but of some *publick-spirited Gentlemen*" (p. 193). Later he shows himself as a door-to-door interpreter, first writing and printing a paper advertising the benefits of keeping the streets clean. "I sent one of these Papers to each House, and in a Day or two went round to see who would subscribe an Agreement to pay" for the service. The popular success of this venture, he adds, "made the People more willing to submit to a Tax for that purpose" (p. 203), that is, made them "good Citizens."

The most literal example of Franklin's mode of public-spirited interpretation occurs in his discussion of his role as mediator in procuring American wagons and supplies for the British troops under General Edward Braddock in 1755. To illustrate his method, he intended to incorporate two texts into his account, the primary "Advertisement," couched in legalistic terms—"Whereas 150 Waggons, with 4 Horses to each Waggon, and 1500 Saddle or Pack-Horses are wanted for the Service of his Majesty's Forces" (p. 218)—and an accompanying letter "To the Inhabitants of the Counties of Lancaster, York, and Cumberland," addressed familiarly to his "Friends and Countrymen" (p. 219).[20] The letter interprets the original document's official language in terms well adapted to the "common People": "You may now do a most acceptable Service, and make it easy to yourselves." As ever, Franklin "improves" on the original text by interpreting the written precept in the best interests of his countrymen, especially those less skilled in the imaginative reading of such texts: "Three or four of such as cannot separately spare from the Business of their Plantations a Waggon and four Horses and a Driver, may do it together, one furnishing the Waggon, another one or two Horses, and another the Driver, and divide the Pay proportionately between you" (p. 220).

In the final section of the *Autobiography* Franklin progresses from the everyday world of "common Life" to the more challenging sphere of colonial politics, in which the interpretive skills he had perfected throughout establish him at last as a model American hero. Part Four was written during the last months of his life and consists of only seven pages of manuscript, but despite its brevity, its thematic relationship to the earlier sections is clear. It recounts three incidents that took place between 1757 and 1760, while Franklin was in England acting as colonial agent for the province of Pennsylvania, and in each he presents himself as a heroic defender of his countrymen's rights.

The first incident consists of Franklin's being brought before Lord Granville, then president of the Privy Council, to answer the charge, "You Americans have wrong Ideas of the Nature of your Constitution; you contend that the King's Instructions to his Governors are not Laws, and think yourselves at Liberty to regard or disregard them at your own Discretion" (p. 261). Franklin responds by explaining the Americans' interpretation of their royal charters; that just as they could not make laws without the king's consent, neither could he make them without theirs. The immediate disagreement could not, of course, be resolved; it would take the Revolution to settle the matter of American "Liberty." But the thematic value of the exchange is that it highlights Franklin as an unyielding defender of his countrymen's right—and ability—to interpret texts.

He is equally unyielding in the second incident, his attempt to persuade the Penn family to provide "reasonable" financial support for the colony's defense against French and Indian assaults along its borders. Again, the conflict hinges on different interpretations of terminology, "each Party [having] had its own Ideas of what should be meant by *reasonable*" (p. 262). But here Franklin's "Character," both personal and written, is challenged as well. After their initial meeting with him, the Proprietors ask him to put the Americans' complaints in writing. When he submits his text to them, they complain of its "want of Formality"; insist that thereafter he negotiate solely with their solicitor, Ferdinand John Paris; and without informing Franklin, write to the Pennsylvania Assembly asking it to send over "*some Person of Candour* to treat with them," "intimating thereby," Franklin explains, "that I was not such." Though he speculates that the Penns' complaint over his "want of Formality or Rudeness" was probably in response to his not having addressed his "Paper to them with their assum'd Titles of true and absolute Proprietaries of the Province of Pensilvania" (p. 264), the larger significance of this incident is that it showcases him as a representative American heroically engaged in a contest with tradition-bound, paternalistic leaders to see who would wield greater textual authority. The link in Franklin's mind between personal and written "Character" is further evidenced in the reason he gives for refusing to negotiate with the Penns' lawyer. Paris was "a proud angry Man," he explains, "and as I had occasionally in the Answers of the Assembly treated his Papers with some Severity, they being really weak in point of Argument, and haughty in Expression, he had conceiv'd a mortal Enmity to me" (p. 263).

Although this specific dispute, in which each side's political position is equated with its style of presentation, ostensibly results in a stalemate, Franklin artfully concludes his discussion of it by showing how his "Character" came to be vindicated, after all. During the delay occasioned by the Penns' refusal to negotiate with him, the Pennsylvania Assembly had persuaded the governor to pass the Supply Act of 1759, "taxing the Proprietary Estate in common with the Estates of the People, which was the grand Point in Dispute" (p. 264). The third and final incident in Part Four recounts Franklin's pivotal role in securing the Privy Council's approval of that act in 1760. The Penns' having petitioned the king for a council hearing in which to contest this legislation, their legal counsel argues that the American tax assessors would be likely to act with bias against the Proprietors, levying disproportionate taxes that would eventually lead to the Penns' financial ruin. Franklin and his counsel respond by defending the character of the American officials, insisting that they are "honest and discreet Men, under an Oath to assess fairly and equitably" (p. 265). It is Franklin's personal endorsement and the weight of his own "Character," however, that finally carry the day. After hearing both sides of the debate, one member of the council, Lord Mansfield, asks to speak with Franklin in private and requests his interpretation of the act and, in particular, his personal and written assurance that "no Injury would be done the Proprietary Estate in the Execution" of it. Franklin gives his word and, as a fitting final gesture in a personal narrative that has dealt extensively with the politics of circumspect naming, signs his hard-won good name. As a result of his actions, the act is finally passed, and the collective American character is vindicated in the person of this American hero, who has shown himself capable of providing "an essential Service" to his country (p. 266).

Tzvetan Todorov has defined *interpretation* as "any substitution of another text for the present text, . . . any endeavor which seeks to discover, through the apparent textual fabric, a second more authentic text."[21] This definition is useful in discussing Franklin's acts of interpretation in the *Autobiography* insofar as it directs attention to the textual substitution and doubling that repeatedly result from Franklin's politicized use of language. His rephrasing of the British "Advertisement" for army supplies into a more persuasive personal letter to his "Friends and Countrymen"; his redefining of traditional moral precepts so as to derive the thirteen "Virtues" necessary to make good Americans; his rewriting of Josiah's biblical Book of Proverbs so as to instruct a distinctly American audience; his renaming of the cannon as a "Fire-engine" so as to ensure its purchase—all show Franklin substituting one "text" for another, in a continuous text-making and remaking for political ends. The problem in applying Todorov's definition to Franklin's verbal artifice arises from Todorov's use of the word *authentic*, which implies that the intent of interpretation is to recover a sort of ur-text, lurking beneath the surface of "the apparent textual fabric." Franklin's intent in the *Autobiography* would seem to be the exact opposite: he invariably begins with an ur-text, a precise specification of a desired goal, such as the legalistic "Advertisement," and then proceeds to transform its appearance, to adapt it to what he considers to be the mental capacities of those whose cooperation is needed to attain that goal.

In Todorov's terms, then, Franklin begins with an "authentic" text and transforms it into an "apparent" one, a politically expedient "fabric"-ation. This is the method of interpretation he promotes, either literally or figuratively, in each of the instructive anecdotes that make up the *Auto-biography*, and it is also his method of composition throughout. As a narrative strategy, however, his privileging of appearance over reality has disturbing formal ramifications. It results, first, in an autobiography in which the authentic self is increasingly obscured and finally lost altogether beneath the fabricated "Character" of the model American. It results at last in a narrative that resists closure, for the gap between life and life story becomes so great that in the final pages of the *Autobiography* it seems virtually unbridgeable. Finally, there is yet another way in which this narrative resists closure or resolution. Like those counterproductive aspects of Franklin's authentic self that must be submerged beneath his exemplary public persona, the views of any who oppose his political endeavors must also be subordinated or suppressed in the narrative to highlight his successful leadership strategies. Thus his repeated privileging of political ideology over historical reality results in a text that tells only one side of the new American story, even as it gives brief glimpses of an underside, a second story lurking beneath the "apparent textual fabric."

Franklin seems to have begun the story of his life with the intention of revealing himself to his son-reader as a fairly well-rounded character; that is, not only as a man whose "Means" of attaining success might be "fit to be imitated," but also as one who had had very human "Faults" (p. 43). In the course of Part One, he enumerates and occasionally shows himself correcting what he calls in printer's parlance the "*Errata*" (p. 70) of his life, youthful insensitivities or errors of judgment such as breaking off his first engagement with Deborah Read without a word of explanation or spending money left in his safekeeping by a friend. Even in that first section, however, Franklin is selective about the questionable traits he is willing to acknowledge, and once he has begun to address a public audience, writing as a model wise man to other would-be wise men of the new republic, the printer's term disappears and with it any serious highlighting of Franklin's human frailty. In "The Art of Virtue" section, for example, although he humorously acknowledges certain of his limitations, he is careful to place his emphasis more on the need to appear virtuous than on the need to become so. The lesson here, as in the subsequent sections, is clear: public facade is all. Thus, just as the young Franklin comes to privilege verbal artifice over literality, so the narrative comes to privilege the exemplary public persona over the all-too-human authentic self, and the result is the large number of verifiable discrepancies between life and life story that historians seem to feel so hard-pressed to explain.

Most, after carefully pointing out specific discrepancies, tend to want to give Franklin the benefit of the doubt. A. Owen Aldridge, for example, explains that although the *Autobiography* depicts Franklin as "an abstemious person, rigidly controlling his pleasures and amusements. . . . The evidence of his biography shows that he wined and dined lavishly throughout most of his life—certainly to the limit of his physical capacity after the age of forty." Aldridge generously allows that "one cannot, of course, be sure whether Franklin's abstemiousness remained fresher in his memory than did his self-indulgence or whether he engaged in conscious shading."[22] Robert F. Sayre is equally generous regarding another instance of Franklin's artful "self"-portrayal. Addressing an anecdote from Part One, in which Franklin humbly claims to have been sought out in London by Sir Hans Sloane and at length persuaded to part with a unique asbestos purse for a handsome price, Sayre points out that the entrepreneurial Franklin had in fact heard that the man was a "Lover of Curiosities" and written a letter offering to sell him the purse. "Either by design or by failure of memory," Sayre allows, "Sloane is forced into the category of influential men attracted to the young Franklin."[23]

Since Franklin readily admits—and repeatedly illustrates—that he was ever successful in contriving the *"Appearance"* of attractive qualities, if not always in acquiring the *"Reality"* of them (p. 159), it seems likely that in both of these instances he was indeed forcing the evidence, fabricating a more admirable self-image. Nevertheless, in noting these factual discrepancies and numerous others, the Yale editors of the *Autobiography* overleap the question of Franklin's artifice even more gracefully than Aldridge or Sayre. Their adverbs alone are models of tactful qualification. "Curiously," they comment, Franklin's "story" of his attempts to obtain reimbursement from Braddock's successor in New York (for the supplies the Americans had provided Braddock's army) does not square with the account he later wrote to the Speaker of the Pennsylvania Assembly, Isaac Norris: in the autobiographical anecdote Franklin stresses his steadfast defense of the

Americans' right to immediate repayment and of his own assessment of what is due them; in the letter he reports only that he readily agreed to seek reimbursement in England at a later date (p. 255, n. 6).

Occasionally, as in their attempt (and inability) to verify Franklin's claim that he was responsible for introducing a street paving bill in the Pennsylvania Assembly, the editors take Aldridge's and Sayre's tack, explaining that perhaps Franklin's memory was "confused" as to who did what when (p. 203, n. 1). At other times, apparently when no respectful explanation seems feasible, they merely report the facts as tactfully as possible. In spite of his "disclaimers of ever asking for a public office," we are told, "Franklin actually did apply for the Assembly clerkship in 1736 and the deputy postmaster generalship in 1751" (p. 185, n. 8). Later, after Franklin has described how he had drawn up and secured the assembly's passage of a voluntary militia bill "without much Difficulty" (p. 230), and after he has stressed that the election of militia officers had gone on "swimmingly" (p. 237), the editors note that "actually," the enactment of this controversial bill "caused great excitement and near riot in Philadelphia" (p. 237, n. 7). Similarly, they must qualify Franklin's claims to have studiously avoided entering into personal disputes when more weighty political issues were at stake, by pointing out, graciously, that "Franklin's mild, even-tempered recollection of Pennsylvania politics and of the negotiations with the Penns in London belies the bitterness of these events revealed in contemporary documents" (p. 213, n. 8).

D. H. Lawrence was neither gracious, respectful, nor tactful when, confronted with such an obviously promotional self-image, he felt compelled to ask, "What's wrong with Benjamin, that we can't stand him?" Lawrence's theories of human motivation and behavior were about as far from Franklin's as is conceivable, and it is perhaps because of that distance that he was able to see so clearly the central motive underlying Franklin's various acts of fabrication: the intent to set up a "dummy of a perfect citizen as a pattern to America." Certainly he saw the implications of self-division inherent in Franklin's personal and political philosophy for arriving at a "uniform Rectitude of Conduct" (p. 148). "Which of the various me's do you propose to educate, and which do you propose to suppress?" Lawrence wanted to know. "The perfectibility of man, dear God! When every man as long as he remains alive is in himself a multitude of conflicting men. Which of these do you choose to perfect, at the expense of every other?" Finally, after deriding Franklin for trying to deny the "vast forest" of the soul in favor of a "neat back garden" to be held in check by a "barbed-wire fence" of expedient virtues, Lawrence arrived at the answer to his own question: "Now I, at least, know why I can't stand Benjamin. He tries to take away my wholeness and my dark forest, my freedom."[24]

Lawrence could hardly be called a disinterested commentator; he was as intent as Franklin on promoting a specific credo for his contemporaries. Nevertheless, his reading of the *Autobiography* still provides valuable insights into Franklin's personal and written "Character." First in importance is the suggested link between Franklin's self-promotion and his seemingly paradoxical strategy of self-denial. "I . . . put my self as much as I could out of sight" (p. 143), Franklin says of his strategy for persuading the common people to be good citizens and to support his various schemes for local and national improvement and avoided "as much as I could, according to my usual Rule, the presenting myself to the Publick as the Author of any Scheme for their Benefit" (p. 193). In these passages, as elsewhere, Franklin promotes himself as a model of wise leadership who suppresses the literal truth in favor of creating a good—politically beneficial—effect. In the process, however, what Lawrence called various "selves," and what I call various facets of Franklin's authentic self, are also suppressed, put "out of sight." In sociopolitical terms, the result of such conscious fabrication may be a "perfect citizen," but in human terms, as Lawrence points out, the result is a diminution of authentic selfhood, a lack of "wholeness."

Lawrence's assessment of the implicit human cost of Franklin's political strategy is important because it suggests the ultimate narrative cost as well. The *Autobiography* itself lacks wholeness, as evidenced most obviously in that it does not actually end. In 1771, shortly after beginning his personal narrative, Franklin had jotted down an outline of events to be included. At the time of his death in 1790, he had not reached the end of his list. His narrative goes only sparingly into the year of 1760, and there is no real sense of closure. Although his success in securing British acceptance of the Supply Act of 1759 effectively resolves one particular conflict with the Penns, for example, the last thirty years of his life and the affairs of the Revolution have yet to be recounted. Moreover, Franklin devotes the last few lines of Part Four to a brief description of the Penns' subsequent anger at William Denny, the provincial governor who had allowed the Pennsylvania Assembly to pass the bothersome Supply Act in the first place. The last we hear of these inconclusive recriminations is that the Proprietors' threats to sue the man for breach of instructions "were never put in Execution" (p. 266).

Although most scholars attribute the *Autobiography*'s truncated ending to Franklin's old age and failing health during the winter of 1789–90 (he died on April 17, 1790), that alone does not account for certain narrative decisions he made at the close of Part Three. That section ends with his arrival in England in 1757, and Part Four dramatizes what I have called his representative, heroic persona, but details none of his personal life during this period—for good reason. As Michael T. Gilmore has pointed out, during these years Franklin had "systematically if privately betrayed the social and moral philosophy he was propounding in the *Autobiography*." Once in England, for example, he had begun what would become an eighteen-year romantic liaison with his landlady, Mrs. Margaret Stevenson, and he had resumed friendly relations with the ne'er-do-well friend of his youth, James Ralph. Thus, Gilmore claims, he "could not go into detail about his life abroad without betraying his personal recidivism, and to do so, of course, would have been to defeat his very purpose in writing."[25] In other words, Franklin had reached a narrative impasse: even if he had lived to continue writing, it seems unlikely that the pronounced split between the real and the fabricated self, between life and life story, could ever be resolved in narrative form.

There is one other important way in which the *Autobiography* lacks wholeness. Just as it eventually comes to depict only one side of Franklin's life, so too it finally tells only one side of the new American story. Specifically, Franklin's continued success as a model American is shown to be dependent on his ability to subordinate not only his own ego but also the "Objections, and Reluctances" (p. 143) of any who oppose his political objectives, and the carefully fabricated *Autobiography* does the same. It promotes Franklin's side of the story—what he considers the proper political lessons to be learned—in any given sociopolitical conflict. It privileges verbal artifice over literality; political expediency over open dialogue and debate; paternalistic wise men over the shortsighted and self-interested "common People." And it subordinates, defuses, or suppresses opposing political views, any counterarguments or counterevidence that would suggest another version of the events being recounted, a second story.[26]

As a literary craftsman, Franklin was adept at holding that second story at bay, even if his artful and confident interpretations often belie a reality that we now know to have been fraught with conflict and challenges to his authority. Nevertheless, to dramatize his successful leadership strategies in the *Autobiography*, he had to allude to such opposition, to acknowledge, for example, that the Quaker-filled assembly objected to his plan to purchase a cannon; that the inhabitants of Lancaster, York, and Cumberland counties had to be persuaded to comply with Braddock's request for supplies; that the Proprietors did not accept his interpretations of American rights and interests. Thus readers are apprised of a second story even as their attention is repeatedly diverted from it. We are made to focus on the expedient solution to any sociopolitical conflict, not the conflict itself; on the political ideology, not the historical reality. And it is this built-in tension between the promotional surface narrative and the implicit second story which is finally the *Autobiography*'s most distinctive feature. Generations of scholars have responded to that tension by trying to recover the various facts Franklin "confused" or "forgot," but to accept those terms is to overlook the many instructive instances of intentional substitution or omission by which Franklin shows his hand: the "Fire-engine" ruse; the expedient omissions of his proper name to achieve specific political objectives; even his design of "The Art of Virtue," whose pages allow for deviant strains of behavior to be briefly noted and then erased, in the hope of eventually eliminating them altogether. The cumulative evidence argues that if the *Autobiography* lacks wholeness, both as a personal and a national narrative, it does so by design: the second story that seems ever to lurk beneath the apparent textual fabric is one Franklin chose not to tell.

In essence, the *Autobiography* illustrates the political principles of the new patriarchy ushered in by the American Revolution: a political system led by father figures, like Franklin, whose authority was not inherited but derived from education and from the high level of verbal proficiency that enabled them to use language as a means of social control. As Jay Fliegelman has pointed out, for example, in his study of family and politics in this era, one major "revolutionary insight" was that "the title of father was transferable," and this insight was "reinforced by the new definition of a true parent as one who forms a child's mind rather than one who brings that child into the world."[27] The verbal skills that Franklin recommends for wise men of the new republic are indeed, as he tells us, intended to "prepare the Minds of the People" (p. 200), to make them good citizens. In literary terms, however, when it came to telling the new American story, the patriarchal politics of language that Franklin advocates in the *Autobiography* resulted in a politics of form as well: a surface narrative whose continued existence depended upon the repeated suppression of dissident voices and dissident points of view.

2

Second Thoughts and a Second Story: Brackenridge's *Modern Chivalry*

Early in the first volume of *Modern Chivalry*, the hero, Captain John Farrago, is precipitously invited to become a member of the American Philosophical Society, and when he declines, humbly "conceiving himself unqualified for a place in such a body," the honor is extended on his behalf to his servant, Teague O'Regan, who is, in the Captain's words, "but a simple Irishman, and of a low education," indeed "totally illiterate."[1] The Captain, a man "of good natural sense, and considerable reading" (p. 6), is of course aghast at this suggestion, the more so as the "philosopher"-recruiter explains: "At the first institution of the society by Dr. Franklin and others, it was put upon a narrow basis, and only men of science were considered proper to compose it; and this might be a necessary policy at that time, when the institution was in its infancy, and could not bear much drawback of ignorance. But it has not been judged so necessary of late years. The matter stands now on a broad and catholic bottom. . . . There are hundreds, whose names you may see on our list, who are not more instructed than this lad of yours" (p. 25). The Captain is able, in this early instance, to dissuade Teague from accepting such a dubious honor, and as happens throughout the novel, Brackenridge follows the picaresque incident with authorial commentary. He stresses, for any who have missed his point, that his criticism is leveled against the current farcical makeup of the society so that a "spurious brood of illiterate persons . . . have been admitted indiscriminately with the informed," and not against the society as it was originally conceived: "The institution of the American Philosophical Society, does great honor to the founders; and what has been published by that body, comes not behind what has appeared from societies of the same nature elsewhere" (p. 28).

Brackenridge's praise and his humbly qualified nationalistic pride, like his interpolated acts of interpretation, suggest his ideological link with Franklin and the revolutionary generation of Founders. But his satirical depiction, in miniature, of a society that has suffered a loosening of its once high standards, a "democratizing" at the hands of the uninformed, attests to his advanced historical perspective and, specifically, to his personal encounters with the defiant and often (as eighteenth-century American intellectuals would term them) "irrational" popular energies that had surfaced in resistance to that republican ideology in the few short years since the nation's founding.[2] *Modern Chivalry*, the first two volumes of which appeared in 1792, only two years after Franklin's death, offers a less idealized, less optimistic vision of the potential character of American society than that which had informed the *Autobiography*. It speaks with more urgency of the need for a social hierarchy based on education; of the need for class manipulation at the hands of a paternalistic leadership drawn from the educated elite; and of the role language must be made to play in America to effect such social control.[3]

The major difference between the *Autobiography* and Brackenridge's novel, however, is that the latter work's urgency carries with it an increasingly haunted sense of its own futility, for despite Brackenridge's best efforts to the contrary, *Modern Chivalry* leaves modern readers with disturbing second thoughts about the practical effectiveness of the ideology its author promotes. Unlike Franklin's heroicized persona, for example, whose leadership qualifications are so frequently portrayed through Franklin's central role as a pacifying, unifying agent, Brackenridge's hero is an outsider, a picaro. This would-be father figure is commonly viewed by society as an officious interloper, and late in the book, as governor of the New Settlement, where his attempts at authoritative leadership are "unfavorably received" (p. 659), he is usually "obliged to yield" (p. 701) to the antic demands of "the people." Similarly, Franklin's seemingly tireless confidence in the ultimate stabilizing force of his various ad hoc interpretive strategies is denied to this later hero. In contrast to Franklin's fixed prominence as sage and mediator, Brackenridge's Captain, who uses markedly similar verbal artifice in his efforts to resolve sociopolitical conflicts, figures nevertheless as a mere traveling repairman, servicing a disdainful, uncooperative society and having only discrete and fleeting moments of success. By the latter half of *Modern Chivalry* the artful language of leadership has failed altogether: Captain Farrago is accused of deceiving the people, and he becomes the first of a long line of American heroes who have had to light out for new territories farther west.[4]

Finally, the form of this multivolume satire is equally telling of its troubled political vision. Brackenridge intentionally divided the book into alternating chapters of plot and authorial commentary, suggesting that he felt it imperative to highlight the lessons Franklin had so artfully integrated into his many didactic anecdotes: the need for authoritative interpretations of American interests and, in particular, the need to persuade— to entice—potentially uncooperative audiences to accept such interpretations. "Intending solid observations," Brackenridge explains of the novel he hopes to see "made a school book," "*we interlard pleasantry to make the boys read*" (pp. 77, 443). But as *Modern Chivalry* progresses, another, more unwieldy split becomes evident within the chapters that carry the plot. Brackenridge chooses to satirize in exaggerated, farcical detail the sociopolitical "Objections, and Reluctances" that Franklin had glossed over in the *Autobiography*, and the result is that the promotional story of the Captain's attempts to maintain order eventually becomes overshadowed by the rival story line of his challengers, whose dissident voices grow in strength as they grow in number. Moreover, as Farrago's authority wanes, Brackenridge oversteps the formal bounds he had originally set for himself and intrudes his authorial voice into the fictional chapters to defend his hero and himself against imagined charges of demagoguery. What had begun as an amusing, carefully modulated political allegory thus gives way to a second story, dictated by the author's growing awareness of and attempts to conciliate opposing views. By the last volume of *Modern Chivalry*, Brackenridge seems to have lost all aesthetic control over his text, and readers are left with the sense that by 1815, the new American story has suffered an irreparable division.[5]

The first three volumes of *Modern Chivalry*, published in 1792–93, seem closely to translate the revolutionary generation's attitudes and values into fiction. In these early pages, the Captain as a matter of course takes on the leadership responsibility for righting the wrongs, preventing the misdoings, and especially, correcting what seem to be the inevitable misperceptions of his less-educated countrymen. Like Franklin's heroicized public persona in the latter sections of the *Autobiography*, Brackenridge's hero is presented as a paternalistic authority figure, a surrogate or adoptive father.

In his first speech Captain Farrago broaches the issue of fathers and sons in terms that suggest the postrevolutionary rationale for the adoptive-father metaphor. "Gentlemen," he lectures a group of jockeys mistakenly and greedily trying to determine the bloodlines of a mere nag, it is a strange thing that you should suppose that it is of any consequence what may be the pedigree of a horse. For even in men it is of no avail. Do we not find that sages have had blockheads for their sons; and that blockheads have had sages? It is remarkable, that as estates have seldom lasted three generations, so understanding and ability have seldom been transmitted to the second. . . . I will venture to say, that when the present John Adamses, and Lees, and Jeffersons, and Jays, and Henrys, and other great men, who figure upon the stage at this time, have gone to sleep with their fathers, it is an hundred to one if there is any of their descendents who can fill their places. Was I to lay a bet for a great man, I would sooner pick up the brat of a tinker, than go into the great houses to chuse a piece of stuff for a man of genius. [pp. 7–8]

The ideology is clearly and newly American. Hereditary aristocracy, and thus monarchy, is mocked; a more democratic meritocracy is championed; and merit, the text humorously suggests, is to be determined by those like the Captain, "of good natural sense, and considerable reading," who are best able to "chuse" and to tutor future great men. The lecture characterizes the Captain as a future-minded patriot, intent on reeducating a self-interested people, and it prefigures, in particular, his role as adoptive father to his servant, the illiterate Teague O'Regan, who is certainly no better than a tinker's brat and who, under Farrago's tutelage, will slowly climb the social and political ladder on his way to becoming a "great man." As the book progresses, Captain Farrago will continually advise Teague on his career choices and aptitudes, at one point will offer a small marriage allowance, and as a general overseer of his affairs will in all ways act like a father toward the young man.

The Captain's concluding remark in this passage, "Was I to lay a bet for a great man," also alludes to the more practical considerations underlying his paternal role. In its immediate context, for example, his choice of the betting metaphor appears to be a rhetorical strategy addressed specifically to his audience of greedy, shortsighted jockeys, an attempt to reason with them in terms they will understand. Farrago's simple rhetoric in this scene, however, like his general attempt to dissuade money-minded men from their impractical speculations and to spread a little republican ideology along the way, fails miserably, for we are told that "the jockeys thought the man a fool, and gave themselves no more trouble about him" (p. 8). Furthermore, in the ensuing rush to place bets and then to determine the race's outcome, the Captain not only feels "a good deal hurt with such indecency amongst gentlemen" but is also literally hurt, "jostled by some one in the croud, and thrown from his horse" (pp. 8–9): his "higher" authority as an educated man is threatened by the unruly mob.

In the chapter that follows, "Containing Some General Reflections," Brackenridge comments first on "the good sense of the Captain" in trying to dissuade the gamblers from their unrealistic expectations about a horse unfit for racing. The moral, he points out, is sound and one that will be more fully illustrated in the remainder of the work. The social order, like the natural order, is hierarchical: "Every thing in its element is good, and in their proper sphere all natures and capacities are excellent. . . . Let the cobler stick to his last." If Farrago's ideology is sound, however, his mode of inculcating it, his sensible if simple rhetoric, is not, for Brackenridge's second reflection is on the laughable "simplicity of the Captain; who was so unacquainted with the world, as to imagine that jockeys and men of the turf could be composed by reason and good sense; whereas there are no people who are by education of a less philosophic turn of mind" (p. 11). In other words, though the Captain is properly equipped and motivated to become a spokesman for American values, his task at the outset of the novel is to learn how to enact his rightful authority in a postrevolutionary culture where learned authority is so easily overridden by mob rule. He must learn how to appeal to the people more effectively; and he must learn, in a money-minded culture where all seem obsessed with their own interests, how to "deal" with them. Taken together, the lecture scene and the subsequent authorial commentary suggest that the task of this early American hero will be to adapt and to improve his language skills so as to maintain social order, which is to say, an orderly social hierarchy. And learning to speak with more authority, it is implied, will mean trading his "simplicity" for duplicity.

Finally, the Captain's use of the betting metaphor also alludes to the practical dynamics underlying his paternalistic relationship to Teague, a relationship that is economic, not familial or even sentimental.[6] Farrago acts like a father and fulfills paternal functions, but he is of course an employer, an overseer, with a personal investment in his servant's future. Early in the novel it becomes clear that by keeping Teague's affairs in order—and keeping Teague in his proper place—the Captain is looking after his own interests as well as the nation's. The merging of those interests is especially evident in the second incident of the picaresque journey. The Captain and Teague arrive "at a place where a number of people were convened, for the purpose of electing persons to represent them in the legislature of the state" (p. 13). When these citizens insist on "giving

Teague their suffrages," the Captain resists their efforts as an attempt "to invade my household, and thus detract from me the very person that I have about me to brush my boots, and clean my spurs" (p. 16).

The phrase "invade my household" synthesizes the various aspects of Farrago's role as spokesperson for a patriarchal society. It establishes him as acting head of a "household," a father figure in a microcosmic social unit; it signifies that such leadership is based on economic power; and it equates any threat to that symbolic social unit with political interference—"invasion." Furthermore, the Captain's resolution of his personal predicament, the imminent loss of an underling, functions at the same time as a stopgap solution to the larger problem, the popular promotion of unqualified legislators. "Composing his voice, and addressing him in a soft manner" (p. 16), he artfully dissuades Teague from being a candidate. Thus Farrago serves his country in microcosmic fashion by keeping his own household in check, and his relationship to Teague serves as a fictional model of the new American patriarchy.

A closer look at the behavioral patterns that develop in that gentleman-servant relationship shows more clearly the duplicitous nature of Farrago's paternalistic authority and its effects on this American hero's use of language. As a symbolic representative of the public's best interests in this novel, the Captain, like Franklin before him, quite literally enacts Madison's description in *Federalist* No. 49 of the proper role for a government representative. He is presented as one of those "confidential guardians of the rights and liberties of the people," and in that capacity one of his main charges is to "repress" the unrealistic demands and ambitions of his countrymen, and of Teague O'Regan in particular, on the grounds that (as the Captain himself puts it in the foregoing scene), "it is sufficient to possess the right [for example, to run for office]; not absolutely necessary to exercise it" (p. 15).

Repress is a word Brackenridge habitually uses to describe the Captain's attempts to keep Teague in his proper station. As their journey continues, for example, several incidents occur in which Farrago must discourage Teague's ill-conceived plans for social and political advancement, dissuading him from leaving his own menial employment for more attractive professions, for which he is obviously unqualified. At one point, however, Teague's ambitions take the form of paying court to a landlady's daughter, a young woman of more culture and more wealth than himself, and here, we are told, "the Captain having been a good deal troubled, heretofore, with the pretensions of this valet, in wishing to be a member of the legislature, a philosopher, a preacher, and now a lover, thought he had now a good opportunity of repressing his presumption for the future" (p. 66). As Teague's confidante and confidential guardian in all matters, the Captain, "counterfeiting every possible disposition to serve the bog-trotter," advises him to enlist the aid of the young lady's brother in his suit. As usual, the Captain knows more of the matter than his servant does, and the brother, considering "Teague's advances to his sister as an insult upon the family" (p. 66), chastises him accordingly with a whip. Teague's presumptions are indeed repressed, for the moment if not for the future. In a later scene in a tavern, Farrago will again have to "repress . . . the disposition of the bog-trotter" (p. 216), this time to enter into political debates on issues too complex for his understanding: "The Captain think-ing [the] subject [the postwar assumption of state debts] above the com-prehension of the Irishman, was not willing that he should speak" and "obliged him to be silent" (p. 217).

That such forms of repression—physical restraint and the silencing of potentially disruptive voices—are intended to have larger political signifi-cance is evidenced both in the Captain's story and in Brackenridge's au-thorial commentary. As a "new way of quelling mobs," for example, Far-rago will endorse throwing water on them: "The Captain said he had seen something of the kind attempted in repressing bees, when they swarmed . . . and that the riots of men were analogous" (p. 374). Brackenridge's use of the term is even more explicit. "The fact is," he comments on one of the tavern debates just mentioned, "that the command of Lake Erie, by posts established upon it, and from thence to the Wabash, are the only means of repressing the Indians; not so much from the actual force of these estab-lishments as from the effect upon the imagination of the enemy" (p. 227).

The implicit definition here, that repression is a political means of checking the "imagination" of subversives, reveals that Brackenridge's use of the term is closer to our own than might have been expected. Repress-ing in *Modern Chivalry* means subordinating wayward psychic energies, manipulating and diverting them into more politically acceptable chan-nels; and this emphasis on having to apply "restraint to the common mind in the violence of its emotions" (p. 441) provides the key to Bracken-ridge's political philosophy. "There is nothing so difficult as to manage the public mind," he admonishes his readers. "It must be done by the lever, or the screw, or other mechanical power; to speak figuratively, and not by direct force" (p. 602). Such psychic "management" is most often depicted as "correcting the imagination," as when, in the above scene, we are told that the Indians' "imagination is not corrected" by well-reasoned "negociations" (p. 225) as much as by flamboyant shows of force. But the prime means of "correcting" minds not in concert with the prevalent sociopolitical order is language.[7]

The Captain learns this lesson very quickly as the book progresses. We have seen Brackenridge criticize him for his simplicity in the opening pages. Shortly afterward, when Teague is invited and would join the American Philosophical Society, Farrago turns—necessarily, his author would insist—to duplicity: "The Captain finding that it answered no end to dispute the matter with him, by words of sense and reason, took a contrary way to manage him" (p. 25). By convincing Teague that membership in such an organization would be no less than "rack and torture" (p. 27)—"they would think no more of throwing you into a kettle of boiling water, than they would a tarapin; and having scraped you out to a shell, present you as the relics of an animal they had procured, at an immense price, from some Guinea merchant" (p. 26)—he is able to keep the young man in his proper place. Soon it becomes Farrago's "usual method" to address the "hopes and fears" of his underling "with all possible art" (p. 38), and the result is a satirical form of psychological coercion. In another instance, we see the Captain "counterfeiting . . . an approbation of [Teague's] project of becoming a lawyer" (p. 148) but sending him to the workhouse instead, where he has paid the keeper to teach "his refractory servant" a lesson. "For *the idea was to be imposed upon Teague*, that this was an office, or as it were an inn or court, or chamber of the Inner Temple; and that the several flagellations, and grindings, and poundings, were so many lessons, and lectures, to qualify him for the practice of law" (p. 149; my emphasis). Teague's ambition is, of course, soon repressed.

The Captain's task in each instance is to correct Teague's imagination and thus to promote and maintain the desired sociopolitical order, and he does so essentially by renaming reality. In the workhouse scene, for example, when Teague is "sentenced to an hour or two's hard labor, at grinding plaister of Paris, this [is] called Coke upon Littleton"; "when the employment [is] varied, pounding hemp, or picking oakum, it [is] called Hawkin's Pleas of the Crown, or Foster, or 4th Blackstone, &c." (p. 150). Brackenridge's treatment seems a farcical dramatization of Jefferson's claim that "the new circumstances in which we are placed call . . . for the transfer of old words to new objects," but the point is clear. Renaming reality is here the task of the educated interpreter of American values, and literality is rejected in favor of language that creates the desired political effect on the "common mind."

The Captain's antiliterality stance as an interpreter is emphasized, as above, in the many times he is shown "counterfeiting" his verbal support of Teague's intentions with words that carry double meaning. It is also apparent in the stylistic advice he, like Franklin, gives to other would-be wise men in his travels. Early in the book he advises a jilted young man that if he would succeed in his next suit to a lady, he must "impress" on her the "idea" that by accepting his proposal she is acting in her own best interests. In particular, he must use words that will merely "hint a little" at his intentions; that will "bring her to [the] suspicion" that she might lose him; and above all, that will "make her think" that marriage is her own idea. "Imagination governs the world," the Captain instructs him, and the political principle is that the man who would govern the world, or even his small share of it, must control the imagination of his subordinates (p. 65).

The same principle surfaces a bit later when Farrago conspires with a father to dissuade his daughter from her romantic attachment to the sweet-talking Teague O'Regan; here the issue is clearly whose language will wield the greater authority over the daughter's mind, that of the self-interested suitor or of the more socially responsible fathers. The Captain, acting as "guardian of the young gentleman" (p. 235) in question, advises the distressed father that "art accomplishes more than force" and that rather than opposing the girl, he should "affect" to speak of Teague with respect, meanwhile leaving it to Farrago "to say such things to the young lady, as under pretence of recommending her lover, will be effectual to disgust her, and remove her attachment" (p. 236). Farrago then "praises" Teague to his mistress for such accomplishments as having recently learned "to blow his nose with a handkerchief, and keep from breaking wind in company, a practice to which he was a good deal addicted at his first setting out" (p. 237). The young woman's ardor is effectively dampened.

The two older men have thus preserved order in their respective households by resorting to duplicitous rhetorical ploys, and as a final touch to the scene, Brackenridge steps in to press his point, that "as the bog-trotter is making an attack upon the honour and happiness of the family, it is self-defence, and justifiable to counteract him by stratagem, when open force will not avail" (p. 242). Moreover, he seems to want to emphasize in particular the Americanness of his—and the Captain's—"justifiable" authority in such matters. He has laid down such "rules for a prudent father, or guardian, to correct the imagination of a young lady," he claims, because "the greater part of our romances and comedies in the English language are calculated to depreciate the respect which a young lady ought to have for the opinion of aged and grave persons; and to confirm her in taking the Teague O'Regan of her own choice" (pp. 241–42). The passage implicates Brackenridge, the American artist, in the conspiracy of "fathers" intent on correcting the imagination of younger and less discriminating members of the American "family." Specifically, it equates literary with sociopolitical authority and establishes both the new American hero and the new American artist as civic-minded con men who use verbal artifice as a means of social control to further the interest of the patriarchy.

These Americanized notions of authority all converge in a scene in which the Captain is shown "authoring" a text that will channel Teague's thoughts into endeavors that will make him a better citizen. In this instance Farrago tries to get his illiterate servant "to acquire some small things which [are] necessary to the creditable and convenient discharge of a public function; such as learning to write his name if possible" (p. 243). While Teague is working at this task, however, social invitations arrive, and the Captain, "instantly reflecting that this correspondence with the gay world would undo all that he was doing, and draw off the bog-trotter from his lessons . . . saw it necessary to read the billets as from different persons, and containing language different from what was in them." Here, in a move reminiscent of Franklin's inclusion of the original "Advertisement" for military supplies and his interpretive "Letter" to his less-educated readers, Brackenridge includes both the original "billet" and the Captain's newly authored version.

As written by the Lady.

Would wish to have the pleasure of Major O'Regan's company this evening at tea. Lawyer Crabtree and Doctor Drug will be here; and you know we shall split our sides laughing at the ninnies. You're so full of your jokes that I want you here. . . .

Yours sincerely,
Patty Muslin

As read by the Captain.
     Sir,
     You will instantly do one of two things, either relinquish your attention
to Miss Muslin, and be no more in her company; or meet me this evening
precisely at six o'clock . . . with a brace of pistols, and a second, to take a
shot. I shall have a coffin ready, and a grave dug, for which ever of us shall
have occasion to make use of it.
                                   Your humble servant,
                                   Benjamin Johnston
                                   [p. 244]

Teague, of course, is terrified of such a challenge; gives the Captain leave
to write an answer declining in his behalf, and returns, as intended, to his
studies. "By these artifices, certainly innocent as the object was good; for
it can be no injury to deceive a man to his own advantage; by these
artifices, the Captain succeeded, in preventing a correspondence with the
gay world" (p. 246)—and in furthering more politically useful endeavor.

     Brackenridge's definition of *deceit* here is very close to Franklin's defini-
tion of *sincerity* in "The Art of Virtue"; that is, "deceiving a man to his
own advantage" apparently means the use of "no hurtful deceit." The
difference between the two authors' naming of tactics—*deceit* versus *sincerity*—is significant, however, in that it helps to explain why Brackenridge's
authorial voice and authorial choices, unlike Franklin's, came to be so self-
consciously defensive as his narrative progressed; or why, as Lewis Leary
has described the problem, the second half of *Modern Chivalry* came to be
"spoiled with second thoughts and evasive, politely phrased rewritings."[8]
First, despite his detached satirical stance in the opening pages, by choosing to promote verbal deceit as the most expedient means of social control
in a society where rational discourse fails, Brackenridge put himself in the
position of having to defend, with increasing vigor, a model of sociopolitical authority that—as he would learn from personal experience—was
becoming increasingly suspect. In addition, by choosing to highlight in
farcical detail the challenges to leadership that Franklin had so optimis-
tically glossed over in the *Autobiography*, Brackenridge introduced into
his text narrative complications that could not be resolved: "second
thoughts" concerning the model of authority he chose to promote and,
finally, a second story altogether, one in which the problems of representative democracy no longer admitted of any sane solution.
     From the outset of *Modern Chivalry*, Brackenridge makes explicit what

Franklin had only implied—that the sociopolitical authority he promotes for heroes, leaders, and American artists is based on deception. In the first volume, for example, deception is introduced as an explicit theme to justify the Captain's move from simplicity to duplicity. Meeting with men who masquerade as Indians to defraud the government of treaty money, the Captain is at first appalled: "Is it possible that such deception can be practised in a new country?" (p. 56). He soon learns to counter such self-interested tricks with public-spirited ones, and the didactic import of the incident is that the popular misconception of freedom, after the Revolution, has called for artful checks and balances. The humorous "billets" scene, in which Farrago deceives Teague to his own advantage, occurs in Volume 3, published in 1793. The need for authority based on deceit seems to be the main theme of this volume, for Brackenridge opens it with a reminder that his object has been "the giving an example of a perfect stile in writing," and he playfully stresses the means by which such a style must be accomplished: "I acknowledge that no man will ever possess a good stile that has not well studied, and exercised himself in writing, selecting with a most perfect delicacy, in all cases, the proper term; but he must go beyond this, and be able to deceive the world, and, never let it come into their heads that he has spent a thought on the subject" (p. 161).

In subsequent volumes Brackenridge becomes less playful in his portrayals of the need for deceit in maintaining social order, and with good reason. A year after publishing Volume 3, he had tried unsuccessfully to act as mediator between the rebels and the government in the Whiskey Rebellion, a popular revolt against federal taxation. On this occasion, his artful rhetoric had neither stopped the insurrection nor saved his own hide, for although he was finally absolved, he had suffered the ignominy of a formal hearing to determine whether he should be tried for treason. Thus it comes as no surprise that in Volume 4, published in 1797, Brackenridge spitefully—in true sour-grapes fashion—allows the rascal Teague O'Regan to begin his farcical (and short-lived) rise to power as a duly appointed excise officer. The sharply derisive tone of this volume is set in the opening chapter, where the author explains this untoward turn of events: the Captain had momentarily given over to the misguided spirit of the times; he had not been "willing to be the means of deception" in thwarting the Irishman's appointment (p. 253). The consequences of Farrago's failure to impose his better judgment are clearly and grimly delineated. When the new excise officer is beset by a mob, the Captain belatedly tries to intercede on Teague's behalf, but again, mistakenly, forgoes the verbal artifice that has served him so well in the past: "Let me endeavour to save him from your odium," he beseeches the angry gathering, "not by falsehood, but by reason" (p. 304). The Captain, however, and the novel's readers apparently, must learn anew that the people will not be reasoned with. The "outrage" Brackenridge allows to be committed against Teague is the most mean-spirited and prolonged to date: the young man is stripped, tarred and feathered, and forced to hide out at night in a forest, where his life is threatened by maurauding citizens and wild animals (pp. 304–5, 317).

By the time Brackenridge wrote Part II [Volume 1], published in 1804, Farrago's patriotism—that is, his willingness to deceive—had revived, but Brackenridge's good humor had not and would not again. In this section and for the remainder of the novel, the authorial voice intrudes with increasing preachiness into the narrative proper to promote the mode of authority the Captain represents. In this volume in particular, what Leary has called Brackenridge's defensive "second thoughts," his anxieties that readers understand the motives underlying his hero's artful deceptions, lead him to distinguish very carefully between his authorial use of the term *deceit* and sheer "demagoguery." For example, in a chapter that contains one paragraph of the Captain's fictitious reflections on government and six of the author's corroborating remarks, Brackenridge first claims that Rome had been "mistress of the world . . . owing to a few great men that happened to rise in it," then immediately anticipates the reader's suspicions: "Were these men demagogues? Not in a bad sense of the word. They did not deceive the people for their own ends" (p. 414). The confident, flippant tone is gone, and the lengthy disclaimer prepares us for the Captain's similar argument, and similar self-defense, in the next volume, published in 1805.

By now, the people's assertion of their "democratic" rights and privileges can no longer be countered by the revolutionary generation's language of social control, and the Captain is brought before a town meeting to answer for his duplicity. He defends himself with the republican ideology of the Founders, on the grounds that it was not *democracy, that I have meant to expose; or reprehend, in any thing that I have said; but the errors of it: those excesses which lead to its overthrow.* These excesses have shewn themselves in all democratic governments; whence it is that a *simple* democracy has never been able to exist long. An experiment is now made in a new world, and upon better principles; that of *representation.*" In particular, he claims, he has been acting not out of self-interest but as representative of the people and the principles set forth in the Constitution: "The demagogue is the first great destroyer of the constitution by deceiving the people. He is no democrat that deceives the people. He is an aristocrat; and seeks after more power than is just. He will never rest short of despotic rule. Have I deceived the people? . . . who wish nothing more than to inform their understanding, and regulate their conduct?" (pp. 507–8).

Brackenridge's sympathy for his "well intended" hero is as obvious as his contempt for Farrago's shortsighted opponents (p. 509). They respond that it is "presumption" for Farrago to have decided what was right in any matter of public interest, but more significant than their anger at being patronized is the rhetoric Brackenridge has them use to unseat Farrago as their representative. "It is too much to bear," one protester argues. "I am for repressing all such presumption. It leads to aristocracy" (p. 508). Here, "the people" have taken away the Captain's prerogative of naming—of saying what is aristocratic and what is not—and they have turned his strategy of repressing other voices back on himself. Finally, and in line with this farcical role reversal, the crowd of ruffians attains its ultimate "authority" by agreeing with his only defender in the crowd that Farrago "has got some kink in his intellect, that gars him conceit strange things" (p. 508). The verdict against learned leadership, spoken appropriately enough in the vernacular, is that it is the Captain's, and not the "common mind," that needs "correcting."

The upshot of this conflict is that the Captain abandons his attempts to counsel the mob and leaves town "in the capacity of an exile" (p. 510), in search of a new, less intractable community where he might still do some good. The thematic and formal repercussions of the trial episode, however, cannot be passed over. In trying to elicit sympathy for Farrago, Brackenridge has highlighted for readers a situation in which the revolutionary generation's concept of sociopolitical authority has clearly failed to impose a rational order on American society. In other words, he has provided readers with detailed second thoughts about the very leadership model he wants to promote. He has also jeopardized his own textual authority, for although the trial episode tells a cautionary tale, it also ushers in seemingly insurmountable tactical problems for hero and author alike: dissident "voices" that will not be silenced by the literary-legal language of the educated elite and a psychological terrain where there is no longer any discernible solution to America's growing sociopolitical conflicts.

In his subsequent exaggerated endeavors to show that it is the untutored mob and not his hero who is mad, for example, Brackenridge abandons even the most satirical attempts at social realism and engages in out-and-out fantasy. He guides the Captain to the Lack-Learning settlement, where people literally raise arms to protect themselves from scholars, lawyers, and authority figures in general; to the Mad-Cap settlement, whose inhabitants consider it a point of honor to challenge forest animals to duels rather than shooting them outright as fair game; and finally to the founding of Farrago's own New Settlement, where, as governor in name only, he is repeatedly "obliged to yield" to the antic wishes of citizens who so misunderstand the principle of universal suffrage that they angrily debate whether to give their animals the vote (p. 701). The Captain never fully regains the authority he held in the novel's opening pages, a fact Brackenridge obviously intends his readers to regret. But as we see the fallen hero repeatedly try—and fail—to outwit such witless mobs by artfully engaging them in extended debates over absurd matters, we come to feel that Brackenridge has failed to win his case regarding Farrago's sanity. In addition, as we see Brackenridge abandon his discrete chapters of witty authorial commentary and intrude his voice with increasing seriousness and urgency into the plot, to defend his hero's ideological motives, we come to feel that he has lost control of his own text—and perhaps even to ask whether this author might not be as mad as his hero.

The latter question is finally the most useful in understanding the formal disintegration of *Modern Chivalry*, for Brackenridge's growing obsession with the folly of the people in rejecting learned leadership creates two disturbing—and perhaps unforeseen—narrative complications. The first and most obvious involves the novel's hero. Farrago's heroism, his patriotism, consists of his willingness and ability to deceive the people to their own advantage. For the people themselves, Brackenridge stresses, the cost of such deception should be regarded as negligible: they are in need of sociopolitical leadership to save them from their mad, self-interested delusions of freedom and power and to instruct them in their own best—collective—interests. But what is the cost to Farrago, to a leader who, to serve the people, must trade his natural simplicity for artful duplicity, must ever conceal his true thoughts and feelings—indeed, his true self—beneath a carefully fabricated verbal facade?

Franklin, also promoting self-denial as a leadership strategy, had assured his audience of would-be wise men that such "Sacrifice" of their "Vanity" would "afterwards be amply repaid," and he had effectively proved his claim by highlighting his "frequent Successes" and suppressing any evidence to the contrary (*Autobiography*, p. 143). In contrast, Brackenridge's Captain is only sparingly repaid in the early volumes, where his strategies for keeping Teague in his proper place are only stopgap at best, and he receives increasingly diminishing returns on his selfless efforts to serve the people in the second half of the book. Starting in Part II, Brackenridge repeatedly has his hero insist that "*humility and self-denial*" are the basis of "republican virtue" (p. 392). "Three things are necessary to constitute a great man," we are taught: "Judgment, fortitude, and self-denial" (p. 423). In spite of such recurring axioms, however, readers cannot help but be aware that Farrago's own rewards for such altruism consist of public humiliation and personal deprivation. He is repeatedly ostracized for his learning and his artful language, and he leads a painfully solitary existence, ever alone in his views of republican virtue and ever having to move on, looking for new opportunities to do good. By the time he finally settles down at the end of the book, as nominal governor of the New Settlement, he seems to be the last of a dying breed, for although his "senate thought that he ought to marry," Brackenridge's last words on his hero inform us that Farrago "does not seem to have succeeded; for he remains yet unmarried" (pp. 795, 800).

The narrative conflict between professed ideology and the portrayal of lived experience in the second half of *Modern Chivalry* thus leaves us with serious doubts regarding the reasonableness of Farrago's endeavors, for his limited and short-lived political successes hardly seem adequate recompense for his ultimate loss of selfhood.[9] A similar conflict develops and similar doubts arise concerning the reasonableness of Brackenridge's own endeavors to serve the people, for his depiction of himself as an American artist becomes, in the novel's latter volumes, as fraught with images of diminished authority and self-sacrifice as his depiction of the American hero.[10]

In the first half of the novel, Brackenridge makes it clear that the new American artist's task is not easy, but he repeatedly shows himself equal to it. Early on, for example, he establishes the similarity between his artistry and the Captain's verbal artifice by claiming that "my business is to speak nonsense; this being the only way to keep out of the reach of criticism" and to "please fools" (pp. 36, 37). The implications are, first, that the American artist is at odds with his readers, who fail to appreciate "sense," and second, that to hold their attention, he must act the fool himself or, as Brackenridge will later describe his task, must "deceive the world, and, never let it come into their heads that he has spent a thought on [his] subject" (p. 161). The breezy self-irony in such statements leaves the impression that Brackenridge feels confident of his ability to hold his audience, and even his later, poignant depiction of a fictitious fellow artist who died in poverty and obscurity does little to negate that impression.

Brackenridge begins that imaginary anecdote by comparing his compatriot's meager living accommodations with the more spacious quarters of famous London authors. They have traditionally lived in the "upper stories" of "mansions," we are told, but M'Comas, the writer he had hoped to visit in Philadelphia, had lived in the rat-infested "second story" of a "low building": "The roof was low, and did not permit a tall man as I am, to stand upright on my entrance" (pp. 171, 172). The architectural symbolism suggests both the paucity of the American artist's materials, which constrains him to write second-rate rather than top-flight "stories," and the unaccommodating attitude of his audience, who would have him lower himself to its level and who, when he persists in his writing, considers him "a raving crazy brained creature." Brackenridge expresses his resentment at such an "undervaluing manner" in M'Comas's miserly landlady (p. 172), and in commiserating with the intellectually starved author, he suggests yet another reason for the man's untimely demise: the paucity of "American" artists in general. "I have no doubt," Brackenridge explains, "that want of food, reducing him to great weakness, together with pain of mind from his desolate situation, in a new country, where there were but few in the same line with himself, with whom he could share his joys, or communicate his griefs, might hasten the dissolution of his frame, prematurely" (p. 195). The obvious similarities between Brackenridge and the dead artist, a Scottish immigrant who spent his life writing a "playful satire" on American follies, suggest finally that Brackenridge was indulging in a bit of artful self-portraiture, and he reinforces our suspicion of likeness when he includes the man's long poem in his own text: he regrets that some readers will assume that he has written it himself and that his prefatory anecdote is an "invention" to make the poem more interesting and "to keep myself out of sight and behind the curtain" (p. 173). Readers who take the bait, however, and who read this anecdote merely as an appeal to their sympathy—and patience—miss its larger significance, for the artist who tells this sad tale is himself a survivor. Brackenridge is so clearly in control of his materials in these early pages that he can, in fact, have it both ways. He can elicit our sympathy for the common plight of American artists, and he can win our admiration for his own uncommon ingenuity in overcoming that plight. Unlike the "unfortunate Scotchman" of the anecdote, our author is free to move on.

By the time he came to write the first volume of Part II, published in 1804, Brackenridge's sense of his own imaginative freedom and of his own authority seems to have diminished considerably. In an early scene, for example, he imagines for us another undervalued American artist, but here the distance between our author and the failed artist he portrays appears virtually nonexistent. The scene begins with the Captain visiting an insane asylum, wishing to see a "mad poet" who lives and works in the "second story." Unlike M'Comas, this second-story artist is not merely (and mistakenly) thought mad but is mad, "confined here by his relations" because he has become "so absent in mind, that he [is] incapable of taking care of himself" (p. 386). Moreover, this poet has made Farrago "the hero of his Poem" and is thus busily engaged in "travestying" Farrago's adventures (p. 386). The brief incident ends with the Captain leaving the asylum "affected with melancholy" and with Brackenridge's cheerless promise that the madman-artist's "manuscript having fallen into our hands, we shall select parts of it, and according as the reader seems to like that which he gets, we shall give him more" (p. 387).

Brackenridge and the mad poet are writing on the same subject and the remainder of *Modern Chivalry* will contain the madman's work interspersed with the present author's, suggesting that these two artists and their texts are indistinguishable. Consequently, it would seem that by 1804 Brackenridge felt himself to be writing a mere "travesty," an inferior and farcical imitation of life, a second-rate story. Even more revealing of his frustration in this stage of the novel is the notion that the American artist's madness consists of his being "incapable of taking care of himself," for Brackenridge presents himself, here and elsewhere in this section, as sacrificing his own aesthetic preferences to those of the untutored people, whose childlike attention can be held only by indirection, "nonsense," "deceit." It is the people, then, or more specifically, the American artist's altruistic loyalty to them, that constrains him to write "travesty," as our author explains in a later scene in which he depicts a company of village players engaged in a pantomime, with Harlequin playing the role of "a politician with the people on his back" (p. 440). There Brackenridge defensively anticipates the objections of any mature readers in his audience: "The critic will say, what use can there be in such representations? We do not write altogether for grave, or even grown men; our book is not for a day only. We mean it for the coming generation, as well as the present; and intending solid observations, *we interlard pleasantry to make the boys read*" (p. 443).

It is the American in Brackenridge that makes him want to serve a rising people by continuing to find new and ever more fantastical ways to make them read. But the artist in him regrets the constraints thus imposed on his imagination and makes him want to defend his authorial choices. He does so again at the end of this section, admitting that though "my inclination leads me to metaphysics, chiefly, . . . I have confined my self in this volume, to mere narrative" (p. 463). Although he attributes this decline in the scope and caliber of his work to old age, the cumulative evidence in this volume and in the subsequent ones suggests that he may be deceiving himself; at least it suggests another explanation. Like his hero, Brackenridge never stops promoting the republican virtue of self-denial; indeed, one of the last chapters of the 1815 volume consists entirely of a diatribe against the "*want of self-denial*, or want of sense" in the nation's public bodies (p. 801). The second half of *Modern Chivalry*, however, provides detailed evidence of the cost of such self-sacrifice to the American hero, the American artist, and, consequently, to the new American story. The formal deterioration of this text is finally attributable to Brackenridge's having sacrificed his first "inclinations" as an artist and having "confined" himself at last to a "second story," a "mere" travesty from his point of view, but as Franklin would have understood, a useful means of communicating instruction to the common people.

Modern Chivalry is, after all, a satire.[11] I began by claiming that the discrepancy between the mode of sociopolitical authority Brackenridge intended to promote at the outset of his novel and the picture of failed authority that has emerged by its end is the logical, if unforeseen, result of his decision to highlight what Franklin had chosen to downplay: the folly of the people in rejecting the learned counsel of an educated elite. Northrup Frye's analysis of literary modes provides yet another set of terms for explaining Brackenridge's ultimately self-defeating narrative strategy, but one that is equally useful. The philosopher, Frye explains, in terms readily applicable to Franklin's authorial stance in the *Autobiography*, "teaches a certain way or method of living; he stresses some things and despises others; what he recommends is carefully selected from the data of human life." The satirist, on the other hand, "may often represent the collision between a selection of standards from experience and the feeling that experience is bigger than any set of beliefs about it. The satirist demonstrates the infinite variety of what men do by showing the futility, not only of saying what they ought to do, but even of attempts to systematize or formulate a coherent scheme of what they do. Philosophies of life abstract from life, and an abstraction implies the leaving out of inconvenient data. The satirist brings up these inconvenient data."[12]

If satire represents a collision between professed standards and perceptions of lived experience, Brackenridge's lack of aesthetic control over his multivolumed satire suggests perhaps the degree of impact in that collision. It suggests, at the very least, his inability to resolve with uniform effectiveness the growing conflict between ideology and actuality, between the control strategies of leadership and the retaliatory assertiveness of the people in the first ten or fifteen years following the signing of the Constitution. By the end of *Modern Chivalry*, the "inconvenient data" that were so confidently ridiculed in the opening pages have overridden hero, author, and text alike: the language of social control has failed in its job, and a second story has established itself as an ever-present and ever-growing threat to the revolutionary generation's promotion of a new patriarchal world view.

ꙮ 3

"The Folly of Precipitate Conclusions": Brown's *Wieland*

Neither Franklin's *Autobiography* nor *Modern Chivalry* leaves the reader with any proper sense of an ending. The *Autobiography*, for example, does not end in literary fashion at all; it merely stops. Franklin's projected outline for the work would have taken the narrative up to the late 1780s, that is, to the "present" in which he was writing. But the narrative breaks off around 1760, and it seems logical to attribute the truncated ending not solely to Franklin's failing health but also to the fact that in the years next to be recounted, the gap between Franklin's actual life and the fictional life story he was presenting to his readers as a model had become too great to be bridged by his usual artful methods. Brackenridge's novel is plagued by a similar gap between professed ideology and lived experience, and although his text deteriorates in quality and plausibility as a result, there is evidence that he, too, had intended to carry his project to greater lengths. "I do not know that I shall write more," he admits in the last paragraph of *Modern Chivalry*, "though I have some transactions in my mind, that I could wish to chronicle; and characters that might be drawn" (p. 807). If readers are left with a sense of anything after reading these two texts, it is that the authors are ultimately unreliable storytellers: in both narratives the language of authority becomes more and more cut off from reality, and no literary resolution of this problem seems possible—there are still aspects of the new American story that "might" be told.

Charles Brockden Brown raises this implicit narrative concern over the ultimate effectiveness of verbal artifice and the resulting tendency toward unsatisfying narrative endings to a formal principle. Specifically, Brown carries the psychological implications of Franklin's and Brackenridge's language of social control to its logical limit and portrays language as a means of mind control. In his Gothic renderings of the new American story, he explores the consciousness of Americans trying to survive in a world in which human motives are ever inscrutable and unpredictable, and the sort of verbal artifice—including counterfeiting, forgery, and verbal "shorthand"—that his predecessors had used to repress anarchic social elements is used literally to repress the anarchic elements in the human psyche. Thus in *Wieland; or, The Transformation*, renaming experience is portrayed as a necessary means of self-denial, of forgetting, driving out of consciousness the darker truths about one's human nature, and the art of renaming, which *Wieland*'s narrator learns from the various father figures in her life, is equated with the art of telling a one-sided story, one that reveals only half the truth. What makes this "American Tale" and Brown's others so terrifying, however, is his final insistence on the limited temporal effectiveness of such artful stories, and he teaches readers this lesson by structuring his narratives around the impossibility of ever safely drawing a conclusion. In *Wieland*, the type of "inconvenient data" that Franklin had so carefully glossed over and that Brackenridge had allowed to get the upper hand surface repeatedly and ever unexpectedly to challenge the narrator's deductions about herself and others, and her survival depends on her ability to revise her own story at a moment's notice and thus to defuse any rival second story that threatens her life, her peace of mind, or her authoritative control over her text. And as we witness the urgent and continuous "transformation" of her narrative, we come to learn the "folly of precipitate conclusions."

Starting with William Dunlap, author of the first critical biography of Charles Brockden Brown, critics of Brown's novels have persistently resorted to external data—especially Brown's "headlong rapidity of composition"—to account for apparent inconsistencies in the texts, the most prominent of these being the characteristically "muddled" ending.[1] Critical readings of *Wieland*, for example, have offered various extratextual explanations—apologies—for its conclusion: on one hand, Brown is portrayed as a "careless writer" whose inattention to revision forced him to concoct an improbable "*deus ex machina* denouement"; on the other, his opportunities for revision are shown to have been severely limited by the page groupings of the proofs and thus "the very professionalism of the printer" is blamed for the various abruptnesses of the final chapter.[2] Only in the last fifteen years have critics begun to shift some of the blame for the bothersome ending onto the narrator, Clara, and yet what is seen as her final "artistic confusion" is still shown to be the inevitable result of "Brown's own indecision," his "contradictory and unresolved" notions about the role of fiction.[3]

Granted, *Wieland*'s conclusion *is* bothersome, not only because of
Clara's rapid attempt to tie up all loose ends but also because of its rather
cavalier optimism after some two hundred pages of deepening moral
chaos and especially because of its heavy dependence on what Leslie
Fiedler has rightly called "broad coincidences hard to credit."[4] But to
attribute such blatant aesthetic deviance to Brown's lack of forethought,
discipline, or aesthetic principles is to overlook certain salient features in
the catalog of his fiction. That is, it seems noteworthy that five of his six
novels are written in an epistolary format, an authorial decision which
signals that the narrator's point of view should constitute a thematic concern and which also, as Henry Fielding pointed out, effectively frees an
author from the obligation to create "regular beginnings and conclusions."[5] Furthermore, Brown left two novels, *Stephen Calvert* and *Memoirs
of Carwin the Biloquist*, unfinished, and a third, *Arthur Mervyn*, was published in two parts, its ending delayed for over a year. On the basis of this
evidence, we should at the very least allow that Brown was aware of, if not
actively concerned with, the problems entailed in making satisfactory
endings.

Evidence of the latter possibility, however, may be found in the texts,
where, if intentionality be at issue, Brown seems to have gone out of his
way to impress those problems on his readers. All of his novels have
endings that call attention to themselves—that call into question not only
their own credibility but also the belief in the possibility of endings per se.
Edgar Huntly, for example, ends with a letter describing the assumed
death of the arch villain Clithero Edny, after which the writer, Sarsefield,
concludes: "With the life of this wretch, let our regrets and our fore-
bodings terminate. . . . May this be the last arrow in the quiver of adversity! Farewell!"[6] I say "assumed death" because what actually happens is
that Clithero jumps from a boat into the water and is "seen no more"
(4:293). Only fifty pages earlier Sarsefield had seen Edgar plunge "into a
rapid stream, from a height from which it was impossible to fall and to
live." "You sunk to rise no more," he told the miraculously surviving
Edgar, and yet, "My eyes, my ears bear testimony to your existence now, as
they formerly convinced me of your death. What am I to think? What
proofs am I to credit?" (4:242).

Such questions recur throughout the book—"What should I think?"
(4:11), asks Edgar. "How was I to consider this act[?] . . . What are the
conclusions to be drawn by dispassionate observers?" (4:91–92)—and cut
to the heart of a novel replete with "consequences . . . that cannot be

foreseen" (4:90); outcomes that are "contradictory to precedent events" (4:194); "exception[s] to all the rules that govern us in our judgments of human nature" (4:45–46); and in particular, stories, such as the one Clithero tells Edgar, which are "completely the reverse of all . . . expectations" (4:90). Given this emphasis on the extreme difficulty of drawing conclusions and this backlog of thwarted expectations, readers who credit —or discredit—Brown with his villain's convenient "suicide" in the final chapter surely do so with as much credulity as Sarsefield, who foresees an end to adversity. In other words, it is this narrator's sanguine sense of an ending, not Brown's, that warrants our skepticism: there is no absolute proof of Clithero's death, and in light of Edgar's survival in a strikingly similar situation, we are obliged to suspect that both Clithero and the contingent threat of further adversity are still at large in a naive America. If we are left with any certainty at all, it is that Edgar is correct in exclaiming, near the end of his portion of the narrative, "How little cognizance have men over the actions and motives of each other! How total is our blindness with regard to our own performances!" (4:278).

The pervasiveness of this dual theme—for it appears in various forms in all the novels—necessarily fuels our skepticism regarding the credibility of Brown's other narrative endings and his other self-satisfied narrators. In *Ormond*, for example, Sophia Westwyn bases her conclusions and her optimism for the future solely on her estimation of Constantia's character, though in fact neither she nor the reader has actually seen what transpired between her friend and the villain Ormond behind closed doors. We are left with the suspicion that Sophia's case parallels Constantia's—that perhaps "a bias . . . swayed her thoughts, though she knew not that they were swayed"—thus that her admitted faith in the "ultimate restoration of tranquillity"—in happy endings—has made her an unreliable narrator (2:157, 292). Both *Jane Talbot* and *Clara Howard* end with seemingly resolved misunderstandings, claims of undying love, and pledges to marry, and yet throughout these novels, which are structured as series of impassioned and hastily dispatched letters, we have witnessed decisions and revisions which mere minutes have reversed, including reversals of sentiment within any given letter: "Skip the last couple of sentences," writes Jane, "or think of them as not mine: I disown them"; in another instance, her lover concludes, "In this long letter I have not put down one thing that I intended" (5:234, 268). Indeed, what proofs are readers to credit when characters know their own hearts and minds so imperfectly and when we have been specifically warned in *Jane Talbot* that "passion may

dictate large and vehement offers upon paper, which deliberating prudence would never allow to be literally adhered to" (5:265)? The very
tidiness of such endings calls attention to itself and to the possibility that
the narrators have been and will continue to be blind to their own performances, for Sophia, Clara, and Jane have all repeatedly witnessed the
ubiquity of the "unexpected" and the "unforeseen"—two frequent epi-
thets in Brown—and seem yet to be unwary of "the folly of precipitate
conclusions" (3:57).

The last phrase is used by Arthur Mervyn near the beginning of his tale,
and although he seems, in the early stages, to be circumspect enough to
realize that "it may by no means be uncommon for men to *fashion* their
conclusions in opposition to evidence and *probability*," he quickly goes the
way of all Brown's characters, developing a myopic pride in his own
"power of arranging . . . ideas and forming conclusions" (3:76, 116).
Throughout the novel Arthur is repeatedly shown to misinterpret the
actions and motives of others—of Welbeck, Wallace, Mrs. Fielding, his
(perhaps) future wife, to name but a few—and to be blind to his own
performances. His professed good intentions more often than not cause
others anger or anguish and at times physical harm. Again, in light of this
character's overwhelming lack of insight, we must doubt his self-professed
powers of deduction. And not surprisingly, in the last paragraphs, after
musing with ambivalence over his planned marriage—to one of the first
Dark Ladies in American literature—he comes to an impasse: "This is but
the humble outline of the scene; something is still to be added to complete our felicity. What more can be added? What more? . . . But why am I
indulging this pen-prattle?" His final act as narrator is to abjure his pen
"till all is settled" regarding his future, "till Mervyn has been made the
happiest of men" (3:446). In other words, there is no "regular" conclusion. Like the villainous Clithero, Arthur's ambivalence is merely seen no
more—the moral conflict is repressed rather than resolved—and though
the written narrative stops, the action quite obviously does not. It seems
unlikely that a con—and conned—man like Arthur will ever be the happiest of men, but the larger issue here is determined by the final metaphorical act. We are forced to consider whether a narrative ending is ever
significant of anything more than an "Arthur"/author's[7] laying down of
the pen for lack of knowing "what more can be added"—that is, whether
endings are possible when "Life," as Arthur's situation has shown, "is
dependent on a thousand contingencies not to be computed or foreseen"
(3:135).

What I have been trying to show is that the unsatisfactoriness of Brown's endings is consistent with the vision of reality that emerges as these various texts progress. His novels blatantly and repeatedly challenge the reader's sense of an ending. Specifically, Brown's fictional worlds are governed by coincidence, "contingencies"; as a result, unforeseen complications are ever imminent, and thus narrative closure, the tying together of all the loose strands of a story, is impossible. Moreover, since human actions and motivations are always shown to be ambiguous, then hindsight is ultimately as unreliable as foresight, and thus denouement, the *un*tangling of the various strands of a story, is equally impossible.[8] In such worlds the human condition is that suggested by Ormond when he berates Constantia, "Thou seest not an inch before thee or behind" (2:255). Narrators are constitutionally unreliable because no one can ever know the whole story.

Yet nearly all of Brown's characters eventually take on the role of narrator or, more specifically, of "author." The role allotted to the hero by Franklin and Brackenridge is democratized in Brown's fiction (in *Edgar Huntly* alone, Edgar, Clithero, Mrs. Lorimer, her brother Arthur, and, by virtue of their letter-writing, Sarsefield and Waldegrave are all "authors") to the extent that storytelling appears to be an aspect of the human condition. Contrived narratives, whether oral stories, letters, journals, manuscripts, or books, abound in these novels as representations of their authors' attempts to impose order on an anarchic reality. We have already witnessed Arthur Mervyn's pride in his talent for "arranging . . . ideas and forming conclusions"; similarly, at the beginning of her tale, Clara Howard informs her correspondent that she has put "the enclosed letters into a regular series" (5:187). Brown's emphasis is always on the contrivance of regularity, the artificiality, of such narratives, which emphasis gives rise to his frequent metaphors of verbal trickery: forgery in *Ormond* and *Jane Talbot*, counterfeiting in *Arthur Mervyn* and *Ormond*, and ventriloquism in *Wieland*. But he is also careful to show that the success of such trickery is dependent not only on the talent of the storyteller but also, as Clara Wieland will come to understand, on the "errors"—the credulity—"of the sufferers" (1:244). Thus to be human is to create and to believe in stories that must inevitably be false, partial and biased renderings of events that are ultimately inscrutable. "Disastrous and humiliating is the state of man!" exclaims Edgar Huntly. "By his own hands is constructed the mass of misery and error in which his steps are forever involved" (4:278).

Brown's novels bespeak a theory of fiction similar to that described by

Frank Kermode, whose apt phrase, "the sense of an ending," I have been using throughout: "Men in the middest make considerable imaginative investments in coherent patterns which, by the provision of an end, make possible a satisfying consonance with the origins and with the middle."[9] "Men exist more for the future than the present," we are told in *Clara Howard*. "We are busy marking the agreement between objects as they rise before us, and our previous imaginations" (5:201). Very simply, Brown's characters hope to foresee, or to "fashion," endings to their various stories so as to give stability to their lives and meaning to the fearfully random events in the middest; they need fictional structures; they need to believe in their own "authority." What makes Brown's work unique, however, and singularly appropriate for an American author writing only twenty-odd years into the "middest" of the American experiment, in his insistence on the extreme danger attendant on any rigid belief in the finality of human stories and thus of human authority over the temporal flow of events. His characters suffer (and occasionally die) as a result of relying too heavily on their own sense of an ending.

In discussing *Wieland*, I will try to delineate more fully the complexities of this theory of fiction which focuses so fearfully on misperceived endings. In particular, I will discuss Clara Wieland's role as unreliable narrator, her spurious "conclusions," and what they tell us about stories and storytellers; in closing, I will try to derive, from the evidence of this text, what Brown considered to be the proper uses of fiction, for when contrived endings are used so consistently and self-consciously to represent palpable threats to human well-being, two of the more obvious questions to arise are, why write fiction and, perhaps more important, why read it? Indeed, these questions are raised to thematic concern in Brown's works. "Why do I write?" asks Clara Howard's would-be lover. "For whose use do I pass my time thus?" (5:189). Clara Wieland questions her own responsibilities as storyteller—"Why should I rescue this event from oblivion?"—and elsewhere, after reading from the text of her brother's confession, will ask, as a reader to readers, "Will you not . . . be astonished that I read thus far? What power supported me through such a task I know not" (1:228, 174). Some critics have argued that, strongly influenced by the Scottish Common Sense school of thought, "the conventional wisdom of his age," Brown "feared that fiction would unsettle the mental balance of novel-readers" and therefore wrote novels to dramatize "the dangers of novel-reading."[10] I do not believe this to be the case, however, for in worlds such as the ones Brown creates, in which *all* reasoning is shown to

be fictitious, mere storytelling, the gravest danger lies in immediate action. As a result, written stories serve both their authors and their readers
as precautionary mediations, never finally foolproof but useful nevertheless, if for no other reason than for their very duration. *Wieland* presents a
hierarchy of fictional forms and thus a hierarchy of dangers, but its characters encounter the greatest perils when they stop writing and stop reading—when they engage actively in "the folly of precipitate conclusions."

Clara Wieland begins her narrative with statements of bleak despair,
revealing that since "every remnant of good" has been wrested from her
life "and exterminated," she has resigned herself to "a destiny without
alleviation" (1:6). In recalling the dire events of her recent past, first the
loss of a lover as a result of a con man's tricks, then the death of her
immediate family at the hands of a brother who believed he was obeying
divine commands, she becomes more and more confirmed in her hope-
lessness and foresees no alternative but death: "Why not terminate at once
this series of horrors? . . . I will die, but . . . only when my tale is at an
end" (1:228). Eventually, after she has described her brother's similarly
inspired attempt on her own life, his awakening to remorse, and his suicide, we read, "And now my repose is coming—my work is done!" (1:233).
But if we have taken her at her word and expect her to die after this final,
breathless exclamation point, we are mistaken, for on the next page we
find a continuation of her work, "Written three years after the foregoing,
and dated at Montpellier," and of her life, which has regained its "ancient
tranquillity" (1:234, 237).

Setting aside for a short while the specifics of the questionable conclusions drawn in this sequel, what we have in effect is a narrator who has
projected two distinct endings, neither of which comes to pass, and who
has produced a third, the sequel, which, as Clara herself admits and as
critics have wholeheartedly concurred, bespeaks "events the least probable" (1:234). What has not been generally recognized, however, is that
Clara's inability to satisfy her audience's expectations with a consummate
ending has been prefigured throughout as a family trait, passed on to her
by fathers and father figures. Clara's uncle, for example, tells the story of
her maternal grandfather, who literally jumped to a hasty and mortal
conclusion (and I should probably say here how strongly I agree with
Arthur G. Kimball, who feels that "Brown has been underrated as an
ironist"[11]). While on a picnic the grandfather had suddenly "betrayed

alarm," but instead of enlightening his companions as to the details, he had briefly reported that he had just received a "summons" from his dead brother, and "before their surprize would allow them to understand the scene," he had rushed to the edge of a cliff and thrown himself over, leaving his immediate audience and future audiences, such as Clara, "unacquainted with particulars" of what he actually heard. Moreover, the uncle's personal conclusion to this story, that his father had "unquestionably" suffered "maniacal" illusions, is unsatisfactory to Clara: "I was far from accounting for [such] appearances in my uncle's manner" (1:178–79). Thus we are presented with an inconclusive story within an inconclusive story, a dubious heritage for any author. Nor is the Wieland side of the family any more fortunate or its endings any less precipitate. Clara's questionable success as narrator is specifically foreshadowed in the early authorial, or storytelling, experience of her brother, in whom Clara sees an "obvious resemblance" to her father, and of her father himself (1:23).

Early in the novel we learn that the younger Wieland had begun work on a book about "that mysterious personage, the Daemon of Socrates." His "skill in Greek and Roman learning was exceeded by that of few, and no doubt the world would have accepted a treatise upon this subject from his hand with avidity; but alas! this and every other scheme of felicity and honor, were doomed to sudden blast and hopeless extermination" (1:48). On a purely phenomenal level, we are presented with a written text that does not end according to plan (that never ends) and with the image of a reading audience left with no conclusive knowledge. Thematically, Theodore's unfinished treatise provides a more specific analogy to his sister's ultimately inconclusive narrative, for the "Daemon" in question was perceived to be a personal demon by his accusers and a Satanic visitation by the later Church Fathers.[12] This unresolved historical debate virtually resurfaces in *Wieland*. Once the disembodied voices begin, Theodore maintains "the probability of celestial interference" (1:75), and Clara entertains both the possibility of "evil geniuses" and of a "mysterious monitor," whom she calls "*my* heavenly friend" (1:132, 85, 94). Furthermore, Theodore's accusers impute his acts to "the influence of daemons," and Carwin the biloquist will declare that "some daemon of mischief seized me" (1:176, 201). Any final interpretation of *Wieland*'s plot depends on the reader's evaluation of the nature of the "daemonic" voices, and Clara's seemingly complete book is hardly more helpful than her brother's unfinished one in enabling us to draw our own conclusions. That is, even though Brown himself ostensibly weights the evidence in favor of Carwin's guilty agency with a scientific, authorial footnote explaining "Biloquium, or ventriloqution" (1:198), readers are never given any direct proof of what young Wieland hears on the night of his crime: the source of the voice that orders him to kill his family remains shrouded in mystery.

Readers are not permitted to witness the incidents immediately leading to the crime, for example. We get all our information from stories told after the fact: Wieland's confession is first delivered orally in a courtroom, then copied down by an unknown person, and finally copied down again by Clara, who incorporates only a part of the text into her own story; she stops "in the midst of the narrative" and picks up again "near the conclusion" (1:175, 176). Her action alone suggests the material "transformation" that stories undergo in the telling, and we are led to suspect, as one of Brown's later heroines declares, that "second-hand" narratives have "all the deductions and embellishments which must cleave to every story as it passes through the imaginations" (5:215)—and the pens—of its various tellers.

The unreliability of the story evidence Brown provides is confirmed once Wieland and Carwin begin to change their own stories, to revise their former conclusions. Originally, Wieland says (and unquestionably believes) that he had heard a "direct communication" from God ordering him to kill his wife and children (1:167); Carwin says that he was not in the house at the time the voice was heard. Later confronted by both Clara and a fierce Wieland, who demands, "whose voice—was it thy contrivance? Answer me," a shaken Carwin admits, "it is too true—I did appear—in the entry—did speak. The contrivance was mine, but—" (1:220). Wieland here concludes that he had been "guilty of . . . error" in believing he had heard God's voice, that he had "been made the victim of human malice." Within seconds, however, he revises his story a second time. He apparently receives a new "illumination" regarding Carwin's agency, which he communicates to Clara: "The form thou hast seen was the incarnation of a daemon. The visage and voice which urged me to the sacrifice of my family, were his. Now he personates a human form: then he was invironed with the lustre of heaven. . . . He from whom his commission was received is God" (1:225–26). Wieland is once again confirmed in his belief, but readers presented with such conflicting and urgently revised stories are farther than ever from being able to draw a conclusion. Then arises a final source of contention, "new sounds . . . uttered from above." Carwin having withdrawn from the room after his truncated confession, a voice tells Wieland that "not heaven or hell, but thy senses have misled thee to commit these acts. . . . Be lunatic no longer." Although Clara admits that her brother "reflected not" that this voice might be as spurious as the original murderous commands, she says that Wieland has been "restored to the perception of truth" and describes his overwhelming remorse and the resulting suicide, which he effects "with the quickness of thought" (1:230, 231). The phrase suggests yet another hastily drawn conclusion.

Given this multiplicity of story evidence, how can one determine what Theodore Wieland actually heard on the night of his crime? Bell's reading recapitulates Clara's conclusions and seems representative of the critical consensus, that "Carwin is only indirectly responsible for Wieland's madness," that his previous vocal tricks have "only unsettle[d] Theodore's ability to distinguish between fact and fiction, leading him [on the night of the crime] to accept the reality of voices produced by his own imagination."[13] But to say that Wieland was insane and imagined hearing voices is to overlook certain unanswered questions such as Carwin's admission that he was in the house and "did speak" to Wieland on that night. "The contrivance was mine, but—": his confession remains significantly inconclusive. Since we never know the extent of his "contrivance," and since he had previously admitted his betrayal of Clara's lover, Pleyel, a man of "exquisite sagacity," by a vocal "imposture" that "amounted to proof which the most jealous scrutiny would find to be unexceptional" (1:209–10), it seems probable that the voice that ordered Wieland to sacrifice his family was real, was Carwin's. Probability is all Brown allows us, however, and even to say the voice was Carwin's does not resolve the final problem: what is the source of Carwin's vocal powers?

Brown himself provides a seemingly authoritative footnote to acknowledge the existence of "ventrilocution," but buried among the scientific information is the admission that "unsatisfactory speculations are given on the means by which the effects are produced. . . . This power is difficult to explain" (1:198). In the midst of the confrontation scene, Clara declared that whether Carwin were "infernal, or miraculous, or human, there was no power . . . to decide" (1:227), and readers are left similarly powerless to determine the source of Carwin's "voice." He himself knows "not by what name to call it" (1:198). He can only explain ambiguously, "the mode in which heaven is said by the poet to interfere . . . [is] somewhat analogous to my province" and elsewhere admits to being controlled by a "daemon" (1:203, 201). Therefore, lacking absolute knowledge of what Wieland heard, we cannot reject the possibility that he heard the audible enunciation of God's will (cf. the "story" of Abraham). More important, we are forced to realize that Clara's "treatise" on daemons is as inconclusive as her brother's because, as one of Carwin's former acquaintances affirmed, the biloquist's powers are "such as no human intelligence is able to unravel" (1:130).[14]

If Theodore's unfinished book foreshadows the ultimate functional inadequacy of Clara's narrative, its inability to communicate the reality behind events, her father's "imperfect tale," which is the first "story" in *Wieland*, suggests another, more integral cause of narrative imperfection: not only does external reality remain inscrutable, but storytellers are shown to be unreliable. The elder Wieland's fate was similar in many particulars to that of his son and remains, for future generations, as inexplicable. He had been an extremely religious man, who spent his final night expecting a direct communication from his God, a dire retribution, the reasons for which he would not reveal to his family. He was found alone in his place of worship, his body "scorched and bruised," his clothes "reduced to ashes," and when he was asked for an explanation on his deathbed, "the sum of the information which he chose to give" added up to an "imperfect account." "There was somewhat in his manner that indicated an imperfect tale," and Clara's uncle "was inclined to believe that half the truth had been suppressed" (1:18). "What are the conclusions that we must form?" (1:19) asks Clara, an ironically appropriate question for a woman who has inherited from her father the same dubious authority as a storyteller.

It seems incredible that critics have so long taken Clara at her word, faulting Brown rather than her for *Wieland*'s doubtful ending, when she admits that her "narrative may be invaded by inaccuracy and confusion," that her "opinions were the sport of eternal change," and at one point, that her "mind seemed to be split into separate parts, and these parts to have entered into furious and implacable contention" (1:147, 180, 140). Moreover, she is repeatedly shown to suppress information as a result of having had second thoughts about the cost to herself of telling the truth. Early in the novel she describes her duplicitous treatment of Pleyel, her willful withholding of the "true state of [her] affections" (1:79) to make him jealous enough to make his own declaration. After considering the possibility of making her "confession in a letter," she decides against it on the grounds that it would reveal a side of her womanly nature that would appear unseemly: "A second thought shewed me the rashness of this scheme" (1:82). Even though, writing in retrospect, she is willing to admit the errors of such self-serving contrivances, there is further evidence to suggest that her conscious suppression of the truth in these instances may be merely the external manifestation of her repressed nature throughout. In the sequel, for example, we learn that during her separation from Pleyel, during his marriage, though she tried to view him as a "friend," her "passion" was merely "smothered for a time": "My passion was disguised to myself" (1:237–38).

A number of critics have commented on Clara's thinly disguised incestuous desires for her brother, and this tendency to obfuscate "passions" and motives even to herself is figuratively reinforced by the many instances when Clara describes her narrow escapes from dangers which she perceives to emanate from a dark *recess*, a word she often associates with her closet (e.g., 1:87, 207). Kimball has written persuasively that "Clara's symbolic private closet" serves as "a striking metaphor for Locke's 'dark room of the mind'": "Like Edgar Huntly's wilderness cave, it harbors the shadowy night-side of the id. . . . The closet contains at different times the 'memoirs' of her father, the incarnate irrationality which is Carwin, a 'lancet and other small instruments' with which Clara contemplates suicide [and murder], a manuscript of her innermost secrets, . . . and a host of other vague terrors of physical violence, death, seduction and incest, which . . . remain in obscurity."[15] That she keeps her father's manuscript locked in her closet metaphorically strengthens the idea that she has inherited his dubious mode of authority, and that her own journal of secret transactions is also linked with this dark recess provides more specific insights into her authorial psychology. Pleyel says that Clara always wrote much more than she permitted her friends to read and that when interrupted, she "hurried the [journal] out of sight" (1:125). More figuratively, Clara's journal is written in shorthand. On a phenomenal level, we perceive that the original information, "disguised" as *it* may be, is virtually transformed into a symbolic representation that offers only partial data to readers. Thematically, we are given metaphorical evidence that this narrator habitually uses language to conceal the truth. Thus Clara Wieland shows herself to be, by nature and by design, an eminently unreliable narrator.

The next question must be, then, what has Clara suppressed or repressed in the telling of *Wieland*? The distinction is necessary because two of her "conclusions" remain suspect by virtue of these closely aligned tendencies. The first is her final testimony regarding Wieland's death, which takes place, symbolically, in the second story of Clara's dwelling (see 1:56, 217). Clara describes her brother's death as a suicide, but because she and he were the only ones in the room at the time, we only have her word for it; and other of her "words" in this section cause us to doubt whether we really know what happened in that second story. In describing her preparations for the confrontation scene, for example, Clara revealed herself capable not only of premeditated "self-defense" against Carwin— "in a fold of my dress an open penknife was concealed"—but also of murderous passion (1:223). Convinced that Carwin had willfully tricked Wieland into murdering his family, she admits that she "thirsted" for the biloquist's blood and was "tormented by an insatiable appetite for his destruction" (1:221). In addition, she admits to having been capable of killing her brother to save her own life, of entertaining "any means of escape, however monstrous," and this memory precipitates an outburst of the inveterate desire for self-censure: "O, insupportable remembrance! hide thee from my view for a time; hide it from me that my heart was black enough to meditate the stabbing of a brother!" (1:222–23).

Like Wieland and Carwin during this final sequence of events, Clara revises her "story" frequently, and although she contends that she had been finally incapable of "self-defense," the rapid changes in her state of mind undermine our certainty. For example, what exactly does Clara mean when, in reviewing her account, she exclaims, "I listen to my own pleas, and find them empty and false" (1:223), and what motivates her to account for having Wieland's blood on her hands when she is found (1:232)? The inclusion of this detail is reminiscent of Carwin's artful "narratives": "Those that were . . . most minute, and, of consequence, least entitled to credit, were yet rendered probable by the exquisite art of this rhetorician. For every difficulty that was suggested, a ready and plausible solution was furnished" (1:74). Certainly, one conclusion readers would be warranted in drawing is that just as Wieland's death is caused by Clara's penknife, "plunged . . . to the hilt in his neck" (1:231), so might his "suicide" have been effected solely by Clara's pen—that Clara might have killed her brother and suppressed half of the truth in the later telling.[16]

I am, however, arguing only the possibility that Clara murdered her brother, and I argue thus because, first, it is the unreliability of conclusions per se that demands our attention in *Wieland*, rather than any one of Clara's conclusions; and second, the issue of whether Clara is a murderer is itself subsumed in her conclusion regarding Carwin. Her final word on this man who has been variously described as "an imp of mischief" and an "enemy of God and man" is that he is "probably engaged in the harmless pursuits of agriculture" in "a remote district of Pennsylvania" (1:123, 216,

239). This is the story Carwin told Clara and which she believed. But when he first appears in the book, it is stated that "he had formerly declared that it was his purpose to spend his life" in Spain (1:68). The point is stressed: Pleyel "was *taught* to believe that Carwin should never leave that country" (1:72; my emphasis), and yet Carwin has shown up to perpetrate his deceptions on the American scene. The biloquist himself admits that he is "destined perpetually to violate [his] resolutions," that "the temptation to interfere" is, for him, "irresistible," and he is described as a villain who "sets his engines of destruction . . . against every object that presents itself" (1:206, 200, 130). The Satanic overtones are not gratuitous, for as one critic has shown in delineating the parallels between *Wieland* and *Paradise Lost*, Carwin has brought "death and sin into the garden of *Wieland.*" In Brown's "American Tale," Carwin may be seen as evil incarnate, and if he is, and if, as Clara contends, he has turned his energies to harmless gardening, then surely evil has died out in America— a highly unlikely conclusion.[17] Like Milton's Satan, that first "author of evil" (*Paradise Lost*, 6:262), Carwin is presented as an "author" of "evils," of "unheard-of disasters" (1:50, 160). His specific evil, however, is that he is an artful storyteller, one who fashions tidy fictions with endings that seem absolute; and Clara Wieland has a constitutional need to believe in such stories, which, by the provision of an end, make a satisfying consonance with her interpretation of what has gone before.[18]

But if to accept a happy ending is to satisfy a need for order, it is also to repress knowledge of a truly anarchic reality, to indulge, however momentarily, in the comfort of "better thoughts." In the midst of her difficulties, Clara had admitted the extent of Carwin's demonic hold over her with images that showed him quite literally lurking in her mind: "Carwin was the phantom that pursued my dreams"; "the image of Carwin was blended in a thousand ways with the stream of my thoughts" (1:157, 148). But "better thoughts grew up in my mind imperceptibly," she says at the beginning of her sequel, and she emphasizes that the change was not the result of conscious effort: "Perhaps it merely argues a fickleness of temper, . . . a defect of sensibility" (1:235), that is, an unconscious desire to forget the darker implications arising from her past experiences, the second story that lurks beneath the surface of her present narrative. Clara's willingness to believe in Carwin's seductive tale shows that she has substantially repressed her former horror regarding his power to effect evil, a power that might at any moment resurface; and by extension, that she has repressed the horrifying extent of her own capacity for evil, perhaps her ability to kill even a brother. Her removal to Europe at the end heightens the sense that she has cut herself off from any direct knowledge of the evil potential that still lurks in America and in her own Americanness. Clara's various conclusions—that Wieland was merely mad, that she was a power-less bystander, that Carwin has repented of his storytelling—are indeed the comforting products of her better thoughts, but *Wieland*'s "happy" ending leaves any credulous readers on the brink of a dangerous future, unprepared.

Two of the central issues raised by this text are, what is the benefit for Clara in writing her "story" and for the reader in reading it? It is not enough to say that Clara writes to achieve peace of mind, for surely the more important aspect is how obviously that peace is founded on shaky ground. But it is also not enough to say that readers achieve a healthy distrust of reading fiction, for it is not reading but acting that generates the gravest danger in this book. *Wieland* presents a hierarchy of fictional forms and a variety of writers and readers, and to understand more fully the proper uses of fiction—and of language—as suggested by this novel, we must turn our attention back to the "middest."

First, it seems clear that Clara's writing and her ability to revise her story have kept her alive and relatively sane. Friends tried to withhold from her "the implements of writing; but they quickly perceived that to withstand would be more injurious than to comply" with her wishes (1:235). Clara firmly believed that she would "die . . . only when [her] tale [was] at an end," and one of her authorial outbursts reveals what she saw as the terrifying alternative to writing: "Why not terminate at once this series of horrors?" she asks, "—hurry to the verge of the precipice and cast myself for ever beyond remembrance and beyond hope?" (1:228). For Clara, the image of the precipice is equated with both death and insanity, and insanity is portrayed as having to encounter, without mediation, the dark side of the human psyche: the "heart . . . black enough" to entertain "insupportable desires." Thus her fervent drive throughout to suppress and to repress and her insistence on maintaining her own "authority," which is threatened from without but even more fearfully from within.

Wieland, more fearfully than the *Autobiography* or *Modern Chivalry*, presents a subtle and highly sophisticated defense of verbal artifice as a means of keeping an anarchic human nature in check. An early dream reveals Clara's fears of encountering what Kimball has called "the shadowy night-side of the id" (in this instance incestuous desires) and her salvation from such an encounter: "A pit, methought, had been dug in the path I had taken, of which I was not aware. . . . I saw my brother, standing at some distance before me, beckoning and calling me to make haste. He stood on the opposite edge of the gulph. I mended my pace, and one step more would have plunged me into the abyss, had not some one from behind . . . exclaimed, in a voice of eagerness and terror, 'Hold! hold!'" The voice, which turns out to be Carwin's, quoting from *Macbeth*, awakens her to "images so terrific" that they disabled her, "for a time, from distinguishing between sleep and wakefulness, and withheld from [her] the knowledge of [her] actual condition" (1:62). The final phrase holds the key to what might seem at first mere Gothic melodrama, for the scene acts as a metaphor for the psychological complexities of the creative process and, in particular, its dependence on sublimation. Clara has been saved from experiencing the primal depths of her incestuous desires, her "actual condition," by a poet's words projected out of the dark "recess" (1:61) where her dream originates.

The word *recess* is used elsewhere by Clara to describe the closet where her writings are kept and from which they eventually emerge. It is also used by Brown, in an earlier poem in which he had depicted his own (less urgent) experience in "Fancy's . . . enchanting maze": "In this recess I sat / And saw, or dream'd I saw, an airy shape, / And heard aerial notes, a voice" that he would also call "my genius, my divine / Instructress, better angel, heavenly friend . . . my Muse."[19] Later in the novel, Clara will call the voice that warns her away from the dangers brewing in her psychic closet "*my* heavenly friend" and after one vocal warning will wonder whether the phenomenon exists "in [her] fancy or without" (1:94, 147). It would seem that, among his numerous functions in this book, Carwin also serves as a creative impetus, a stylistic mentor. Just as he "taught" Pleyel to believe in stories, his fictions instruct and inspire Clara in the art of storytelling as a means of self-defense. The dream scene shows how Clara's poetic imagination, under Carwin's tutelage, enables her to transform potentially harmful energies into compelling "images," into a fictional surface narrative less harmful to herself and to others than the truth would inevitably be.[20] Similarly throughout, though her narrative of sublimation keeps her from acknowledging her true capacity to do evil, it also keeps her, for the duration of her tale, from so doing. We must remember that it was when Clara was trapped in an actual encounter with the murderous Wieland that she began to see no alternative but to become a murderer herself; the immediacy of the danger had forced her to a hasty conclusion. And Clara's case is not isolated: once Theodore leaves off writing his book on Socrates' Daemon, he must encounter the dangers of daemons face to face. Without benefit of mediation, his violent passions surface all too tragically, with "the quickness of thought."

Quickness of thought is the true culprit in *Wieland*, for although Clara's authorial experience provides intriguing insights into Brown's theory of creativity—a theory similar to his predecessors' theory of social control—the larger significance of the writing metaphor lies in the time factor. The thematic complement to the defense of literary art as mediation is the warning against unmediated response, against action based on precipitate conclusions, and this helps to illuminate the psychological seductiveness of Carwin's treacherous "authority." This multifarious character is dangerous as an artist figure in his own right because of the immediacy of his art: he is literally a *teller* of tales. In the world of *Wieland*, unsatisfactory narrative endings represent the insufficiency of conclusions derived by unreliable mental processes; consequently, in such a world the only safety lies in postponing those conclusions, metaphorically, in lengthy narratives committed to paper—prolonged "stories" that can be revised again and again to meet the needs of a moment. Carwin's vocal fictions, however, induce the most immediate misperceptions in (as in one of Clara's experiences) "interval[s] . . . too brief to be artificially measured" (1:85). Similar and more enlightening phrasing occurs in Brown's "The Man At Home," published the same year: "Our curiosity is proportioned, among other circumstances, to the shortness of the interval, and thus slightness of the bar between us and knowledge."[21] "Seeming slightness" is surely more accurate (for the Man is, of course, another of Brown's victims of credulity). Throughout *Wieland*, the human mind is shown to be infinitely fallible, and yet characters are driven to *know*, to jump the bar—or to strike through the mask, as a later American writer would call it. Carwin's vocal fictions are effective precisely because they allow his conclusion-seeking victims insufficient time for doubtful reflection; they seem to provide direct knowledge.

Finally, to follow the logic of Brown's metaphorical fictions one more step; if the written word is privileged over the spoken one, then a reading audience must be privileged over a listening one by virtue of the longer mental "interval." And as usual, *Wieland* delineates this moral by inversion. Theodore, for example, not only abandons his writing, but he also becomes "less disposed than formerly to . . . reading" (1:35) once Carwin's vocal tricks begin: thus an end to reading helps pave the way into the chaotic abyss of direct experience. Pleyel is the most noteworthy reader in this novel, however, and his behavior serves as a warning to *Wieland*'s readers in three respects, each showing by contrast the value of circumspect reading.

First, Pleyel's situation is somewhat analogous to the reader's, in that he becomes motivated to discover the real nature of Carwin's character and the information he reads has undergone several narrative transformations. The Philadelphia newspaper article, a notice of an escaped convict named Carwin, had been "copied from a British paper" (1:133). When Pleyel tracks down the printer, he finds that the article had been forwarded by a Mr. Hallet, who had received the clipping in a letter from one Ludloe, which letter, a damning accusation against Carwin, Pleyel also reads. At this point he believes he has discovered the truth about Carwin, but readers of *Wieland* must suspect the veracity of such emphatically secondhand narratives. The second way Pleyel serves as a warning is that, like Wieland, he is seduced from reading to acting. Armed with what he believes to be absolute proof of Carwin's villainy, he departs for Clara's house and on his way hears the false scenario that convinces him of her degeneracy. He later admits that though "hearing was the only avenue to information," his "uncertainty vanished": "I yielded not but to evidence which took away the power to withhold my faith" (1:134–45). Blinded by jealousy, Pleyel thus fails the test of experience in one of Brown's fateful intervals.

Finally, the jealousy I have just mentioned provides the most important clue to Pleyel's credulity in accepting the printed evidence against Carwin and to his main significance to the reader. His research into Carwin's background was originally precipitated by his misreading of Clara's journal. Glancing over her shoulder at a text written in shorthand, of which he caught "only parts of sentences" and random words—"*summer-house, midnight, . . . another* interview" (1:125)—he immediately harbored suspicions of her involvement with the biloquist: he jumped to a hasty conclusion. Although he saw the "necessity of resorting to other means of information" (1:126), his vision was already distorted by unconscious motives, and he never questioned his further reading. At the outset, then, Pleyel is shown to be a poor reader, and the end result is that Brown's readers, having learned from indirect experience, are forewarned against "the folly of precipitate conclusions."

I began this chapter by asking, what are the proper uses of fiction as suggested by *Wieland*? It should be obvious by now that this novel presents a world in which all mental processes are shown to be fiction-making because external realities such as the motives and actions of other people are ever inscrutable, and thus any interpretations of them must remain inconclusive "stories"; more important, because the human mind itself, in trying to interpret experience, is ever subject to unconscious impulses, "insupportable" passions, which must be repressed if life and "story" are to go on in orderly fashion—again, the result is sheer fiction. Because these are the lessons Clara Wieland learns from stories authored by the various father figures in her life, and because she does survive with her sanity intact to establish a happier household and to append a happier ending to a narrative that first appears to have ended in despair, it seems logical also to conclude that Brown was supporting his predecessors' patriarchal world view, even if he chose to take an extremely fearful and convoluted narrative route to do so. Even this conclusion must be revised, however, or at least qualified, because Clara is, after all, the daughter of this American family, and because Brown himself has long been credited not with patriarchal but with feminist sympathies as a result of his "advanced views as to the rights and education of women" in the new republic.[22] How can such "advanced views" be reconciled with such seemingly authoritarian ones? If Clara Wieland's narrative transformations are any indication, it would seem finally that Brown's feminism consisted of the belief that women are equal to men in their capacity to experience and to act upon the full range of human passions and that American daughters have much to learn from their fathers' ability to conceal the darker side of their nature beneath artful fictions.

PART II

Revision and Reform

Introduction: "The Fraud Is Manifest"

"The most common expedient employed by democratic nations to make an innovation in language consists in giving an unwanted meaning to an expression already in use. This method is very simple, prompt, and convenient; no learning is required to use it correctly and ignorance itself rather facilitates the practice; but that practice is most dangerous to the language. When a democratic people double the meaning of a word in this way, they sometimes render the meaning which it retains as ambiguous as that which it acquires."[1] It seems ironic that Tocqueville's predictions about American literature often fell so far short of the mark when his description of the problem of expedient and ambiguous language in this country so closely describes the concerns of those nineteenth-century authors whose works have come to be canonized as our earliest American classics. The previous chapters traced how the practice Tocqueville comments on came to be represented in three early American fictions, virtually as a political platform; in particular, how the revolutionary generation's postwar semantic strategies, which displaced the production of meaning from words themselves to qualified interpreters, like Franklin and Brackenridge's Captain, became assimilated in Brown's fiction to the point that all Americans were shown to be self-interested "authors" of fictions and all words to be unreliable—inconclusive—signifiers. In Part II I focus on works by Cooper, Poe, Hawthorne, and Melville to show how truly dangerous these nineteenth-century sons felt their Fathers' linguistic politics to be. As Emerson, one of the most outspoken and rebellious sons of his era, would warn his audience, "In due time the fraud is manifest, and words lose all power to stimulate the understanding or the affections."[2]

The attitudinal distance between these eighteenth- and nineteenth-century authors' views on language may be roughly measured by contrasting the virtual motto of Jefferson's generation, "the new circumstances under which we are placed call . . . for the transfer of old words to new objects," with the watchword of Emerson's, "old words are perverted to stand for things which are not."[3] It can almost be said that the revolutionary generation's respect for the political expediency of juggling semantics died with Jefferson. At least it seems one of American history's ironies that in the same year Jefferson—and John Adams—died (both on July 4, 1826), James Fenimore Cooper published what would become his best-known novel, *The Last of the Mohicans*, in which he would vicariously, in the guise of an indignant Indian, condemn his countrymen for their characteristically politicized language: "the pale-faces . . . have two words for each thing." Again, in *The Prairie*, published a year later, he would stress the theme that runs throughout the Leatherstocking Tales: "Is a Pale-face always made with two tongues? . . . He has said one thing when he meant another."[4]

I highlight the accusations made by Cooper's Indians, not only because he is the first American romancer I will study in this section but also because they establish the terms by which the language of paternalistic authority figures is represented and criticized throughout all of the fictions treated here. First, the duplicity of language, the elasticity so valued by the previous age, is consistently derided and rebuked. That is, the Founding generation's language of social control is portrayed in these nineteenth-century works as a language of patriarchal domination, perpetrated by white, educated, Anglo-Saxon, Protestant males who use words politically to further their own interests, which is to say, the interests and values of the dominant culture: "Such are the pale-faces," we read in *The Last of the Mohicans*, "[their] cunning tells [them] how to get together the goods of the earth."[5] The confidential guardians of the postrevolutionary period become, in Cooper, imperialistic white fathers who have arrogated the power of naming to themselves and, in the process, corrupted the names given by the original proprietors of the New World. They become, in Poe, tyrannical guardian-narrators who use language to exclude subversive foreign elements from closed rooms, closed minds, and closed—male-dominated—texts. They become, in Hawthorne, fraudulent socially sanctioned guardians—the physician, the minister, the judge—who control with equal proprietary interest names, souls, and property. And they become, in Melville, the ethically depleted father figure, once honored but now unmasked, who has omitted a sister—and so much else—from the text of his son's life.

There is, of course, more than one explanation for the animosity toward father figures that pervades these texts. Surely on one level it is personally and psychologically charged: all four of these authors had highly conflicted feelings toward their own fathers. The financial failures and early

deaths of Poe's, Hawthorne's, and Melville's fathers deprived these sons
not only of a secure social standing but also of strong, positive male role
models during their formative years.[6] Though Cooper's situation was ostensibly the opposite, in that he witnessed and benefited from his father's
rise to power as a successful businessman and a prominent politician, the
psychological effect seems to have been similar. Recent psychoanalytic
studies have shown, for example, that during much of Cooper's early
manhood, and especially during the years in which he wrote the first three
Leatherstocking Tales, his conflicted relationship with his domineering
father fueled both his negative characterizations of the "manly" authority
he felt the elder Cooper represented and his creation of the Leatherstocking himself, whom one critic sees as a psychic alternative to Cooper's
own father.[7]

More telling of the political dimension of these authors' animosity toward patriarchal authority figures, however, is the fact that, during the
same years in which George Washington was being popularly mytholo-
gized as a national hero, each of them wrote at least one work of fiction
targeting revolutionary "fathers"—heroes, leaders—for criticism.[8] Cooper
wrote three, The Spy (1821), in which Washington is portrayed with great
ambivalence as a master of disguise and deception; The Pilot (1824), in
which John Paul Jones's patriotism is shown to mask a variety of suspect
personal motives; and Lionel Lincoln (1825), in which the new American
son is credited with the social and political conscience that is ominously
lacking in his revolutionary father.[9] Hawthorne's "My Kinsman, Major
Molineux" (1832) also tells the tale of a representative son, a young man
who must learn to see beyond the falsity and failed authority of revolutionary father figures, Whig and Tory alike apparently. As several critics
have pointed out, although modern readers tend to interpret the title
character as a "justly deposed royal governor of Massachusetts," to Hawthorne's contemporary readers, "the name Molineux would probably have
called to mind an actual figure of that name in revolutionary politics,
although one who was not a royal governor at all, but rather a patriot
hero—one of the fathers. By appearing . . . to recount what the fathers
did to the British, Hawthorne actually reveals what the sons would like to
do to the fathers."[10] Similar animosity can be discerned in Hawthorne's
Biographical Stories for Children (1842); the author's particular contempt
for Benjamin Franklin is "barely disguised by a mask of qualified respect."[11] Franklin's fatherly character would fare much worse at the hands
of Melville and even Poe. In Pierre (1852) Melville portrayed his hero's

revolutionary sires as having vociferously fought for their own liberty while robbing American Indians and African blacks of theirs. In *Israel Potter: His Fifty Years of Exile* (1855) he singled out Franklin's paternalistic duplicity for special scorn: "Every time he comes in he robs me," the young Israel soon realizes, "with an air all the time, too, as if he were making me presents. If he thinks me such a very sensible young man, why not let me take care of myself?"[12] Poe also stressed the fraudulent nature of Franklin's "Virtue" in "The Business Man" (1845), which, as J. A. Leo Lemay argues, viciously "portrays Franklin's practical advice on conduct and discipline as the philosophy of a scoundrel who prides himself on being a methodical businessman." Peter Proffit, the "low crook" of the title, is "a version of Franklin," "a caricature of man without ethics and spirituality."[13] If these authors harbored resentment against their natural fathers for their failure to act as proper guardians, this group of texts suggests that they felt equally alienated from the nation's Founding Fathers, whom they unmask as mere confidence men, or at least from the dubious patriarchal "ethics" those men endorsed. Implicit in all of these works is the idea that America's model Fathers enacted a hidden agenda, that they concealed their own selfish motives behind a diversionary verbal facade, or, to return to the words of Cooper's accusers, that they characteristically said one thing when they meant another.

The animosity with which Cooper and his fellow romancers imaged— personified—their criticisms of the Founding Fathers may have set them apart from the mainstream, but they were certainly not alone in feeling that the professed goals of the Revolution had not been realized. In daily life, the sorry split between the revolutionary generation's professed ideals of freedom and equality, on one hand, and the serious inequities of lived experience in the United States, on the other, was becoming increasingly evident as the nineteenth century progressed. "Privilege based on ability rather than inherited status, upward mobility for all groups of society, and unlimited opportunities for individual self-fulfillment had become ideological goals, if not always realities," for white men but threw into bold relief the social, economic, and political limitations imposed on such marginalized members of the national "family" as Native Americans, Negro slaves, and women.[14] By mid-century numerous reform organizations had sprung up to champion these disfranchised groups and others— laborers, debtors, prisoners, children, the sick, the insane—whose voices had been silenced in the wake of the new nation's explosive economic development.

In literature, other "reforms" were taking place. The American story was being recast. As Emerson described the new and now apparently genuine democratic fervor, the "literature of the poor, the feelings of the child, the philosophy of the street, the meaning of household life" were becoming "the topics of the time."[15] New literary voices were also making themselves heard; new storytellers were finding an ever-increasing audience for their perspectives on America's sociopolitical inequities. Between 1820 and 1870, for example, fiction written by and about women became "by far the most popular literature of its time," and as one critic has described them, these "many novels all tell, with variations, a single tale. In essence, it is the story of a young girl who is deprived of the supports she had rightly or wrongly depended on to sustain her throughout life and is faced with the necessity of winning her own way in the world. . . . Her dilemma, simply, was mistreatment, unfairness, disadvantage, and powerlessness, recurrent injustices occasioned by her status as female and child" in a patriarchal culture.[16] In his prefacing remarks to Frederick Douglass's autobiographical *Narrative* (1845), prominent abolitionist Wendell Phillips specifically referred to the Founders' shadowy handiwork to remind readers of the truly revolutionary nature of any black American's attempt to break the silence imposed upon him by the country's white patriarchal politics: "In all the broad lands which the Constitution of the United States overshadows, there is no single spot,—however narrow or desolate,—where a fugitive slave can plant himself and say, 'I am safe.'"[17] And in *Woman in the Nineteenth Century*, published the same year, Margaret Fuller linked the plight of the American woman with that of "the Red Man, the Black Man," and exhorted Americans to make good on the revolutionary generation's professed ideals, to make their words meaningful at last: "Though the national independence be blurred by the servility of individuals; though freedom and equality have been proclaimed only to leave room for a monstrous display of slave-dealing and slave-keeping; though the free American so often feels himself free, like the Roman, only to pamper his appetites and his indolence through the misery of his fellow-beings; still it is not in vain that the verbal statement has been made, 'All men are born free and equal.' . . . The New World may be called clearly to perceive that it incurs the utmost penalty if it reject or oppress the sorrowful brother"—or sister.[18]

Cooper's, Poe's, Hawthorne's, and Melville's efforts to revise and reform the American story is finally my subject here. As their fictional treatments of revolutionary father figures briefly suggest, their criticisms of the patriarchal politics of language in America led them to want to tell the other side of the nation's story, to unmask the fraud that they felt had been perpetrated on the national family. In their major fictions, they would do something else as well: they would imagine a second story altogether, giving voice to those victimized, disempowered, and silenced by patriarchal culture. Each employs the idea of a second story slightly differently, but whether they use the metaphor explicitly or implicitly, the second story in their texts represents a realm of experience, values, and attitudes that has been suppressed or—as they often express it—conveniently forgotten by those who control the terms of cultural representation.

In the early pages of *The Last of the Mohicans*, for example, Cooper has Natty Bumppo acknowledge to his revered Indian companion Chingachgook that "every story has its two sides." In context, the remark refers to the Leatherstocking's willingness to listen to the Mohican's version of American history, which is obviously different from the tale of heroic conquest told by Natty's own fathers. But the remark has larger significance, for the task Cooper sets for himself in this literally two-sided novel is to recover the second half of the American story, the side white culture's history books failed to tell. Poe's attempts to recover the second story led him eventually to create his own new form of sociopolitical allegory. In his early Gothic tales about women, he makes it the reader's task to see that the male narrator tells a one-sided story, that the woman's story has been criminally suppressed—and repressed—by the man's self-serving fiction; later, in the three detective tales featuring C. Auguste Dupin, he images the suppression of the woman's story as a crime perpetrated by male-dominant culture as a whole, and he assigns the task of solving the crime and recovering the lost story to a detective-storyteller with a cultural awareness that is shown to be lacking in the men around him. Hawthorne takes that task and that burden of awareness upon himself. He announces in the autobiographical sketch that prefaces *The Scarlet Letter* that he had found the materials for his romance in "the second story" of the Custom House and that to bring Hester Prynne's long-forgotten story before the public eye he had had to remove himself from that symbolic bastion of patriarchal politics and androcentric thinking. He uses the same architectural-narrative metaphor in the opening pages of *The House of the Seven Gables*, when his narrator ushers the long sequestered Hepzibah Pyncheon down from her lonely room in the second story and over "the threshold of our narrative" to meet the unreceptive public eye. Hawthorne's purpose in publicizing the suppressed second story is less cultural restoration than cultural renovation, however, for both novels are cautionary tales, warnings to first- and second-class Americans alike against the self-divisive psychological and ethical conflicts that come of living in patriarchal society. Melville also tells a cautionary tale in *Pierre*. While growing up, we are told, his young artist-hero had lived in the "repose of a wide story tenanted only by himself," but shortly after the novel begins, his repose is shattered by the introduction of a second story, that of his illegitimate sister, which has been omitted from the family history. Pierre's task as an American author is to find a new narrative form that will include both stories, but unlike his own author, he fails miserably, and his failure is specifically attributed to his inability to overcome the imaginative limits imposed by his fathers.

Finally, in addition to the second-story metaphor, all of these fictions are linked not just by their authors' decisions to highlight and heroicize the challenges to patriarchal authority that Franklin, Brackenridge, and Brown had tried to censure but also by the striking similarities in their symbolic depictions of such challenges—and challengers—as "feminine." The subjects of these second stories are all "women," and the most admirable male storytellers within the framing texts are those who enact a feminine or an androgynous sensibility. Cooper's androgynous Mohicans, for example, who are descended from "the greatest and most civilized of the Indian nations," are called the "women" of their race, and they are especially characterized by the high degree of ethical sensibility that Cooper attributes to white women but that he shows to have all but atrophied in white men. These dark-skinned and graceful Indians are thus early versions of Poe's Dark Ladies, such as the raven-haired, "idolatrous" Ligeia, whose "incomprehensible lightness and elasticity" of movement and whose "Hebrew" features, her narrator assures himself, set her apart from "our own race." They are surely akin to Hawthorne's outcast Hester Prynne, "the people's victim and life-long bond-slave," who feels "hardly more reverence than the Indian would feel for the clerical band, the judicial robe," and to Melville's Isabel Banford, who is marked by an "unknown, foreign feminineness." Like the Mohicans, Cooper's artist figure, David Gamut, is also characterized by androgynous qualities, and he is shown to be genuinely heroic only when he forsakes the patriarchal tradition of Old World psalmistry in which he has been trained and devotes himself to telling the story of America's lost sisters. Poe's androgynous heroes, Roderick Usher and "the double Dupin," are similarly capable of recovering the lost second story, and Hawthorne and Melville focus on the moral blindness of male artist figures—Arthur Dimmesdale, Clifford Pyncheon, Pierre Glendinning—who fail to do so because they finally give in to the long hereditary habit of one-sided patriarchal thinking that keeps the "better half" of their nature in psychic bondage.

Why would Cooper, Poe, Hawthorne, and Melville, none of whom was ever more than at best ambivalent toward the women's rights movement that was growing during their lifetime or even toward women authors, equate their artistry with the recreation of "women's" stories? Just as there are a number of reasons for their negative fictional treatments of father figures, so too are there various possible explanations for the deference and sympathy they show to female or feminized characters. Recent studies of nineteenth-century authors' responses to the country's growing consumer culture suggest an economic factor at work. Like the women novelists with whom they were competing in the marketplace, the male authors treated here were well aware that women were making up an increasingly large segment of the book-reading and book-buying public; thus in equating superior moral virtue with femininity, they may have been deferring to the presumed self-interest of their potential audience and to their own need to earn an adequate living.[19] Their fictional criticisms of "manly" and unimaginative men lead to an equally plausible explanation for their seeming identification with wronged and suffering femininity: they may well have felt themselves at odds with the men in their audience, or rather, with the prevailing popular assessment of proper manly endeavor that marked their own artistic efforts as socially deviant, effete, and effeminate.[20]

That the male American author's social and cultural status was as marginal and precarious as his financial one suggests psychological explanations for these four writers' sympathetic portrayals of femininity. It could certainly be argued that the women in these fictions do not represent real women as much as they symbolize "otherness," and that, consciously or unconsciously, their creators used them to convey their personal grievances against the oppression and suppression of their own otherness in rigidly business-minded, androcentric society. I refer, of course, to Simone de Beauvoir's formulation in *The Second Sex* that "no group ever sets itself up as the One without at once setting up the Other over against itself." Beauvoir stresses what these authors seem to have understood so well, that although "'otherness reaches its full flowering in the feminine,'" "whether it is a race, a caste, a class, or a sex that is reduced to a position of inferiority, the methods of justification are the same."[21] Cooper's, Poe's, Hawthorne's, and Melville's astute and imaginative depictions of the politics of language in male-dominant culture show that they knew only too well the variety of methods by which any expression of otherness might be rendered inaudible.

Last, there is compelling textual evidence for reading these female and feminized characters as having a positive psychological value, that is, for reading them not just as representative victims but also as positive ethical models, symbolizing potential correctives to the exclusive, androcentric thinking that their authors so strenuously condemn. These characters are inaudible, after all, only to those around them who choose not to hear any story but their own. The "women"—sisters, daughters, and androgynous artists—in these texts stand as symbolic alternatives to society's villainous fathers and single-minded brothers, and to that end, their authors imagine for them an alternative to patriarchy's ethically depleted language, an "other" language, in which long-suppressed or conveniently forgotten truths can finally be told. Cooper's Mohicans, Poe's Ligeia, Hawthorne's three Pyncheon women, and Melville's Isabel are all gifted with the ability to communicate in music or musical sounds, rather than mere words, and that male artist figures such as David Gamut, Roderick Usher, and Arthur Dimmesdale have the capacity (if not always the moral courage) to tell the truth is imaged in their curiously dual mode of musical speech. Cooper, Poe, and Melville also stress the foreignness of truth-telling in male-dominant culture by giving their female and feminized characters foreign languages, Indian and French, both of which must be translated into English so that a new, second story might be heard.

Such prolonged and detailed linguistic fantasies suggest the imaginative energy with which these authors tried to break the "sentence" of patriarchal culture both for themselves and for their readers.[22] In the texts treated in the following pages, the fraud perpetrated by American patriarchy is indeed made manifest, and the resulting reformation of the American story in these texts—the imaginative recovery of the second story and the heartfelt attempts to reintegrate otherness into our culture—leaves us with a literary legacy of no small dimension.

𝒜 4

Two Sides to Every Story:
Cooper's *The Last of the Mohicans*

In the confrontation scene that precipitated his exile in *Modern Chivalry*, Captain Farrago had been challenged by a self-styled representative of the people who was described as a westerner, "a factious man, in a leathern pair of breeches, who had never had the opportunity before of making himself heard" (*Modern Chivalry*, p. 505). The brief characterization is prophetic of the character subsequent generations of readers would consider the first quintessentially "American" hero, Cooper's Leatherstocking. Making his first appearance in 1823, in *The Pioneers*, and appearing in five Leatherstocking Tales altogether, including *The Last of the Mohicans* (1826), *The Prairie* (1827), *The Pathfinder* (1840), and *The Deerslayer* (1841), Natty Bumppo emerged as a spokesperson from those elements of American society that had not yet been dignified in its literature. He was a social outcast, an uneducated and itinerant hunter, a lawbreaker, a companion and confidant of Indians—all qualities that would have excluded him from any serious consideration in the Early National period, but which, at the beginning of the nineteenth century, gave him the right to speak out as a critic of the encroaching white civilization that would drive him ever to the West.

In the course of the five novels, Natty's criticisms of white ways are many, ranging from the unnaturalness of their laws to their abusive treatment of the landscape and its "original proprietors," the Indians.[1] One of his favorite targets is the white man's use—and abuse—of language. Cooper gets a good deal of humorous mileage out of his hero's cantankerous squabbles with scholarly types such as Doctor Battius in *The Prairie*, who believe they can master the American wilderness by the power of naming alone. "Your notions are a little blinded with reading too many books," Natty tells the pedantic naturalist, who had "wanted to make [him] believe that a name could change the natur' of a beast . . . Why, man, you are farther from the truth than you are from the settlements, with all your bookish l'arning and hard words" (1:988–90). But such humorous debates over language merely serve as comic relief from the more serious criticisms leveled at white naming practices and what they represent, for if Natty is laughably crotchety in such instances, he is elsewhere capable of astute political analysis. In the same novel, he lectures his obtuse scholarly companion on the white practice of manipulating language and texts to justify unconscionable political ends, claiming that white men even "twist and turn the rules of the Lord, to suit their own wickedness" (1:1148). He understands, too, that the whites maintain their sociopolitical authority by invalidating the language of their opponents: "If my brother wishes his words to be heard," he advises an Indian chief, "he must speak with a white tongue" (1:1208). Above all, Natty understands that the white man's desire to rename the New World is but the outward sign of his desire to conquer and control it and that such acts of conquest will have devastating effects on land and peoples alike. "I'm glad it has no name," he says of the uncharted lake that provides the setting for *The Deerslayer*, "or, at least, no paleface name, for their christenings always foretell waste and destruction" (2:524).

It is Natty's critical stance toward the white man's politics of naming that most clearly sets him apart from his literary predecessors. Indeed, through Natty's heartfelt harangues, Cooper openly criticizes the same patriarchal values and linguistic practices that Franklin, Brackenridge, and Brown had promoted, and he does so most obviously by subverting those authors' metaphors for authority. In the Leatherstocking Tales the "white fathers" are ineffective leaders because they rely on verbal artifice to maintain their sociopolitical authority, regardless of the cost to nation or family. Thus the artful, manipulative language of learned leadership is outshone by the earnest and spontaneous speech of a barely literate backwoodsman, a conscientious "guide" who prides himself on being "an honest man" (1:502), and book-learning, formerly the qualification of the few privileged wise men capable of heroic leadership, is replaced with the more democratic image of learning from the Book of Nature. "The only book I read, or care about reading," Natty proudly maintains, "is the one which God has opened afore all his creatur's in the noble forests, broad lakes, rolling rivers, blue skies . . . and other glorious marvels of the land!" (2:899).

To look at the ways Natty Bumppo differs from earlier American heroes, however, is to look at only one side of his character. What he says about language and what he does with it are often strangely at odds, and his speech acts are often markedly similar to those of Franklin's heroicized persona or Brackenridge's Captain. Although he remains a bachelor all his life, and although he frequently decries the folly of the white fathers of a previous generation, aging military leaders, for example, who have failed to adapt their verbal strategies to the circumstances of the New World, nevertheless Natty acts as a father figure himself, offering paternalistic advice to young whites and Indians alike.[2] In *The Prairie* Paul Hover, Ellen Wade, and the Indian chieftain Hard-Heart all bestow on him the honorary title of "father," and in *The Pathfinder* his (understandably re-buffed) marriage proposal to Mabel Dunham takes the form of a promise that he would be a father to her. Like his eighteenth-century predecessors, Natty is presented as a model guardian for those of lesser capabilities, and although his acknowledged status as a wise man derives from his years of surviving the trials of the wilderness, rather than from his reading and writing skills, one of his main functions as a hero is to interpret his chosen "Book" for less skilled "readers," as when, in *The Last of the Mohicans*, he explains the significance of footprints and a cannonball's furrow to those unfamiliar with such inscriptions. Similarly, he acts as interpreter between white and Indian cultures, translating the language of each into terms the other can understand, and it is in this role that he most closely approaches his predecessors, for despite the high value Natty places on honesty, he is frequently forced into situations in which he must be very selective in the meanings he chooses to assign in his translations. He is not above distort-ing or even omitting the truth if he believes the circumstances warrant it. In the *Autobiography* Franklin had instructed wise men in the virtue of using "Discourse . . . well adapted to [the] Capacities" of a dissenting audience. So, too, at the close of *The Last of the Mohicans*, Natty paterna-listically assumes the responsibility of translating for the Delawares only those elements of a white man's speech which he feels they will under-stand and accept: "He made such a communication . . . as he deemed most suited to the capacities of his listeners" (1:874).

This is not to say that Cooper is promoting such duplicitous use of language. Natty himself usually regrets it. In the above scene he is greatly saddened by what he sees as irrevocable differences between the races, which act as barriers to mutual understanding and necessitate circuitous paraphrase rather than literal exchange. In *The Prairie*, before a similar mistranslation, this time in response to a life-or-death crisis, he is moved to appeal to his Creator for forgiveness: "The Lord will forgive me, for playing with the ignorance of the savage, for he knows I do it, in no mockery of his state or in idle vaunting of my own, but in order to save mortal life, and to give justice to the wronged, while I defeat the deviltries of the wicked!" (1:1133). Even more significant than Natty's regret is that Cooper inevitably shows such duplicitous language to come to no good end. It is always a stopgap measure necessitated by whites' having impinged on Indians' rights and having evoked vengeful retaliations that can be countered only with artful verbal strategies, and the number of white and Indian lives lost during such conflicts makes any subsequent victory a hollow one. If what Natty says is at odds with what he does, then, it is because he is torn between his natural tendency to honesty and his acquired sociopolitical allegiance to white culture, which requires him to engage in the politics of language in its behalf. And if Cooper openly criticizes such politicized language through his hero's position statements, he covertly criticizes it by revealing the toll it takes on Natty's integrity and ultimately on white culture.

This duality in Natty's character and the resulting loss of integrity and even humanity are most fully delineated in *The Last of the Mohicans*, where, as Natty himself admits, "every story has its two sides" (1:502). In context, the statement refers to Natty's willingness to listen to the Indians' version of American history, of how the white man's coming had changed the face of the land and upset the balance of power among the various Indian tribes and nations. But the statement has a larger significance, for of all the Leatherstocking Tales, it is in *The Last of the Mohicans* that Cooper seems most intent on telling both sides of the American story, that of white American patriarchy and that of its victims.[3] The sad split in Natty's character is just one of the ways Cooper renders his critique of patriarchal values, attitudes, and linguistic practices in this novel. Another is to pair his flawed white heroes, Natty and Duncan Heyward, with his noblest Indians, Chingachgook and Uncas, so as to privilege an alternative to the white man's cultural orientation to the world.[4] The two Mohicans, whom D. H. Lawrence immediately recognized as having a "curious female quality," represent an alternative model of heroic manhood, and to that end, Cooper imagines for them a curiously feminine language and a linguistic ethic that is clearly superior to the white man's but that is, ominously, on the verge of extinction in the New World.[5] The narrative structure of this novel is divided in two halves, alternative quests through white- and Indian-held territory, and as in the other instances of halving and doubling, the second story, or in Cooper's terms, the second side of the story, brings to light the root cause of this divisiveness: the patriarchal values and attitudes white culture used to justify its silencing of any opposing views.[6] The task for the American artist, as Cooper illustrates in the character of David Gamut, is to break that silence, to learn how to mediate between America's failed "fathers" and their suffering "children." But Gamut, too, is ultimately a victim, and his limited success as an agent of change in this divided fictional world seems to suggest how limited Cooper felt the American artist's authority was perceived to be.[7] Taken together, the "two sides" of *The Last of the Mohicans* constitute an imaginative inquiry into an alternative version of American history but also, finally, a condemnation of the patriarchal ethos which, in Cooper's eyes, had already effectively foreclosed on such an alternative.

The original Author's Preface to *The Last of the Mohicans* establishes that one of the main themes of the book will be the clash between white and Indian languages, and the villains of the piece are the representatives of white civilization, who, as part of their civilizing process, suppressed—or "corrupted," to use Cooper's word—the names given by the "original proprietors of the soil" (1:470). "The greatest difficulty with which the student of Indian history has to contend," Cooper tells us, "is the utter confusion that pervades the names," and the first, and apparently most important, reason that comes to mind is that "the Dutch, the English, and the French, each took a conqueror's liberty in this particular" (1:469). He goes on to give examples. The original proper name of one of the tribes of the Lenni Lenape, the name "Mohican," "has since been corrupted by the English into 'Mohegan,'" and even more recently, "after the English changed the appellation of their river to 'Delaware,' they gradually came to be known by [that] name" as well (1:470–71). The enemies of this tribe "were often called by their Indian neighbours the 'Maquas,' and frequently, by way of contempt, 'Mingoes,'" but the "French gave them the name of 'Iroquois,' which was probably a corruption of one of their own terms" (1:471).

In view of this preliminary emphasis on the politically motivated corruption of language, Natty Bumppo seems, when we first meet him, a new kind of white man indeed, an outsider who has many different—and thus more admirable—qualities than the white civilization he has fled. He is initially characterized by his uncorrupted and uncorrupting nature: "His countenance was not only without guile, but at the moment at which he is introduced, it was charged with an expression of sturdy honesty." Moreover, it soon becomes clear that his honesty serves as a particular contrast to white linguistic practices. The first words he speaks are in the Indian tongue, albeit given by Cooper in "free translation," and his respect for their language sets him apart from the white military leaders in the text (1:501). Later in the novel, for example, the young Major Duncan Heyward speaks French to the Maquas and reproaches them that "none of this wise and brave nation understand the language that the 'Grand Monarque' uses when he talks to his children." Cooper has their hostile chief scornfully point out the hypocrisy in this reproach: "When our Great Father speaks to his people, is it with the tongue of a [Maqua]?" (1:741). Natty himself goes by a name given to him by his Indian comrades, "Hawk-eye," and this implicit criticism of white naming is made more explicit in his comment, "I'm an admirator of names, though the Christian fashions fall far below savage customs in this particular. . . . With an Indian 'tis a matter of conscience; what he calls himself, he generally is" (1:534).

And where did Natty, a white man, come by his honesty? The answer is given in the first scene in which he appears: "I am no scholar, and I care not who knows it." "I am willing to own," he tells his companion Chingachgook, "that my people have many ways, of which, as an honest man, I can't approve. It is one of their customs to write in books what they have done and seen, instead of telling them in their villages, where the lie can be given to the face of a cowardly boaster, and the brave soldier can call on his comrades to witness for the truth of his words" (1:502). Book-learning is thus equated with the dishonesty of white language and with a legacy of corrupt practices handed down by white civilization, and as such, Natty, who values honesty, scorns it every chance he gets. He guides Heyward through a wilderness "where no bookish knowledge," he tells him, "would carry you through, harmless" (1:688); elsewhere, in another dangerous situation, he warns him that he will need "a sharper wit than what is to be gathered in books" (1:736). The greatest danger associated with book-learning, however, is that in America, in the struggle for power between the whites and the Indians, such tradition-bound authority might prove fatal: "If you judge of Indian cunning by the rules you find in books," Natty warns, " . . . they will lead you astray, if not to your death" (1:707). The quote implies that another mode of authority is needed if white civilization is to survive in the American wilderness, and Natty's authority as a guide and as a man who values the truth derives from that other mode—from the genuine knowledge that comes of direct experience. Natty scorns "your young white," for example, "who gathers his learning from books and can measure what he knows by the page. . . . Where experience is the master, the scholar is made to know the value of years [of survival], and respects them accordingly" (1:717–18).

Cooper was the first major American author to use book-learning as a metaphor for misinformation, for a dangerously fallen language inherited from past generations of suspect white fathers.[8] Recent biographical and psychoanalytic criticism has provided two personal reasons for his subversive treatment of traditional authority: the Oedipal resentment and competitiveness he felt toward his own father, who was not only a domineering parent but also a prominent political figure; and his defensive, nationalistic stance toward English authors, those white fathers who, Cooper believed, still dominated American literary standards and minds.[9] As a response to the past, then, the antibook metaphor makes sense; but is it workable as a doctrine for the present and as a prescription for the future of American literature?

The contradiction inherent in such a metaphor, the shadow thus cast on the American writer's own authority, is immediately apparent, and Cooper's solution to this dilemma is to present himself as the author of a new kind of book. Midway through *The Last of the Mohicans*, for example, we find an authorial comment on the dishonesty of history books, which will characteristically, Cooper predicts, suppress the truth, the "cruel apathy" of Montcalm during the massacre of Fort William Henry, and allow him to be "viewed by posterity only as the gallant defender of his country." "Deeply regretting this weakness on the part of a sister muse," Cooper archly notes in passing, "we shall at once retire . . . within the proper limits of our own humbler vocation." Given his detailed descriptions of Montcalm's moral failure and military ineffectiveness in the previous chapter, the implication here is that Cooper is writing an alternative history, a corrective to the ideological gloss that surrounds "heroes with an atmosphere of imaginary brightness" by stressing "policy" over moral "principle" (1:677). *The Last of the Mohicans* is a new kind of book because it reveals the dark underside of American history: the first half of the novel is symbolically set in white territory and highlights white characters' belief that the white father is indeed the hero and gallant defender of his children; the second half is set in Indian territory and reveals another, less flattering side to white leadership, of which, like Montcalm's moral failings, Cooper believes his readers "have yet to learn" (1:677).[10]

Finally, Cooper's emphasis on the need to tell the second half of the American story also helps explain his personal reminder to readers (added in the 1831 Introduction to the novel) that "every word uttered by Natty Bumppo was not to be received as rigid truth" (1:477): despite Natty's claim to be an honest man, his character, too, has another side. For instance, in Natty's criticism of the white custom of writing down in books "what they have done and seen," he champions the authenticity of the spoken word, which, because of its immediacy, can be verified or denied. But for all his "sturdy honesty," Natty's own speech is often ethically suspect, precisely at times when he chooses to act as an agent of white civilization—specifically, as an adoptive father. For example, Natty takes young Duncan Heyward, who has "no father," under his protection by teaching him how to use "subtle speech" in tricking a "bad" Indian (1:586, 580). "Go, ... Talk openly to the miscreant, and seem to believe him the truest friend you have on 'arth." Though Natty considers this an "Indian fashion" (1:514), it is surely one the Maquas learned from their white fathers, for even Natty will later justify such deceitful speech in the white language of legality: "Practyse all your cunning," he will advise Duncan once they are in the Maquas' territory, for rescuing white captives from savages is "a lawful undertaking" (1:776). This is strange—contradictory— phrasing for a lawbreaker, but it follows in the expedient tradition of a Benjamin Franklin or a Captain Farrago. Like them, Natty is shown having to "repress" his pupil's voice in the wilderness when stealth is needed and selectively translating—interpreting—white language for an Indian audience, in words he "deem[s] most suited to the capacities of his listeners" (1:707, 874). His authority at such times is unmistakably paternalistic.

Natty's tutelage of his other "son," Uncas—"the one who might, in some degree, be called the child of his adoption" (1:778)—is even more revealing of the political power associated with his language. Natty seems well aware, for example, of the power inherent in naming, for although he liberally accepts the name given him by the trusted Delawares, he refuses the French name "La Longue Carabine," given him by the hated Mingoes: "I do not admit the right of the Mingoes to bestow a name on one, whose friends have been mindful of his gifts, in this particular; especially, as their title is a lie, 'kill-deer' being a grooved barrel, and no carabyne. I am the man, however, that got the name of Nathaniel from my kin; the compliment of Hawk-eye from the Delawares . . . and whom the Iroquois have presumed to style the 'long rifle,' without any warranty from him who is most concerned in the matter"(1:814). At first glance this speech seems to fit in with Natty's characterization as an "admirator" of truthful names and a critic of dishonest white names. But if we remember from the

Preface that the term *Iroquois* is a corrupted name bestowed by whites and if we look at this speech in context and see how Natty establishes his right to keep his own name, we see more clearly that his use of language is also implicated in the power politics of naming.

In this scene Natty and Heyward have been captured by allies of the Maquas, and Heyward, in the attempt to save his friend's life, claims that *he* is "Hawk-eye." At this point Natty defends his right to that name, and a shooting match ensues to determine who is really the famed marksman. "Stubbornly bent on maintaining his identity, at every hazard," Natty outdoes himself in winning the contest, but the real significance of his act is that he lets his gun speak for him—speak his true name, as it were (1:817). Natty frequently metaphorizes his gunshot as "the speech of 'kill-deer'" (1:846). Earlier in the book, he expresses his anger at the villainous Magua in such terms: "There never will be an end of his loping, till 'kill-deer' has said a friendly word to him" (1:684). Later, in one of the final skirmishes, he admonishes his comrades that until they are victorious "nothing speaks but the rifle" (1:851). Nothing is more politically power-ful, nor more "white," than Natty's "speech" at such moments.

With regard to Natty's other "adopted" son, Uncas, the pride of the Mohicans, the evidence of Natty's politically tainted speech gives omi-nous undertones to the following passage. Hearing a gunshot in the dark-ness, Natty remarks, "I know its crack, as well as a father knows the language of his child, for I carried the gun myself until a better offered" (1:695). The gun, of course, now belongs to Uncas, and in having given this gift to his "son," Natty reveals his irrefutable complicity with the white fathers, linguistically and otherwise.

Such contradictory values in Natty's speech suggest that Cooper was not able to imagine any white man's language that was not already tainted by patriarchal acculturation.[11] He was able to imagine an untainted lan-guage, however, even though he admits that it is almost "impossible to describe" (1:701). The uncorrupted language of the Mohicans is the an-tithesis of the patriarchal language in this novel. It is truthful, nonin-trusive, nonappropriative, and to emphasize its otherness, Cooper charac-terizes it as virtually "silent" to whites and as "feminine."[12] Chingachgook and Uncas are frequently viewed as Natty's "silent associates," for example (1:528). It is their "custom" to "remain . . . silent and reserved" (1:505), and when they do speak, it is in the "music of the Delawares" (1:758), in "low, guttural tones"—tones "feminine in softness"—that communicate "gentle and natural feelings" and render their language "so very musical" (1:504, 701). The musicality is significant, for like the "eloquent" gestures of the Mohicans' sign language (1:700), it establishes the essential nonverbal dimension of their expression: "The meaning of Indian words," we are told, "is much governed by the emphasis and tones" (1:533).

In a fictional world where words, "names," carry such dangerous power, the Mohicans' nonverbal language represents, above all, a linguistic ethic that is unknown to white America, and this is most evident in the major way in which their language is silent.[13] Just as Natty translates it for his white companions, Cooper is forced to "give a free translation for the benefit of the reader" (1:501)—to render it in white words for it to be "heard." He is even apologetic for the obvious cultural limitations of his own authority, for "if it were possible to translate the comprehensive and melodious language" of the Mohicans, he tells us, it "might read something like the following" (1:841). We never experience that truth-speaking language directly, but we are made as aware of its awesome ethical authority as we are of its awesome otherness in a corrupt patriarchal world: Chingachgook's ancestors, as he reminds the less fortunate Natty, "have not lied!" (1:503).

Such imaginative and subtle rendering of feminized, nonverbal otherness is, I believe, the key to what one critic has called this novel's "ideological elusiveness."[14] That is, Cooper's ethical alternative to patriarchal corruption may be perceived as "silent" throughout, but it is nevertheless a politically articulate silence, a metaphor that weighs nineteenth-century feminine values against masculine, matriarchal against patriarchal, and that tips the ethical scales always in favor of the former. For all their manly strength and courage, for example, Chingachgook and Uncas have another side to their nature: they are symbolically androgynous. They not only speak with a "feminine softness," but they are also repeatedly credited with the "womanly" qualities of honesty, integrity, and responsible social caretaking. It is those qualities which Cooper presents for our admiration and sympathy and which his white agents of patriarchy inevitably undervalue or take unfair advantage of. He introduces this latter idea in his Preface, where he explains that the Mohicans' treaty agreement not to fight the Europeans on their own behalf earned them the scornful label of "women" from whites and other Indians alike and that the cost to them of keeping their word was ultimately "the downfall of the greatest and most civilized of the Indian nations": "Robbed by the whites, and murdered and oppressed by the savages" allied to the whites, "they lingered for a time around their council-fire, but finally broke off in bands" (1:471–72). Later he shows the sorry split in Natty's character by having him praise his Mohican companions for their honesty and then in the next breath apply the scornful label himself, regretting their honest adherence to a contract that has made powerful warriors into mere "women" (1:511). Heyward will also use the term with derision and will find great amusement in Uncas's "little departure from the dignity of manhood" when the noble young chief generously chooses to act as "attendant to the females" during one of their party's stops for food and rest (1:525, 532–33).

Uncas's protective alliance with Cora and Alice in this scene is only one of many instances in which Cooper symbolically links the "womanly" Mohicans with his actual women characters.[15] In this book, the Munro sisters are also characterized by their silence in the presence of white men (e.g., 1:547, 567) and by their reliance on a nonverbal mode of communication. "The pale-faces . . . have two words for each thing," an insightful Indian will tell his white adversaries, "while a red skin will make the sound of his voice speak for him"; "you have often heard me avow my faith in the tones of the human voice," Alice will remind Heyward, her white guardian (1:575, 491). Like Uncas, too, Cora is characterized as a generous and able social caretaker to those in need of sustenance. She is a "maternal" figure, sympathetically offering whatever reparation she can for the damage done by neglectful, shortsighted fathers (e.g., 1:595, 602, 650), and she is the daughter of a dark-skinned West Indian mother, one of "that unfortunate class, who are so basely enslaved to administer to the wants of a luxurious people" (1:653), that is, to their white conquerors. Cora's characterization thus suggests other Indian/women associations to be found in Cooper's fiction. The Mohicans, for example, as Cooper knew, believed their tribe originated at the bottom of a lake, and in *The Deerslayer*, the white mother, whose loss is fervently mourned, is buried at the bottom of Lake Glimmerglass (2:622–23).[16]

In addition to these telling details of characterization within his fiction, there is also external evidence that Cooper was personally preoccupied with subverting patriarchal authority—especially the patriarchal prerogative of naming—at this time in his life. James Cooper had his name legally changed to James Fenimore Cooper, to include his mother's maiden name, shortly after writing *The Last of the Mohicans*. Ironically, he petitioned to have his name be James Cooper Fenimore, but the legislature, which contained members who had been friends of his father (who had, during his lifetime, forbade the name change), would go only so far as to allow Fenimore Cooper. The novelist was well aware of the political overtones and repercussions of his act, for as he wrote to a friend, he would use Fenimore Cooper on his book jackets but would reserve his paternal name to be used "in discourse."[17]

For all of these reasons, then, and for one other, it seems logical to read *The Last of the Mohicans* as a psychologically charged account of a quest for a matriarchal alternative to patriarchal power politics, that is, for a set of values that Cooper shows to have been silenced, suppressed in white discourse, and on the verge of becoming repressed out of white consciousness altogether.[18] The final justification for such a reading is provided by the novel's bifurcated plot. The first half of this book is framed as an ill-fated journey to find a reliable father authority. When that quest fails, when patriarchal authority shows itself continuing to value political power and militaristic formality over the immediate needs of humanity, chaos ensues, and the second half of the book charts the quest to retrieve what the Anglo-Americans have lost: the "daughters" and "sisters" of white society and, in particular, the maternal values personified by Cora Munro. At the center of the novel, the failure of paternalistic authority, the impetus that necessitates the second quest, is dramatized in the failure of white language to bridge the gap between such dangerously divided and conflicted cultural values.[19]

In the first journey, the search party consists of the most worthy representatives of Americanness: the virtuous sisters; their guardian, Heyward, who represents the future and potentially better leadership of white society; the singing master, David Gamut, whose practical effectiveness as an artist will be tested; and, of course, their guides and temporary ethical models, Natty and his Mohican comrades. Cooper's hope for America's future seems embodied in this group, and its search for the father symbolizes the need for a cumulative moral force to be developed and consolidated under the auspices of a strong leader. It soon becomes clear that the white father is not such a figure.

Major Munro represents the best of white civilizing forces. When we first meet him at Fort William Henry, when he is momentarily reunited with his daughters, literally under the gunfire of the advancing French army, we are told that his "air of military grandeur had been . . . softened" by time, which allows him to feel genuine "parental agony" over the

endangered status of his "children" (1:637, 667). (Munro's use of the term
my children, in context, refers not only to his daughters but to all his legal
dependents in the besieged fort.) Cooper's emphasis, however, falls on the
good man's inadequacy, his inability to establish an equitable social order
in the New World. Thus we are made to feel that even the best of white
leadership is not enough, for Cooper focuses our attention on "the deep
responsibility they assume, who disregard the means to attain their end,
and [on] all the danger of setting in motion an engine, which it exceeds
human power to control" (1:666). In other words, Munro and the English, no less than the French (or any of the other white fathers), have
intruded their power politics into the American scene, have subordinated,
divided, and corrupted the Indians in the service of competitive white
interests. "'Tis a long and melancholy tradition," Natty admits, "and one I
little like to think of; for it is not to be denied, that the evil has been
mainly done by men with the white skins" (1:733). The result of such a
tradition is that no military resolution of white conflicts, no treaty between English and French, can restrain the Indian hostilities that have
accrued over time.

Thus the hopeful search party arrives at the fort only to find patriarchal
authority on the verge of collapse, and Cooper symbolically equates that
collapse with the ethical and semantic depletion of the white leaders'
language. The white man's word is imaged here as a vehicle of false hopes,
too immured in the politics of usurpation and oppression to ensure any
safe passage into the future. The party arrives just as Munro loses the
battle to Montcalm. A treaty is signed, guaranteeing the English a safe
retreat from the surrendered fort, but because the march of retreat must
take place under the hostile watch of their enemy's Indian allies, Heyward,
who is about to inherit the mantle of authority, advises his men: "It is
possible, that the Indians . . . of the enemy may intrude; in which case,
you will remind them of the terms of the capitulation, and threaten to
report their conduct to Montcalm. A word will suffice" (1:669). White
words will no longer suffice, however, to keep the oppressed at bay, and
immediately all hell breaks loose, in the form of one of the most brutal
massacre scenes ever portrayed in American literature.

Ironically, the white language that speaks of treaties (texts) and chivalric
conduct here appears as silent to the Indians as their language has been to
whites throughout. The clever Magua, for example, who has learned so
much from the pale-faces, is said to be "deaf" to his victims' cries (1:675),

and the dire results of such inherited white tactics are reinforced for any readers who have missed the point in another depiction of silence, rendered in familial terms that might strike closer to home. Once the Indian attack begins, the Munro sisters call to their father for help: "'Father—father—we are here!' shrieked Alice, as he passed, at no great distance, without appearing to heed them. 'Come to us, father, or we die!' The cry was repeated, and in terms and tones, that might have melted a heart of stone, but it was unanswered. Once, indeed, the old man appeared to catch the sounds, for he paused, and listened; but Alice had dropped senseless on the earth, and Cora had sunk at her side, hovering, in untiring tenderness, over her lifeless form. Munro shook his head, in disappointment, and proceeded, bent on the high duty of his station" (1:673).

The sentimentality of this failed exchange, coupled with the sensationalistic brutality on every side, confirms our sense that the white father's dedication to "duty" and "station" has deafened him to the human needs of all his children, just as his prolonged reliance on the duplicitous language of power politics has made him virtually insensible to the truth when he actually hears it. The resulting loss of humanity is both literal—the plain is strewn with "hundreds of human forms" (1:678), "a confused mass of dead" (1:680)—and figurative. White patriarchal culture loses its ethical sensibility, personified by the female members of its family, who are stolen away. Their kidnapping represents both the "bad" Indians' revenge for their maltreatment and Cooper's warning to a country seriously in need of ethical—and psychological—guidance.

I stress the psychological dimension of Cooper's warning because he was the first major American author to image the damaging and divisive effects of patriarchal culture on the mind, and before turning to the second story of this divided novel, "the father in quest of his children" (1:680), it is necessary to look for a moment at that imagery. Because Charles Brockden Brown had depicted the American mind as the scene of volatile and antisocial passions, he relied on artful language as a necessary means of psychosocial control. For Brown and his revolutionary predecessors, words were moment-to-moment, stopgap measures; they played tricks on minds in need of being tricked, and they did suffice. Cooper, in *The Last of the Mohicans*, probes the effects of such linguistic mind control, of what he and his romantic contemporaries would see as unnatural repression of natural instincts, over time, and he images the American mind as the scene of psychic civil war. The massacre at the center of the book functions as an externalization of such deadly psychic conflict and shows that words will no longer suffice to allay fraudulently pent-up human nature. But in each half of the novel, in each distinct quest, Cooper gives us a more specific image of a mind in conflict, and in such instances he reveals the dynamics of repression which must inevitably lead to recurring breakdowns of white authority.

Those images are of the counterpoised caverns, the Glenn's Falls cave where the first search party hides on the way to Fort William Henry and the Indian cave where Cora and Uncas meet their death. These cavern scenes represent the two combative states of mind engendered by patriarchy, that of the dominant culture and that of the oppressed Other, and as such, they are portrayed in distinctly masculine and feminine, patriarchal and matriarchal terms. The first cave, as Natty admits, has been "sadly changed" by time and, in particular, by the corrosive action of the river water, which, "having broke loose from order," "has been suffered to have its will for a time, like a headstrong man" (1:531, 532). In this psychic interior, where "the river fabricates all sorts of images" and where "minutes [flow] by with the swiftness of thought" (1:532, 552), a headstrong man is indeed still in charge, for at the moment of crisis and impending overthrow of white authority, Cooper places Duncan Heyward in the "centre of the cave . . . where he could command a view" of the danger (1:569)—"in the centre of the cavern, grasping his remaining pistol" and obsessed with "the sullen desperation of his purpose" (1:565). There are, of course, two sides to his purpose: he is defending, on the one hand, the "precious treasure" of white culture, the sisters hidden in "the deepest recess of the inner cavern," and on the other, the white, androcentric point of view that maintains its authoritative self-image by keeping them there (1:556, 562).[20]

The second cave, located in Indian territory, is laden with associations of femininity and otherness. It is "a cavern in the bosom of the mountain," where the Indians "brought most of their valuables, especially those which more particularly pertained to [their] nation" (1:763–64). At the center of this psychic interior is a "sick woman" of the tribe, "surrounded by females" (1:764), and in contrast to the willfulness of the young white leader, whose "self-possession . . . did not desert him" (1:570), "she lay in a sort of paralysis, indifferent to the objects which crowded before her sight" (1:764). The metaphor of illness here suggests that the natural will and instinct of the Other has been paralyzed, its rightful moral vision obscured, by patriarchal domination. If the first cavern scene represents the psychology of the oppressor, this interior represents the psychology of the oppressed victim.

Cooper's concern seems to be to show that in a divided America, both sides suffer psychic damage. Specifically, in the seemingly endless cycle of aggression and counteraggression initiated by the white fathers' appropriation of the New World, genuine ethical values are repressed; conflict and the desire for dominance or revenge prevail. And both cavern scenes stress the dire results of such repression. In the first scene, the white leader symbolically tries to hide the sisters in the deepest recesses of the cavern, but the untamable feminine elements, the "bad" Indians, cannot be safely contained in this interior world, and the balance of power shifts, the white order falls into disorder, with the return of the repressed in this new and more dangerous form. It is also important to note in this scene that Heyward assumes his ill-fated authority only when Natty, the translator and negotiator, leaves the cave to go for help and becomes "lost to view" (1:560). This loss of access to the language of the Other precipitates the white leader's loss of authority and prefigures Munro's failure—and the failure of white psychology—at the center of the novel.

In the second cavern scene it is the whites who intrude into an alien psychic world and bring untimely death and destruction into the American wilderness. Again the psychology of white strategy is emphasized. In this half of the novel, Natty is characterized by his "lingering pride of color" (1:700), and it is in this scene that he advises young Duncan, "Practyse all your cunning, for it is a lawful undertaking": the two enter this psychic interior by means of trickery, deceit, and disguise. Dressed as Indian medicine men, they are allowed into the cave to "cure" the sick woman; instead, they search for and find the imprisoned Alice and then imprison Magua, her Indian captor, in her place. The exchange implies the symbolic kinship between the white woman and the red man, but other instances of mutually corresponding imagery—other images of repression—establish the idea of their common treatment at the hands of patriarchy. To steal the "helpless" Alice out of the cave, for instance, Natty tells Heyward to "wrap her in them Indian cloths. Conceal all of her little form" (1:775). Magua is then similarly restrained and silenced to further the white undertaking: "When the formidable Huron was completely pinioned, the scout released his hold, and Duncan laid his enemy on his back, utterly helpless." In addition, when Magua angrily retorts with Cooper's all-purpose Indian expletive, "'Hugh!'" Natty, "his undisturbed conqueror," replies, "'Ay! you've found your tongue. . . . Now, in order that you shall not use it to our ruin, I must make free to stop your mouth.' As there was no time to be lost, the scout immediately. . . gagged the Indian" (1:774–75).

This latter image of the forceful, physical silencing of otherness will become, as we shall see, a mainstay in Poe's tales of psychological repression. Here it is of special significance for two reasons. First, it establishes a metaphorical link between political oppression, psychological repression, and the duplicitous, manipulative language of American patriarchy. Earlier in the second cavern scene, for example, Natty had described his own role as a con man/"conqueror": by dressing as an Indian conjuror, he had told Heyward, he would be as safe in the interior as a traveling "missionary would be at the beginning of a two hours' discourse" in the "settlements" (1:768). Like the metaphorical speech of Kill-deer, Natty's actions in this scene are equated with white discourse, with the artifice of white language that has affected the psyche of the Other like a disease and has repeatedly, as in the case of the "bad" Indians, transformed simple humanity into inhumane monsters, bent on savage revenge. In particular, Natty's actions here, and his disguise, show that white language keeps up the charade of white supremacy by silencing otherness.

The second significance of the image is that it foreshadows the "deep and awful silence" of mourning at the novel's end (1:866) and, specifically, Magua's inevitable retaliation: the deadly silencing of Cora and Uncas, the last and best hopes for America's future. Just as the internal drama of the first cavern scene had prefigured the outcome of the first quest—the return of the repressed and the resulting overthrow of white authority, so too the struggle for dominance in this second psychic interior prefigures the tragic outcome of the second journey. As Cooper has stressed again and again in this American fable, aggression breeds counteraggression, and at the end of the second journey, at the end of the fable, all there can be for those who have disregarded the means used to attain their end is a silencing of all ethical potential.

As I mentioned earlier, Cora is the main symbolic object of this quest. Of the two sisters, she is the more active, the "untiring" ethical force (1:673). In contrast to Alice's "infantile dependency" (1:593), for example, and to their father's obvious inability to protect his children, Cora is distinguished by "the unyielding character of her resolution" to do whatever is best for the common good and for Alice, "the child of [her] affections" (1:674, 595). She is a genuinely heroic maternal caretaker, a personification of redemptive matriarchal values in a world dominated and desecrated by patriarchal power politics. Finally, there is even a suggestion that Cora's relationship to her sister is that of the signified to the signifier, for Cora, who invariably speaks the truth to white and Indian alike, is described as "a beauteous and breathing model of her sex" (1:823), whereas Alice, in a book so insistently concerned with semantic depletion, is more often portrayed merely as the "beautiful emblem" of womanhood, "devoid of animation" (1:596) and literally "senseless" (e.g., 1:562, 673, 675) until revived by her sister. This reading is supported by the bonding of Uncas, the noblest and most trustworthy specimen of his uncorrupted race, with Cora and by the preference of Heyward, who likes to believe that mere words will suffice, for the "fragile form" of Alice (1:773). Moreover, although the "great and engrossing object" of the second quest is "the recovery of the sisters" (1:730), only Alice survives the ordeal, to be carried back to civilization an invalid, an emblem bereft of meaning.

The deaths of Cora and Uncas at the hands of the vengeful Magua—all three finally victims of the ongoing internecine war initiated by white interests—leave the Americans, whites and Indians together, "a nation of mourners" (1:865), and the theme of mutual national loss in the final chapter is rendered in various forms of silence. Representatives of both nations, including Natty, Heyward, and the two grieving fathers, Munro and Chingachgook, gather in the Delaware camp for the joint funeral rites, a "humbled and submissive throng" (1:868): "No sound louder than a stifled sob [was] heard among them" (1:867). At the edge of this group stands a stranger, an unnamed white soldier, an emissary of peace, who had, symbolically, "arrived too late," now "a silent and sad spectator" to the tragedy (1:867). The "principal actors in the scene" are the Indian women, who silently perform their ministrations and who sing in "a low murmur of voices"—and in words ever silent to white ears—"a sort of chant in honor of the dead" (1:873, 868): "During these . . . songs nothing was audible but the murmurs of the music" (1:870). And at "the centre of that ring" are the silent victims, "the ardent, high souled, and generous Cora," "her form . . . concealed in many wrappers," "her face shut for ever from the gaze of men"; and the noble Uncas, "his dull eye, and vacant lineaments . . . strongly contradict[ing] the idle tale of pride" his rich funeral ornaments are meant to convey (1:866). The last of the Mohicans, like his benumbed father, has been reduced to "the form . . . without the spirit of a man" (1:872). Again, the image is that of a signifier depleted of meaning, of its truth value.

That such silence prevails in these last pages testifies to the seriousness of Cooper's warning to his erring countrymen and to the harshness of his criticism of politicized white language. It also suggests, ironically, Cooper's fear that his own attempt to tell the other side of the American story would go unheard, for another mourner here, one who is finally silent like the rest, is David Gamut, the artist who has seen both sides and has tried unsuccessfully to bring a grievously and dangerously divided world back into harmony. Over the course of the novel Gamut changes greatly, and his art, which originally was perceived as effete frippery, comes to be valued, briefly, for its useful and admirable social function. In the end, however, his moral force, like Natty's, has been misappropriated in the service of the New World patriarchy, and though his potential as a cultural mediator is still great, it has been effectively silenced.[21]

Gamut's primary task at the outset of this novel is to become an American, or at least a New World, artist. In the opening pages he appears laughably out of place, not only because of his ill-proportioned physique but also because of his inappropriate Old World attire, which is embellished with silk and "silver lace" that have become "sullied" and "tarnished" during his unhappy trials in the wilderness (1:485–86). The greatest drawback he must overcome, however, is his habitual reliance on Old World models for his art. He is psychologically tied to his "little volume" of Psalms, itself a reduced New England "version" and now, in the colony of New York, several times removed from its historical and cultural origins. Consequently, the language he must use in his songs is not his own but an imitation of his biblical namesake's. "I utter nothing but the thoughts and the wishes of the King of Israel himself" (1:496), Gamut piously declares, but the inappropriateness of the patriarchal tradition and the patriarchal language that he promotes is shown throughout the first half of the novel, where he repeatedly searches his book for "a hymn not ill adapted" to the white fugitives' pressing spiritual and psychological needs and for "some song more fitted to their condition than any that had yet met his eye" (1:535, 566). Cooper specifically attributes Gamut's difficulty in finding a suitable and useful text to the artist's blind adherence to an ideology that causes him to misrepresent and misname reality, for "like other advocates of a system," we are told, "David was not always accurate in his use of terms" (1:604). Small wonder, then, that during the massacre scene, just as the white leaders' words will no longer suffice to maintain their authority, so too this backward-looking artist is "helpless and useless" before vengeful enemies who have been defrauded of rightful representation once too often (1:673).

This is not to say that Gamut is without talent, even in the first half of the novel, for he is another figure whose character has two sides. Like Natty, he is torn between his natural gifts and his unfortunate patriarchal acculturation, and Cooper images this sorry split in Gamut's character by showing that his art has two dimensions. His true talent is evidenced in the nonverbal component of his songs, the compelling musical quality of his voice, rather than in the inappropriate words he chooses to sing. In the Glenn's Falls cavern scene, for example, although Natty scoffs at Gamut's hymns, telling him that he might be "better employed," even the manly scout is moved to tears by the irresistible "sounds" of the artist's voice (1:534, 536). Later in the same scene, Gamut's ability to bring his audience into "open sympathy" and harmony is again credited to his "tones": "The melody . . . gradually wrought its sweet influence on the senses of those who heard it. It even prevailed over the miserable travesty of the song of David, which the singer had selected from a volume of similar effusions, and caused the sense to be forgotten, in the insinuating harmony of the sounds" (1:566).

Gamut's better half, then, which consists of his native ability to communicate true and natural feelings, untainted by white words, symbolically links him with the Mohicans and their musical, prelapsarian language, and, like them, he represents an androgynous alternative to white manhood. His otherness in this respect earns him little but condescension from Heyward, who considers him a "poor fellow" (1:566), and from Natty, who seems to take special pleasure in measuring his long and manly rifle, Kill-deer, against Gamut's "little" pitch pipe, which Natty calls a "harmless . . . tooting we'pon" (1:602, 779). As usual in this novel, however, the white men are blinded by their own cultural biases as to what a man should be; thus just as Natty misperceives and misnames the function of Gamut's pitch pipe, so too he and Heyward mistake the artist's true potential as an agent of harmony in a world divided by weapons and warfare. It is the white women in this book who truly value Gamut's presence and his ministrations, and his obvious sympathies with the women eventually enable him—however momentarily—to attain his true and worthy stature as an artist and transform his art into an active force for good in the New World.

In the first half of the novel, Uncas acted as "attendant to the females."

Following the massacre, Gamut's androgynous nature enables him to assume the function of faithful attendant, for the hostile Indians recognize
immediately that he is no typical white man, consider him mad and thus
untouchable, and allow him to follow the captured white women to the
Indians' camp, where he can come and go at will. In symbolic terms,
Gamut's attention to the women is of major significance, for it identifies
the task of the New World, or American, artist as one of cultural reparation and restitution. At the beginning of the second quest Gamut forsakes
his patriarchal text and makes the sisters the subject of his art. Similarly, in
the course of two pages his language becomes transformed, from the
"unintelligible" "figurative language" of his biblical model to a "simple"
mode of discourse, more appropriate to the urgency of his task (1:729,
730). Like Cooper, he now tells a second story, one that reminds the white
men in his audience what they have lost and how they might recover the
cultural balance and harmony that their one-sided world view has so severely jeopardized. "The narrative of David was simple," we are told, and
as a result, "the pursuers were put in possession of such leading circumstances, as were likely to prove useful in accomplishing their great and
engrossing object—the recovery of the sisters" (1:730).

The sad irony of Gamut's characterization is that after this brief artistic
breakthrough, he never again realizes his potential. On the contrary, his
new-found authority and his potential to restore what white culture has
lost progressively diminish, and the reasons Cooper gives for their loss
suggest his concerns regarding the practical effectiveness of his own attempt to tell a second story. The first of Gamut's problems is that his new
narrative style—his unorthodox naming—does not meet his audience's
expectations and thus evokes negative criticism. That is, although he can
tell the members of the search party that the lost sisters are being held by
different tribes and although he can describe the tribe that keeps Cora
prisoner, the white men want none of his subjective descriptions; they
want to hear a name with which they are already familiar, and when he
fails to name the tribe in question to their satisfaction, they consider his
narrative "imperfect" (1:731). The second of the artist's problems is the
otherness of his subject matter, although again it is his audience's flawed
sensibility that is shown to be at fault. When Gamut courageously tries to
deliver a message from Alice—symbolically, to tell the "sister's" story,
Natty and Heyward fail to perceive his "deeper" meaning, which remains
"hidden" to them: "The words of Gamut were . . . in his native tongue;
and to Duncan they seemed pregnant with some hidden meaning, though

nothing present assisted him in discovering the object of their allusion" (1:766). Natty in particular complacently attributes their failure as "readers" to the artist's lack of talent. "The simpleton was frightened, and blundered through his message," the scout reassures his young white friend (1:769).

The last and greatest of Gamut's problems, and the one that links him most suggestively to Cooper, is his choice to represent a morally ambiguous hero. Near the end of the second quest, Gamut is momentarily overwhelmed by the cleverness of one of the disguises Natty uses to infiltrate the hostile Indians' camp, and shortly afterward he undergoes "utter confusion of the state of his mind" and accedes to Natty's request that the two exchange clothes (1:781, 787). Since Natty's moral limitations have already been made apparent in this novel, we have to suspect that Gamut's symbolic assumption of the scout's identity and, by extension, his acceptance of Natty as a heroic model, can come to no good end. Cooper confirms this suspicion in the remaining pages by having Gamut forsake his role as cultural mediator and message-bearer and, like his new hero, take up the white men's vengeful cause as his own. That the heroic model he has chosen is not really new and that his choice represents a moral backsliding into unconscious and unconscionable patriarchal bias are evidenced in the climactic death scene in which Gamut fights less to save Cora than to repossess her. He fights like Natty, with inappropriate violence; he fights like his biblical namesake, with an inappropriate weapon; and the two models of behavior are equally useless to save the "precious treasure." What Cooper seems to be imaging in this sequence of events is his own fear that his authorial point of view, his values, would be perceived to be indistinguishable from Natty Bumppo's; specifically, that in devoting so much time to Natty's heroic potential and daring adventures, he might merely dazzle his readers with his character's (and his own) originality and prevent them from seeing clearly Natty's other, darker side and Cooper's deeper meaning. It was apparently to forestall such misreadings that when he wrote a new Introduction to *The Last of the Mohicans* in 1831, he referred to Natty as "an important character of this legend," "a conspicuous actor," but never a "hero" (1:475), and he reminded his audience that "every word uttered by Natty Bumppo was not to be received as rigid truth."

In the last chapter of this novel, David Gamut seems a failed artist indeed. Repeatedly misunderstood by his audience and eventually confused in his own mind as to the best way to put his art to use in such a

divided world, he has reverted to his "little volume," and after singing a
final funeral anthem, a lament for what has already been lost—what he as
an artist has not been able to save—he subsides into "grave and solemn
stillness" (1:866, 874). Even though Gamut seems effectively silenced here,
and with him the values he initially tried to represent—cultural harmony,
restitution, and reconciliation—nevertheless, Cooper seems unwilling to
deny the American artist's potential to communicate such "other" values.
Gamut's last song, like those of the Delaware women, is said to have
touched the hearts of both sides of the American "family"—children and
fathers, Indians and whites, women and men. It does so because, once
again, the sound of the artist's voice has broken the silent spell imposed by
patriarchal words: "His full, rich, voice, was not found to suffer by a
comparison with the soft tones of the girls; and his more modulated
strains possessed, at least for the ears of those to whom they were peculiarly addressed, the additional power of intelligence" (1:874). In imaging
such expressive, nonverbal otherness, Cooper was able to break that silence and to convey a second story to those who had ears to hear.

Psychoanalytic studies have shown that in the last years of Cooper's life
(he died in 1851), his attitudes toward his father and toward patriarchal
authority in general underwent a dramatic change. In the same years that
Hawthorne, Melville, and Harriet Beecher Stowe would be drafting their
stirring fictional indictments of American patriarchy, Cooper would become increasingly anxious to promote and identify with the admirable
qualities of those same white fathers he had been so harshly critical of
twenty-five years before.[22] His late change of mind, however, cannot obvi-
ate his advocacy in 1826 of a very different change of the American mind
and a change of sociopolitical authority. *The Last of the Mohicans* stands
today as Cooper's best-remembered work, and like his legal battle to
assume his mother's name, undertaken in the same year, it records a heartfelt and imaginative challenge to the patriarchal politics of language in
America. Above all, it continues to remind us that there have always been
two sides to the American story.

5

Detecting the Second
Story: Poe's Tales

"Here is a poetic world divided into those who have power and those who have it not, with the emphasis falling heavily on the latter. Here are the guardians or mourners, who victimize the other through forgetfulness and feel guilty about it, or who atone for failure after the other is finally 'gone'; and here are the sleepers, helpless beneath the gaze of those other beings who are charged to remember but so often forget." This passage might very well serve as a description of the final scenes of *The Last of the Mohicans*. The sleepers are Cora and Uncas and the sadly silenced red race, and their rightful Americanness, like their authentic naming, are all but forgotten; indeed, already forgotten, Cooper would have us understand, in the pages of American history books. The guardian-mourners are Munro, the "unconscious father," who is bereaved of a daughter whose voice he had "forgotten" to hear (1:872); the young white military leaders, who represent a new generation of guardian-mourners; and Natty Bumppo, the guide, who, too late, tries to atone for his ineffectual guidance—"if ever I forget the lad, who has so often fou't at my side in war, and slept at my side in peace, may He who made us all . . . forget me!" (1:877).

Actually, the passage quoted above comes from David Halliburton's *Edgar Allan Poe: A Phenomenological View*, and it describes the divided poetic world found in Poe's poetry and tales.[1] Poe's writings, with their foreign landscapes, foreign-sounding names, and feudal mansions, have tended to bother those who would assign—or deny—him a place as a distinctly "American" author.[2] But Halliburton's descriptive terminology is especially suggestive of the thematic structures that link Poe's fictional works with those of his male contemporaries. Like the other American romantic authors treated here, Poe depicted conflicting modes of human experience and of power, and, like them, he dramatized these conflicts through different uses of language and different "stories." Poe's guardian-mourners, typically the masculine narrators in his early tales about women, seem directly descended from the "confidential guardians" of the Early National literature: they manipulate language so as to maintain order in their fictional worlds, and to maintain such order, they must suppress any disruptive second story that threatens the narrative proper. Unlike their eighteenth-century predecessors, however, these narrators rarely claim any conscious intent in their repressive acts, nor are they admirable heroes. Rather, like Cooper's inadequate father figures, they are neglectful guardians, obsessed with defending their own authority. Consequently, their repression takes the form of unconsciousness or forgetfulness, and it becomes the reader's task to see that their acts of forgetting are willful, self-interested acts of aggression, paranoid attempts to repress the threat of feminine otherness, to kill out of consciousness any rival claims to masculine authority. What links Poe so specifically with his fellow American romancers is his depiction of how the language of male-dominant culture facilitates that repression: forgetting is enacted by renaming, by translating the potentially subversive language of female characters, and, when all else fails, by out-and-out silencing.

One characteristic of Poe's artistry that makes his work unique is his insistence on the criminal nature of such repressive linguistic politics.[3] Poe was especially prolific in creating images of violently silenced women, their vocal apparatus the apparent target of their male attackers, who, in his earlier tales, are the storytellers. One remembers the forcible and (the narrator asks us to believe) unconscious removal of Berenice's teeth by her professed lover; the premature shroud that "lay heavily about the mouth" of the ostensibly beloved Ligeia[4]—and of Madeline Usher, no doubt; and later, the throat-cutting and strangulations in "The Murders in the Rue Morgue" and "The Mystery of Marie Rogêt." The psychological violence in such tales is no less preemptive. Morella's narrator-husband comes to a point where he can "no longer bear . . . the low tone of her musical language," and after she "dies," he does what he can to obliterate her memory: "Morella's name died with her at death. Of the mother I had never spoken to the daughter" (2:231, 235). Even in "The Purloined Letter," the least violent of Poe's tales about women, the queen who sees her letter stolen before her very eyes cannot speak to save herself for fear of jeopardizing her position with the king, who is unconscious of the crime taking place.

A second, though obviously related, characteristic of Poe's unique vision is his growing insistence on the need to detect and solve such linguistic crimes, to recover the story that has been too conveniently forgotten by androcentric culture. Although I have grouped his tales about women together above, they actually represent three different phases in Poe's search for ways to image and recover that second story. "Ligeia" (1838), which will be the first tale discussed in this chapter, represents the aesthetic and conceptual culmination of the early phase, whose tales bear women's names. Here the crimes committed are covert, and the burden of detection falls on the reader.[5] "The Fall of the House of Usher" (1839) marks the second phase, Poe's search for a solution to such crimes of omission. Starting with Roderick Usher, Poe provided readers with a tentative model of the detecting ability he had previously required of them: an androgynous character whose developing empathy with a woman enables him to reject one-sided male-authored fictions and to imagine a new fictional form—a second story that provides a text for female experience. And in the third and final phase, Poe turned to a new fictional form himself.[6] In the three tales of detection published between 1841 and 1845, Poe moved from the timeless, dreamlike worlds of remote Gothic mansions, turrets, and dungeons to the social realm of neighborhoods, shops, newspapers, and political intrigue. Here the investigation of overt and seemingly isolated crimes against women uncovers a network of covert gender-related crimes that pervades the entire social order, and the task of solving both the obvious and the hidden crimes calls for a detective with an awareness that other men lack. In the androgynous Dupin, Poe created a new and unquestionably heroic caretaker of social and political order, and Dupin fulfills these responsibilities by going beyond the imaginative limits of the male storytellers around him and fully recovering the second story—the woman's story—that has previously gone untold.

To discover the crime that has been committed against Ligeia requires close attention to her storyteller's language throughout, but if we accept Roland Kuhn's claim that "a phenomenological inspection of *forgetting* and *killing* would show up their close inner relations," we can see that the narrator reveals his own murderous psychological traits in his very first words.[7] "Ligeia" begins with the narrator's claim, "I cannot, for my soul, remember how, when, or even precisely where, I first became acquainted with the lady Ligeia" (2:310). The statement foreshadows his coming psychic struggle to forget her once and for all, but it also reveals the role his authorial control will play in that struggle, for the very first sentence of his text divests Ligeia of any social history, social context, or social authority. The latter issue, his subconscious usurpation of her authority, is further suggested by his claim to have "*never known* the paternal name of her who was my friend and my betrothed, and who became the partner of my studies, and finally the wife of my bosom."

This is a strange omission for one whose vast wealth derives from Ligeia's paternal dowry, but as he tries to give an explanation for it, hidden causes and motivations for his mental block are revealed: "Was it a playful charge on the part of my Ligeia? or was it a test of my strength of affection, that I should institute no inquiries upon this point? or was it rather a caprice of my own—a wildly romantic offering on the shrine of the most passionate devotion?" (2:311). Despite his surface professions of wildly romantic devotion, his tentative emphasis on Ligeia's "playful"— say, rather, competitive and demanding—personality reveals that their re- lationship was conflicted and that he recalls her typically as an opponent in a "test" of naming.[8] This sense of struggle and threat is also evidenced in his description of the "*enthralling* eloquence of her low musical language," which made its way "so steadily and stealthily" into his "heart." *Heart*, however, seems to be a misnomer, or characteristically, a self-serving eu- phemism, for we learn shortly that he "was never made aware of her entrance into [his] closed study save by the dear music of her low sweet voice" (2:311). The "closed" room of the narrator's mind is the true seat of the conflict in this tale, and the conflict is precipitated by the intrusive "voice" of a rival authority figure.[9]

Like Cooper, Poe often imaged the otherness that male-dominant cul- ture tried to forget through use of an alternative form of discourse, a fantasy language characterized by its nonverbal and, symbolically, barely audible qualities. The otherness of Ligeia's speech, for example, had been prefigured in the "singularly low tone" of the Marchesa's "unmeaning words" in "The Visionary" (1834, later called "The Assignation") (2:155), and in the "low tone" of Morella's "musical language" (2:227). Ligeia, of course, also has other disturbing qualities of which her narrator is uncom- fortably aware. Not only does she have no "known" paternal name, which surely marks her as a stranger in patriarchal culture, but among the first descriptions we hear of her are that her footfall had an "incomprehensible lightness and elasticity" (2:311); her features were of a Hebrew cast (2:312); her eyes were "far larger than the ordinary eyes of our own race"; and her great beauty was "the beauty of beings either above or apart from the earth" (2:313). Most important, finally, is her prodigious learning. "It was immense," the narrator tells us, "—such as I have never known in woman," but he quickly appends, "I said her knowledge was such as I have never known in woman—but where breathes the man who has traversed, and successfully, *all* the wide areas of moral, physical, and mathematical science? I saw not then what I now clearly perceive, that the acquisitions of Ligeia were gigantic, were astounding; yet I was sufficiently aware of her infinite supremacy to resign myself, with a child-like confidence, to her guidance" (2:315–16).

The narrator's reference to his "child-like" confidence in Ligeia's "infinite supremacy" is repeated—"Without Ligeia I was but a child groping benighted"—and the effect of his metaphorical associations is to point out again the conflicted workings of his mind. Ligeia's authority over him was like a mother's over her child; his language speaks of emasculation. Moreover, interspersed with these mother-child associations is the image of Ligeia as an aggressive sexual "mentor," a willful pleasurer: "With how vast a triumph—with how vivid a delight—with how much of all that is ethereal in hope—did I *feel*, as she bent over me in studies but little sought—but less known,—that delicious vista by slow degrees expanding before me, down whose long, gorgeous, and all untrodden path, I might at length pass onward to the goal of a wisdom too divinely precious not to be forbidden!" Here again Ligeia usurps the traditional male prerogative.

Psychoanalytic criticism has taught us to see the blatant incestuous desires in such passages and prepared us for the inevitable repression of such desires: "I saw that she must die" (2:316). What stands out in this extended description of Ligeia's sexual otherness, however, is the linking of her threatening sexuality with her authority over texts and over this text maker in particular. This theme culminates in the death scene that follows this passage; the dynamics of repression are expressed in texts, in language. Ironically, we are eased into the death scene with the narrator's vehement protestations of his own verbal impotence: "Words are impotent to convey any just idea of the fierceness of resistance with which she wrestled with the Shadow. . . . I have no power to portray—no utterance capable of expressing . . ." (2:317–18). Ostensibly registering his unutterable grief at her passing, his words nevertheless stand as a literal declaration that his language cannot admit, can only exclude, the otherness represented by Ligeia. The death scene demonstrates that exclusion, first by demonstrating the immediate need for it: Ligeia had authored her own text and not the type of narrative that her husband writes, but a poem, which suggests the possibility of other, alternative forms of discourse.[10] In addition, the poem itself, "The Conqueror Worm," attempts to tell the story of culturally sanctioned oppression as best it can under the circumstances. The last lines reveal that the play that has been described "is the tragedy, 'Man,' / And its hero the conqueror Worm" (2:319), but as Joel Porte has rightly pointed out, "From Ligeia's point of view, the play is the tragedy 'Woman' and its hero the conquering male organ."[11]

The threat to her narrator-husband's authority is implicit in his description of how she "peremptorily . . . bade me repeat certain verses composed by herself. . . . I obeyed her" (2:318). And as usual, his choice of words is double-edged, for though he does indeed "repeat" her verses, in effect her text and her language become incorporated into and contained by—repressed by—his. Patriarchal language has the last word, a fact that is heightened by Ligeia's having no last words of her own but rather "the concluding words of [a] passage in Glanvill: *'Man doth not yield him to the angels, nor unto death utterly, save only through the weakness of his feeble will'*" (2:319–20). The two sets of quotation marks show how surely Ligeia's own "low musical language" has been silenced by the rival authority of literary "fathers" and masculine texts.[12]

After Ligeia has been thus killed out of consciousness, albeit momentarily, the narrator tells of the lengths to which he went to try to keep from remembering her: moving to a new country, becoming "a bounden slave in the trammels of opium" as a way of easing his mind (2:319), and finally taking a new bride. The new woman, however, is but "the successor of the unforgotten Ligeia" (2:320), and correspondences between the second marriage and the first become apparent. Rowena, for example, seems to have had firsthand experience of Ligeia's "tragedy, 'Woman,'" with all its sadosexual undertones, for she is described as dreading her husband's fierce frenzies and shunning him during "the unhallowed hours of the first month of . . . marriage" (2:323). Their conflicts are also characterized by their having different states of mind, different perceptions: she "spoke, in an earnest low whisper [reminiscent of Ligeia's low tones], of sounds which she *then* heard, but which I could not hear—of motions which she *then* saw, but which I could not perceive" (2:324); "if this I saw—not so Rowena" (2:325). Characteristically, the narrator attributes such deviance to a sickness in her mind; characteristically, the wife dies, the rival story gets suppressed.

Thus the second death scene may be read as another look into the narrator's conflicted mind, as a repetition of the early scene of Ligeia's stealthy intrusion into his "closed study."[13] Here the room has become, appropriately, the bridal chamber of Ligeia's successor, the wife whose voice is never heard in the text. The psychological conflict has been reduced to its essence, a struggle between masculine and feminine states of mind; and the repression mechanism has become ingrained, for the drops of poison fall "as if from some invisible spring in the atmosphere" (2:325)—the phrasing reveals the unconsciousness of this murderous act.

It seems fitting that before she dies Rowena can hear Ligeia's presence (she speaks "frequently and pertinaciously, of the sounds—of the slight sounds" in the closed room) for surely, ironically, they are sisters under the skin.[14] The narrator admits that he "could not hear" the sounds at first (2:324), just as Munro, in Cooper's novel, could not hear the feminine voices in the midst of *his* struggle for authority. Once the narrator begins to hear his victim's voice, the terror builds: "It might have been midnight, or perhaps earlier, or later, for I had taken no note of time, when a sob, low, gentle, but very distinct, startled me from my revery. . . . I could not have been deceived. I *had* heard the noise, however faint, and my soul was awakened within me" (2:326–27). The movement from revery to an awakened state signals imminent return of the repressed to consciousness, and again, as in the first death scene, the narrator tries to ward off his psychic unease by clinging to a language that will not admit the existence of otherness. He describes his "unutterable horror and awe, for which the language of mortality has no sufficiently energetic expression" (2:327).

Rather than the language of mortality, say the language of masculine texts, for it soon becomes clear that the narrator intends to fight for his authority, to end his tale rather than allow Ligeia's verbal "revivification": "But why shall I minutely detail the unspeakable horrors of that night?. . . Let me hurry to a conclusion" (2:328–29). That Ligeia has been and here continues to be repressed out of language is nowhere more evident than in the final image we have of her. "The bandage lay heavily about the mouth," and as "the thing that was enshrouded advance[s] boldly and palpably into the middle of the apartment," the narrator raises his "voice" as if to intercept, to override, the imminent breach of her silence: he shrieks "aloud" the name "of the Lady—of the LADY LIGEIA" (2:329–30). In that last authorial act of naming, he exerts his ultimate control over the language of the text.[15] And he commits his last crime of omission, for the story Ligeia is obviously dying to tell, in her own words, is now lost.

That a crime has been committed against the Lady Madeline Usher is more immediately obvious: she has been prematurely entombed. Her brother Roderick has traditionally been considered solely responsible for this precipitate burial, but he is but a character in the story, and his actions are at least in part the product of his narrator's construction. That is, though critics have credited him with a variety of personal motives for trying to kill his "tenderly beloved sister" (2:404), including self-defense, euthanasia, and a vampiristic "creative impulse,"[16] the fact remains that he could not have incarcerated Madeline without the narrator's help, as Roderick himself comes to realize: "*We have put her living in the tomb!*" (2:416). Thus it is the male narrator's actions in this story, his influence over Roderick and his misogynist strategies of textual control, that first warrant a reader's attention—and suspicion.

The narrator, a boyhood friend of Roderick, arrives on the scene at the outset to bolster his friend's waning manhood, and from hints variously placed in his narration it soon becomes clear that he views Roderick's acute nervous condition as arising from his sister's presence, perhaps from her overcloseness or her unmanly influence. The long-standing critical consensus is that the narrator is a well-intentioned man of reason, valiantly, albeit naively, trying to make sense of a world skewed by irrational forces.[17] His animosity toward Madeline, however, which is foreshadowed in his first description of the mansion upon his arrival, seems unreasonable and irrational. The "vacant and eye-like windows" (2:398), the "fine tangled web-work" of fungi hanging from the eaves (2:400), and the crack that runs from roof to foundation prefigure Roderick's "luminous" eyes, his "hair of a more than web-like softness and tenuity" (2:401–2), and his oddly split personality, all of which seem ominous enough to the narrator. But he experiences "a shudder even more thrilling than before" when he looks at the reflection of the house in the tarn, the "remodelled and inverted images" (2:398) that represent Madeline, Roderick's physical and psychological counterpart. In particular, the "silent tarn" (2:400) foreshadows Madeline's ill-fated exclusion from the narrator's story, for she will be buried at "a great depth" (2:410) in the house, in a chamber that lies beneath the surface of the tarn and of the narrative.

The narrator's first encounter with Madeline confirms the conflict between the male storyteller and the lady of the house, for he frames the encounter as one between mutually exclusive presences. "I regarded her with an utter astonishment not unmingled with dread. . . . A sensation of stupor oppressed me," he says, and the effect of his presence on her is equally oppressive: "On the closing in of the evening of my arrival, . . . she succumbed . . . to the prostrating power of the destroyer." What is of interest here is the periphrastic description of her lapse into a cataleptic—speechless—stupor and the narrator's passive construction in the phrasing that follows: "The lady, at least while living, would be seen by me no more." Without implicating himself as an agent in her immediate demise, the narrator uses language covertly to relegate Madeline to a passive position in relation to himself, and in the next sentence he tries to exclude her from the text altogether: "For several days ensuing, her name was unmentioned by either Usher or myself" (2:404). Although he ostensibly remarks on this omission to demonstrate his concern and sensitivity for his friend's grief over his sister's deteriorating condition, the effect is to show that the narrator is making sure that Madeline has no place in their masculine language or in this male-authored fiction.

Similarly, on the verge of her return from the tomb, the narrator will try not to hear what he dismisses as her "indefinite sounds" (2:411) as she breaks through steel and a copper-lined vault, sounds that emanate from the tomb "beneath . . . [his] own sleeping apartment" (2:410) on a night when he tries unsuccessfully to sleep. The suggestion here of a guilty conscience, or more specifically, of a consciousness plagued by its repressed underpinnings, is heightened by the narrator's being awakened to such ominous sounds by the nightmare vision of "an incubus," which he wants to believe is "of utterly causeless alarm" (2:411). His word is ill chosen, however, or at least revealing of the psychological processes he has previously tried to conceal, for *incubus* is the archaic name for a male spirit that visited women in their sleep and aroused female sexuality. If his word choice is a conscious misnomer, that is, if he has substituted *incubus* for *succubus*, the female counterpart supposed to visit sleeping men, then the choice is but another narrative strategy intended to exclude any female agency from his text. If, as seems more likely, we are to take *incubus* as an authentic report of a mind that is losing conscious control (for on this night of nights the return of the repressed is imminent), then Poe would seem to be suggesting that the narrator's homoerotic attraction to Roderick has caused him to see himself in some way feminized. If this is the case, then the nightmare status of this identification with female sexuality is no less proof of the narrator's misogyny—of his fear and hatred of the female sexuality incarnate in Madeline Usher.

It is Roderick who finally admits to hearing Madeline, and it is Roderick's growing consciousness of the crime perpetrated against his sister that finally allows her back into the text. Before he can make such an admission, however, he has first to undergo a mighty transformation for a fictional character and free himself of his narrator's control. The conflict between the male storyteller and the female character is internalized in the androgynous Roderick, who, like David Gamut, has two dimensions to his character and his artistry. Roderick's dual gender is depicted in behavior that is "alternately vivacious and sullen" and in a voice that varies "rapidly from a tremulous indecision" to a "species of energetic concision" also described as a "guttural utterance" (2:402). That he is Madeline's twin more obviously implies a merging of gender identities in this story, and there are other suggestions of his partly feminine nature. His composition of a musical ballad is reminiscent of Morella and Ligeia, who had been characterized by their "musical language" (2:227, 311), which their male narrators had also found unsettling. In addition, Poe's physical description of Roderick is, as D. H. Lawrence recognized, very similar to that of the beautiful Ligeia.[18] He has the same large, pale brow; eyes "large, liquid, and luminous beyond comparison"; lips of "a surpassingly beautiful curve"; and "a nose of delicate Hebrew model" (2:401). Thus it is not surprising that the narrator speaks distastefully of his friend's "peculiar physical conformation and temperament" (2:402) or that he will try to cure him of the effeminacy he denigrates as a "mental disorder" (2:410).

We may speculate that it was the masculine side of Roderick's character, or rather, his desire for an exclusively masculine identity, that originally motivated him to summon the narrator to him, "with a view of attempting . . . some alleviation of his malady" (2:398). Once the narrator is in authorial possession of the house, however, and Madeline's effeminizing influence has been dispatched, Roderick begins to have second thoughts about what he will finally come to see as the crime of masculine exclusivity, and his change of mind is imaged in his search for a narrative form that will allow him to express what the narrator has so artfully excluded.

Roderick's first attempt to communicate his inner turmoil after Madeline has been confined to her sick chamber, for example, is through a "perversion and amplification" of a waltz by Von Weber. That Roderick gives an unusual interpretation of this musical score suggests his desire to deviate from male-authored compositions. But the single-minded narrator characteristically refuses to confer such meaning on his friend's deviation from a masculine script and thus labels it merely a "perversion" (2:405). The next of Roderick's creations, a small painting of an interior vault that suggests both Madeline's femaleness and her fate, is illuminated, the misogynous narrator would have us believe, with "inappropriate splendor," and again he resists assigning meaning to his friend's subversive attempt to communicate otherness, claiming that Roderick's subject may be "shadowed forth, [only] feebly, in words" (2:405–6). Roderick's third formal experiment, the musical ballad of "The Haunted Palace," has its own verbal component, which implies Roderick's growing abilities as a storyteller in his own right. But here, perhaps sensing a rival narrative voice for the first time, the narrator escalates his textual control. Acknowledging that there is an "under or mystic current of . . . meaning," he nevertheless exerts editorial authority over Roderick's text in phrasing that hints at partial censorship: "The verses . . . ran very nearly, if not accurately, thus:" (2:406).

"The Haunted Palace," like "The Fall of the House of Usher," tells the story of a mind ("Thought's dominion") assailed and enervated by nameless "evil things," and as in the prose narrative, where Madeline's enshrouded body is graced by "the mockery of a faint blush upon the bosom and the face" (2:410), "the glory / That blushed and bloomed / Is but a dim-remembered story / Of the old time entombed" (2:406–7). The narrator of "The Fall of the House of Usher" has used his narrative strategies to suppress the story of Madeline's victimization, and Roderick's ballad, though it is an improvement over the nonverbal suggestiveness of his music and his painting, is no more explicit about the crime perpetrated against his sister: it tells its tale in symbolism, metonymy, and allegory—all misnomers sanctioned historically by a male-dominant literary tradition. It is Roderick's task finally to retrieve that "dim-remembered story" from the obfuscating language of male-authored fictions, and to do so he must become fully conscious of his own complicity in the crime of excluding by misnaming. It was Roderick after all who had first invited the narrator's misogynistic intrusion into the House of Usher by labeling his "sympathies" with his lady sister a "malady" (2:410).

Roderick's reviving sympathies with and for his sister precipitate her return from the tomb to the text, and in the climactic closing scenes of this tale, when Roderick at last acknowledges and renounces his crime, the narrator struggles to maintain his textual control. As Madeline makes headway up from the lower regions of the house, the narrator, finally showing his true colors, tries desperately to shut out her noisy return with the language of another male-authored fiction, "the only book immediately at hand." Trying to hold Roderick's divided attention with "a gentle violence" (2:413), he reads him the story of Ethelred, a manly hero and "conqueror," who is challenged by a dragon with "a shriek so horrid and harsh, and withal so piercing, that Ethelred had fain to close his ears with his hands against the dreadful noise of it" (2:414). But Roderick here becomes virtually "a resisting reader."[19] He rejects both the model of manliness the narrator has tried to impose upon him and the misnaming of the sound he hears, and he replaces the narrator's death-dealing text with a new, second story in a dramatic act of "re-vision":[20]

> "Not hear it?—yes, I hear it, and *have* heard it. Long—long—long—many minutes, many hours, many days, have I heard it—yet I dared not—oh, pity me, miserable wretch that I am! I dared not—I *dared* not speak! *We have put her living in the tomb!*. . . And now—tonight—Ethelred—ha! ha! the breaking of the hermit's door, and the death-cry of the dragon, and the clangor of the shield!—say, rather, the rending of her coffin, and the grating of the iron hinges of her prison, and her struggles within the coppered archway of the vault! . . . MADMAN! I TELL YOU THAT SHE NOW STANDS WITHOUT THE DOOR!" [2:416]

By momentarily freeing himself of the narrator's control and authoring a second story that explicitly reveals the crime perpetrated against femaleness, Roderick has succeeded in bringing Madeline to the threshold of the narrator's tale. And indeed, the unmasked "MADMAN" in Poe's story is here forced to acknowledge in unambiguous words the irrefutable truth of Roderick's narrative: "Without those doors there *did* stand the lofty and enshrouded figure of the lady Madeline of Usher. There was blood upon her white robes, and the evidence of some bitter struggle upon every portion of her emaciated frame" (2:416). The narrator is still not willing to admit his role in her long struggle for acknowledgment, however, any more than he is willing to wait around for her to speak her mind. Claiming that Madeline and Roderick reunite only to die in each other's arms, this eminently unreliable narrator flees the chamber, the house, and his own misogynistic narrative endeavor.[21] "The Fall of the House of Usher" ends with the narrator's fragmented sentences, the last fragments of his control. But control, nevertheless, for his final act of "sentencing" is to dispatch Madeline and her too-familiar twin into the "silent tarn," out of mind and out of language one last time: "The deep and dank tarn at my feet closed sullenly and silently over the fragments of the '*House of Usher*'" (2:417).

In this tale, Roderick's growing abilities as as "reader" and storyteller are paralleled by his growing terror at the implications of what he must finally do: act as a free agent and virtually rupture the narrative proper with a second story that lays bare the crime of male-authored fictions. The rupture is momentary, lasting just long enough to allow the woman character to get a foot in the door, but it is a significant moment in the evolution of Poe's artistry. Roderick Usher was a new character in Poe's repertoire, an androgynous spokesperson capable of giving voice to female experience and critiquing male-authored fictions which mute that experience, and despite what his madman-narrator must have hoped, his unusual talents were not so easily laid to rest. They would surface again two years later in the service of C. Auguste Dupin, Poe's great detective. The new genre that serves as a vehicle for this androgynous mastermind may be said to be Poe's own "second story," for it too is a new narrative form that critiques male-authored interpretive paradigms that fail—"forget"—to do justice to women. And Dupin, more forcefully than Roderick, provides readers with a model of the cultural detective work that needs to be done to bring such criminal acts of forgetfulness to light.[22]

The epigraph to the first of the Dupin tales, "The Murders in the Rue Morgue" (1841), introduces the idea of crossing gender boundaries to recover the now dim-remembered story of female experience: "What song the Syrens sang, or what name Achilles assumed when he hid himself among women, although puzzling questions, are not beyond *all* conjecture" (2:527). Like Roderick, Dupin exhibits a "Bi-Part Soul," which leads his narrator to imagine "a double Dupin," and he speaks in dual modes, his normal speaking voice "a rich tenor" that rises "into a treble" when he delivers his analysis of a crime, that is, when he recounts the experience of a female victim (2:533). That he represents a second draft of Roderick's character, however, is evident in his greater ability to speak, literally, for the silenced woman, to imagine her story in her own words. In "The Mystery of Marie Rogêt" (1842), for example, Dupin goes so far as to recreate the thought pattern of the murdered Marie in the first person: "We may imagine her thinking thus:—'I am to meet a certain person'" (3:756).

The most significant difference between Dupin's ability to recover the story untold by male-authored fictions and Roderick's, however, is that the detective's skill is presented as the desired model even within the tales in which he appears. Unlike Roderick's closed-minded narrator, for example, Dupin's narrator greatly admires his friend's mental powers (as do the police), and Dupin tries to teach his less-skilled narrator how to read in a new way. In this, the evolution of his character may be traced back to Ligeia, whose deeper knowledge of texts had threatened her narrator-husband by revealing his lesser abilities. In "Ligeia," the narrator had described his attempt to attain to Ligeia's knowledge as being like "our endeavors to recall to memory something long forgotten": "We often find ourselves *upon the very verge* of remembrance, without being able, in the end, to remember" (2:313–14). In "The Murders in the Rue Morgue," Dupin tells his narrator his own partial interpretation of a newspaper text reporting the grisly murders of two women and asks for the man's conclusion: "At these words a vague and half-formed conception of the meaning of Dupin flitted over my mind. I seemed to be upon the verge of comprehension, without power to comprehend—as men, at times, find themselves upon the brink of remembrance, without being able, in the end, to remember" (2:555).

One critic has claimed that readers rightly identify with this "ostensible dummy" rather than with the detective, whom he sees as "grotesquely naive" in this story. He argues that the story is a lesson in the dangers inherent in sexual repression: the overly intellectual Dupin fails to see the obvious sexual nature of the crime and thus tries to rationalize the evidence in a way that the narrator finds incomprehensible, whereas the narrator, who represents "every reader," more naturally sees evidence of rape. "Every reader," this critic explains, knows that "he" is potentially "capable of such actions" and all-too-humanly "finds himself excited by— and identifying with—" the putative rapist-murderer.[23] The similar phrasings above, however, suggest that Poe conceived of Dupin as being like Ligeia, or at least as thinking like her, and it seems unrealistic to fault a character who apparently thinks like a woman for failing to identify with or be excited by the idea of a rapist. Indeed, the point of the similar phrasings seems to be that men and women think and see things differently, specifically, that Dupin, like Ligeia, has mental abilities of which most "men" are unconscious, their conceptions merely "half-formed." He is thus able to read beyond the surface narrative of male-authored texts, to perceive the gap between text and reality, as we are shown in "The Mystery of Marie Rogêt," in which he criticizes virtually point by point a newspaper journalist's attempted reconstruction of the crime. "The sentence in question has but one meaning, as it stands," Dupin instructs his narrator, "but it is material that we go behind the mere words, for an idea which these words have . . . failed to convey" (3:739).

What I have called the gap between text and reality is, of course, a gender gap. In the Dupin tales, male-authored texts exclude femaleness because their authors are incapable of imagining any realm of experience but their own, which is to say that they fail to recognize the various ways in which women are victimized. Such failures of imagination, recognition, and empathy are thus crimes in their own right, for although these male authors are less obviously misogynistic than Poe's earlier narrators, the texts they create continue to leave the woman's story untold, the overt crime unsolved. In "The Murders in the Rue Morgue," for example, Dupin is able to track down the murderer of the old woman and her daughter because he can recognize what has gone unnamed by the newspaper account of the crime: the strange "voice" of the attacker, which none of the "witnesses" could identify, is that of an orangutan. Once this fact is established, the detective is then able to recover the entire scenario—the second story—which reveals at last what the women actually suffered. Not surprisingly, that story presents a grim parody of what in Poe's tales constitutes normative masculine behavior. The trained animal had been acting out a masculine script, first flourishing a razor around the face of one of his victims, "in imitation of the motions of a barber;" then silencing both women when they put up a struggle; and finally trying to conceal all evidence of the crime (2:566–67).

The issue of masculine norms, or rather, masculine conceptions of normative behavior, is continued in "The Mystery of Marie Rogêt." In this tale Dupin criticizes several conflicting newspaper articles on the grounds that they are male-authored "fictions": "It is the object of our newspapers rather to create a sensation—to make a point—than to further the cause of truth" (3:738). Specifically, the truth of a woman's experience gets lost sight of because the language of each text is informed by a rigidly masculine perspective. In discussing attempts to identify Marie's body, for instance, one journalist had argued that the fact that garter clasps had been set back to accommodate smaller legs, as Marie was said to have done, was not admissible evidence that the corpse was the petite Marie because after buying them, "most women find it proper to take a pair of garters home and fit them to the size of the limbs" (3:745). "Here it is difficult to suppose the reasoner in earnest," Dupin comments, revealing the flaw in the male author's generalization: the "elastic nature of the clasp-garter is self-demonstration of the *unusualness* of the abbreviation" which Marie undertook (3:746). That men cannot imagine what the life of a woman is like and that they thus define all experience in masculine terms is more explicitly demonstrated in Dupin's criticism of another newspaper's argument. "It is impossible," this text urges, "that a person so well known to thousands as this young woman was, should have passed three blocks without some one having seen her." But, Dupin explains, this

> is the idea of a man long resident in Paris—a public man—and one whose walks to and fro in the city, have been mostly limited to the vicinity of the public offices. He is aware that *he* seldom passes so far as a dozen blocks from his own *bureau*, without being recognized and accosted. And, knowing the extent of his personal acquaintance with others, and of others with him, he compares his notoriety with that of the perfumery-girl, finds no great difference between them, and reaches at once the conclusion that she, in her walks, would be equally liable to recognition with himself in his. This could only be the case were her walks of the same unvarying, methodical character, and within the same *species* of limited region as are his own. [3:749]

In the third and final tale in which Dupin appears (1845), the "limited region" whose boundaries are set by masculine minds is shown to be the province of the Parisian police. Their failure to recover "the purloined letter" results, as Dupin explains, from the narrow "limits of the Prefect's examination—in other words, had the principle of [the letter's] concealment been comprehended within the principles of the Prefect . . . its discovery would have been a matter altogether beyond question" (3:986). In this tale the plot lines we have seen previously are reduced to their essence, and the political dimension of such gender conflict is highlighted, for the crime is the theft of a text that rightfully belongs to the queen; the thief is the Minister D————, "who dares all things, those unbecoming as well as those becoming a man" (3:976); and "the power thus attained," as even the prefect of police recognizes, "has . . . been wielded, for political purposes, to a very dangerous extent" (3:977). Once again Dupin, acting according to his "political prepossessions" as "partisan of the lady" (3:993), is able to recover the lost text (and replace it with a clever substitute) because he alone can decode the artifice by which the woman has been disempowered: the male criminal had merely disguised her letter to look as if it were his own. And once again this second story acts as a gloss upon the first. The Minister's conscious concealment of the queen's letter is but the external manifestation of the police's interpretive paradigm, by which they unconsciously define all human action only according to "their *own*"— masculine—"ideas" of it. In Dupin's words, "They have no variation of principle in their investigations." Their unchanging principle is "based upon . . . one set of notions regarding human ingenuity" (3:985), and one set of notions, as the "double Dupin" demonstrates, is not enough to accommodate both halves of humanity.

This tale has a new ending, suggesting perhaps that Poe felt he had taken his critique of male-authored fictions to its logical conclusion: the victimized woman lives to benefit from Dupin's recovery of the second story, and the male criminal faces imminent retribution. As Dupin reveals at the end, for "eighteen months the Minister has had her in his power. She has now him in hers; since, being unaware that the letter is not in his possession, he will proceed with his exactions as if it was. Thus will he inevitably commit himself, at once, to his political destruction" (3:993). Dupin's criticism of the police's interpretive paradigm, however, is obviously not new; it merely rounds out the metaphorical arguments begun in "The Fall of the House of Usher." The police's "one set of notions," like the earlier depictions of "half-formed conception" and male-authored texts that failed to convey "but one meaning," represents a blind spot in masculine interpretations of reality that keeps men from seeing how women are victimized. What the men in these tales cannot see, they cannot include in their own story of events, but the crime metaphor that provides the basis for Poe's detective tales insists on the criminal nature of such oversights. The death-dealing misogyny of Roderick Usher's narrator differs from the half-formed conceptions of Dupin's newspaper writers and police only in degree, not in effect. The second story or, finally, the second half of the human story must be recovered by a mind capable of "looking back, of seeing with fresh eyes, of entering an old text from a new critical direction,"[24] and Poe's solution to the problem of such much-needed "re-vision" is the androgynous mind that had first so terrified Roderick Usher and had finally so distinguished C. Auguste Dupin.

I have twice referred to Adrienne Rich's definition of feminist "re-vision" to help explain Roderick's and Dupin's recovery of the second story, so it seems only proper to repeat it here as she originally articulated it: "Re-vision—the act of looking back, of seeing with fresh eyes, of entering an old text from a new critical direction—is for women more than a chapter in cultural history: it is an act of survival. Until we can understand the assumptions in which we are drenched we cannot know ourselves. . . . We need to know the writing of the past, and know it differently than we have ever known it; not to pass on a tradition but to break its hold over us." Judith Fetterley's description of the imaginative act performed by the resisting reader is equally useful in describing the new narrative point of view and new ethos that evolved in Poe's fictions about women between the time he wrote the early tales, those which ironically bear the silenced woman's name, and the years he wrote his detective series:

> To expose and question that complex of ideas and mythologies about women and men which exist in our society and are confirmed in our literature is to make the system of power embodied in the literature open not only to discussion but even to change. Such questioning and exposure can, of course, be carried on only by a consciousness radically different from the one that informs the literature. Such a closed system cannot be opened up from within but only from without. It must be entered into from a point of view which questions its values and assumptions and which has its investment in making available to consciousness precisely that which the literature wishes to keep hidden.

Read in sequence, "Ligeia," "The Fall of the House of Usher," and the three Dupin tales suggest that Poe saw the danger—to art and to culture—of the androcentric tradition Rich and Fetterley address and that he was indeed experimenting with the idea of a radically different consciousness, one that would be capable of imaginative re-vision. The androgynous Dupin accomplishes what Roderick Usher so tentatively began, a fully specified critique of what Fetterley elsewhere calls "the imaginative limits" of one-sided male-authored fictions.[25] The end product of such a critique is the recovery of the lost story, which, in the last tale in the sequence, breaks the hold of male domination and finally ensures the woman's survival by restoring her honor and her sociopolitical power.

Am I arguing, then, that Poe should be considered a feminist author? Certainly there is precious little biographical evidence of any behavior that we would consider even remotely feminist today.[26] Neither is there any question that his fictional depictions of acts of physical violence committed against women are particularly gruesome, and some feminist readers might feel that having to encounter such grisly surface details is too big a price to pay to get to the final acts of recovery and restoration Poe seems to have had in mind. A last stumbling block to any acceptance of Poe as a feminist writer must surely be his now infamous statement that "the death . . . of a beautiful woman is, unquestionably, the most poetical topic in the world." At first glance these words would seem to contradict any argument that his tales show an evolving feminist ethos, a growing awareness and renunciation of death-dealing, male-authored fictions, and indeed, it appeared a year after "The Purloined Letter," in "The Philosophy of Composition," published in 1846.

When feminist critics cite the statement, however, they tend to leave off the second half of the sentence: "—and equally is it beyond doubt that the lips best suited for such topic are those of a bereaved lover."[27] Although I do not intend to justify the images of death which Poe habitually chose as a vehicle for his vision, I do believe that the halves of this statement constitute a conceptual whole which is not inconsistent with his use of the androgyny metaphor, and to argue this final point, I will extrapolate from one of Nina Baym's readings of Hawthorne, all of which, taken together, constitute a very persuasive case for that (male) author's feminist sympathies. The "domain" of Hawthorne's work, Baym writes, is "the male psyche, and throughout his writings 'woman' stands for a set of qualities which the male denies within himself and rejects in others. . . . The ability to accept woman—either as the 'other' or as part of the self—becomes in his writing a test of man's wholeness."[28]

The domain of Poe's work is also the male psyche, and the loss of "woman" throughout his writings represents a halving of "man's" soul, his human potential, and—for the male artist—his imagination. Telling the story of that loss seems to have been for Poe a compelling need, for he told it obsessively again and again and clearly derived a perverse pleasure from doing so. Nevertheless, that such works are cautionary tales is confirmed by the heroic stature of his androgynous heroes. Roderick Usher does come to accept woman both as the "other" and as part of the self, but it is Dupin who stands finally as Poe's greatest achievement. The "double Dupin" represents his creator's fullest expression of the need for wholeness and the need to tell not only the story of loss but the second story as well: the story of recovery and restoration, the woman's story. I have to conclude that Poe's ability to tell both stories, or both halves of the human story, is, therefore, the sign of what we would today call feminist re-vision.

℀ 6

Inhabiting the Second Story:
Hawthorne's Houses

In *A General Introduction to Psychoanalysis* Freud describes the process of repression in architectural images that by now should have a familiar ring to Poe's readers. "The unconscious system," he explains, may be compared to an "ante-room."

> Adjoining this is . . . a sort of reception-room, in which consciousness resides. But on the threshold between the two there stands a personage with the office of door-keeper, who examines various mental excitations, censors them, and denies them admittance to the reception-room when he disapproves of them. . . . The excitations in the unconscious, in the ante-chamber, are not visible to consciousness, which is of course in the other room, so to begin with they remain unconscious. When they have pressed forward to the threshold and been turned back by the door-keeper, they are *'incapable of becoming conscious'*; we call them then *repressed*. But even those excitations which are allowed over the threshold do not necessarily become conscious; they can only become so if they succeed in attracting the eye of consciousness.

The image of "the two chambers, the door-keeper on the threshold between the two, and consciousness as a spectator at the end of the second room"[1] is, of course, particularly and rather literally reminiscent of the final scene of "The Fall of the House of Usher," in which Roderick sits with his "eyes bent fixedly before him" on the "door of the chamber" and Madeline appears "trembling and reeling to and fro upon the threshold" after her "bitter struggle" for admittance (2:244–45). According to Freud's description, the most significant feature of Poe's fictional world is that the repression mechanism is no longer operable. The narrator-door-keeper is at this point in the story unable to turn Madeline back; he can only suppress her tale by manfully ending his own, keeping her out of language if not out of mind.

As we saw in the last chapter, Poe went on to create the modern detective story, turning his focus from the repressive interior worlds of single-minded male narrators to a radically different form of consciousness and giving that androgynous mastermind full play in a newly conceived social realm. Nathaniel Hawthorne's interest in the fictional possibilities of a second story took a different direction (although to tell that story he too would turn to a literary form new to him, the novel), but his concerns with the inner life of those socially and culturally programmed to think in patriarchal terms seem to have begun where Poe left off. That is, *The Scarlet Letter* (1850) begins with the very image which Poe had abandoned at the close of "The Fall of the House of Usher," that of an outcast woman crossing "the threshold of our narrative" and attracting the eye of cultural consciousness.[2] The action of this novel opens with the Puritan community clustered with anxious attention around the small jail, "all with their eyes intently fastened on the iron-clamped door" (1:49). There is indeed a doorkeeper, appropriately the town beadle, upholder of patriarchal law but ultimately as ineffectual as Poe's misogynist narrators in controlling Hester Prynne: "On the threshold of the prison door, she repelled him, by an action marked with natural dignity and force of character, and stepped into the open air, as if by her own free will" (1:52). Hawthorne would employ the same architectural-narrative metaphor in his second novel.[3] The action of *The House of the Seven Gables* (1851) opens with another willful and previously sequestered female figure, Hepzibah Pyncheon, coming forth over "the threshold of our story," to meet "the public eye" (2:31, 39). Here, however, the presence of a doorkeeper is denied. The narrative voice presents itself as a wryly deferential attendant to this ancient lady, and we are initially made to "await Miss Hepzibah at the threshold of her chamber" (2:30). After two pages of Usher-like "listening" for her emergence, we see her come forth to open her cent-shop, in what seems almost a parody of one of Poe's ghastly entrance scenes: "Here, at last . . . here comes Miss Hepzibah Pyncheon! Forth she steps into the dusky, time-darkened passage; a tall figure, clad in black silk, with a long and shrunken waist, feeling her way towards the stairs" (2:32). Both novels then proceed to tell the life stories of these women characters and of their personal victimization by patriarchy.

One of the crucial differences between Poe's early tales about women and Hawthorne's novels is that Hawthorne's narrative personae in these two novels reject the repressive role of paternalistic guardian or doorkeeper, and Hawthorne makes it clear with another architectural-narrative metaphor that their function and his function as an American artist is rather to facilitate the reader's imaginative reentry into those areas and aspects of American life which have been kept from us, which have gone too long unnoticed and unremarked. We are told in the autobiographical sketch that prefaces *The Scarlet Letter*, for example, that it is "in the second story of the Custom House" that he finds the long-forgotten materials for constructing his narrative (1:28), and the discovery scene recapitulates the Freudian psychic structuring just described. In the second story, "in a recess" at the far end of a large room that "remains unfinished"—unsettled, surely—"to this day," he finds "a certain affair of fine red cloth," a letter A, rendered in "a now forgotten art" (1:28, 31). "Certainly, there was some deep meaning in it, most worthy of interpretation. . . . On Hester Prynne's story, therefore, I bestowed much thought" (1:31, 34). Not surprisingly, he finds that he must abandon patriarchal structures altogether to bring his "thought"—and the forgotten second story of American history—to fruition: "So little adapted is the atmosphere of a Custom House to the delicate harvest of fancy and sensibility that, had I remained there . . . I doubt whether the tale of *The Scarlet Letter* would ever have been brought before the public eye" (1:34).

The idea that the American story needed to be restructured and thus redeemed was not exactly new to the author of *Twice-Told Tales* (1837). That "peculiar" title, as F. O. Matthiessen called it, referred not only to Hawthorne's having assembled the collection from tales published previously but especially to his having derived his materials from the "dim-remembered" stories of history and local legend.[4] Neither did the second-story metaphor get left behind in "The Custom House." In *The House of the Seven Gables* the movement from cultural obscurity to narrative publicity is similarly mapped out: the action opens with the narrator escorting Hepzibah from the "strict seclusion" of her room in the second story of the Pyncheon house (2:31) down the stairs and into the shop "fronting the street" (2:34), where she takes "down the bar from the shop-door, leaving the entrance free—more than free—welcome, as if all were household friends—to every passer-by" (2:40). Throughout the novel, Hawthorne frequently alludes to the second story of the family mansion, which seems to haunt the first, the locus of patriarchal business dealings, by its very presence: "The second story, projecting far over the base, . . . threw a shadow and thoughtful gloom into the lower rooms" (2:12). It is specifically associated with the female members of the family—with its former occupant, Alice Pyncheon, for example, whose presence in her "room in the second story . . . imparted an indescribable grace and faint witchery to the whole edifice" (2:191)—and with their nonverbal mode of self-expression. Just as her ancestor Alice had "sat beside the harpsichord, and filled the house with music" from her second-story apartment, so too "the sweet, airy homeliness" of Phoebe Pyncheon's singing comes "down from the upper chambers" (2:209–10, 138). The second story also represents a revivifying, salvific perspective on American life, on the democratic flow of "life in the street" in particular (2:159), for it is from the second-story arched window in the Pyncheon house that Phoebe attempts to reintegrate the effeminate Clifford, an ex-convict, into the "surging stream of human sympathies" (2:165) and to restore his vision of community.

Finally, these three themes—housebound femininity, nonverbal expression, and the offer of a new perspective—come together in an image that compares and contrasts tellingly with Hawthorne's own endeavor in this work of romance. At the end of the chapter titled "An Arched Window," Clifford sits blowing soap bubbles,

> scattering airy spheres abroad, from the window into the street! Little, impalpable worlds, were those soap-bubbles, with the big world depicted, in hues bright as imagination, on the nothing of their surface. It was curious to see how the passers-by regarded these brilliant fantasies, as they came floating down, and made the dull atmosphere imaginative, about them. Some stopt to gaze . . . some looked angrily upward. . . . A great many put out their fingers, or their walking-sticks, to touch withal, and were perversely gratified, no doubt, when the bubble, with all its pictured earth and sky scene, vanished as if it had never been. [2:171]

Like Clifford, Hawthorne constructs a fictional "little world," as he says in the Preface, "of materials long in use for constructing castles in the air" (2:3), and like Clifford's, those imaginative materials come from the neglected second story of American life, so often passed by or shunted off. Unlike Clifford, however, Hawthorne is able to bring the second story out of its ineffectual nonverbal sphere and over the threshold of language. Most important, by bringing that story to the world's eye and by admitting otherness full-fledged into American texts and contexts, he equates his own verbal art not with the repressive forces of culturally sanctioned language but with unofficial and subversive accounts of American experience—at times, literally with "feminine" modes of creative expression. In the Preface to this novel, for example, he equates his own verbal art with the traditional feminine arts of cookery and weaving. The work that follows, he says, is a "dish offered to the Public"; it is also a narrative "woven of so humble a texture" that it might, like a "legendary mist," "float almost imperceptibly about the characters and events" it delineates (2:1–2). Hawthorne thus presents himself as a spokesperson for otherness and his second-story art as a vehicle for the suppressed feminine voice in American culture.[5]

This is not finally to claim, however, that Hawthorne's romances offer any rosy picture of cultural restitution. To say that Hawthorne seems to have identified with feminine otherness, to have had firsthand knowledge of the "second story," is to say that he knew the damaging psychological effects of living in a seriously polarized culture, and therein lies the real newness of his stories. The psychology of the silenced Other, which had merely been symbolically suggested in Cooper's second cavern scene and which, even in Poe's detective tales, comes second-hand, through a sympathetic mediating consciousness, is developed in Hawthorne's romances into complex and detailed psychological characterizations that show the harmful effects of patriarchal culture on individuals and language. Hawthorne might give female characters equal representational space, for example, as a way of signifying ethical challenge to patriarchal domination, but he cannot help but show these characters ultimately as damaged as their male counterparts by their lifelong acculturation. That is, neither Hester nor Hepzibah is fit to be an agent of ethical reform in these stories, as we might have hoped from their brave entrances, because they must be ethically rehabilitated. Forced into self-defensiveness and moment-to-moment survival strategies, they see no alternative but to withdraw from society, which reinforces their sentence of otherness, or to become authority figures, "guardians" over those weaker than they, and thus, ironically, oppressors in their own right. Hawthorne brings them over the threshold to dramatize the psychology of otherness, of victims, in a repressive culture, and he does so by showing them entrapped in an either/or frame of mind, in psychological limitations imposed by the American past. It is only at the end of their stories, when they give up their stalemated, shortsighted struggles with the inequities of the past and give up their "authority" over other lives that they are able to assume their proper "feminine" attributes of sympathy, generosity, and humility—which are the highest ethical values in Hawthorne's fictional worlds.

In these ways Hawthorne shows that the greatest harm done by patriarchy is that it perverts even the best of natures into attitudes of embittered hostility and counteraggression. It leads them to use the very tactics that have been used against them to get even, and the greatest tactical weapon is language. The most unsettling irony in both *The Scarlet Letter* and *The House of the Seven Gables* is that when Hester and Hepzibah finally break their embittered silence, there is no sense of lasting release. Their speech recapitulates the psychology of authority that has kept them so long in bondage. Throughout these two romances, Hawthorne shows language itself to be an ethically suspect force in American lives. It reinforces, as he suggests in *The Scarlet Letter*, the "long hereditary habit" of patriarchal domination and oppression, "which has become like nature" (1:165), and the task he sets both for his characters and himself, as a second-story artist, is to "erase its deep print out of our own brain, where long meditation"—long resentment—"has fixed it in very undesirable distinctness" (1:259). In my closing remarks I will comment on how far I believe Hawthorne succeeded in that task.

What I have been describing comes close to what William H. Shurr has called the "yes but" quality of Hawthorne's style[6], which is nowhere more evident than in the author's complex rendering of Hester Prynne's inner life in the opening scenes of *The Scarlet Letter*. It is obvious, for example, that Hawthorne is greatly attracted by and sympathetic to this darkly beautiful woman who is released from prison only to be made to stand before "a thousand unrelenting eyes," "staring at the features that should have been seen only in the quiet gleam of the fireside, in the happy shadow of a home, or beneath a matronly veil, at church," and readers are made to experience that genuine sympathy (1:57, 63). But we are also asked to regret "the desperate recklessness of her mood" that has caused her to summon up "all the combative energy of her character" and to embrace her ostracism with a vengeance (1:53, 78): "She had fortified herself to encounter the stings and venomous stabs of public contumely" and thus had rendered her scarlet letter so "fantastically" that it had "the effect of a spell, taking her out of the ordinary relations with humanity, and enclosing her in a sphere by herself" (1:57, 54). This mixture of sympathy and regret establishes Hawthorne's stance toward Hester's plight throughout, and one of his main vehicles for conveying this dual perspective, from beginning to end, is the metaphor of silence.

The initial significance of Hester's silence in the opening scenes is that it is culturally imposed: she is silenced at the outset of her ordeal on the scaffold by her legal status as a woman and a wife. One of the many unrelenting spectators is her long absent, now cuckolded husband, Roger Chillingworth, and when "he found the eyes of Hester Prynne fastened on his own, and saw that she appeared to recognize him, he slowly and calmly raised his finger . . . and laid it on his lips" (1:61). Later, when she is back inside the jail and they meet privately, he demands her public silence regarding his identity in ringing patriarchal imperatives: "Breathe not, to any human soul, that thou didst ever call me husband! . . . Thou and thine, Hester Prynne, belong to me. . . . Betray me not! . . . Swear it!" (1:76). What is most shocking about this early encounter, however, is that Hester, who has walked so bravely from the jail and rebuffed the town beadle in his attempt to guide her, allows herself to be guided—silenced—by Chillingworth in this instance: "she took the oath," "shrinking, she hardly knew why, from this secret bond" (1:76).

Hester's acquiescence here provides the "but" clause in Hawthorne's "yes but" vision of her victimization. Yes, patriarchal authority does silence women in its own self-interest, but, he seems to be saying, the coercion and the exclusion are all the more damnable because they become internalized, self-imposed—"she hardly knew why." In other words, Chillingworth may be a personification of the legalistic cultural heritage that makes this woman "the people's victim and lifelong bond slave" (1:227), but Hawthorne's greater concern, as he had stressed in "The Custom House," is with "Hester Prynne's story"; with the regrettable state of her inner life, which is kept in "secret" bondage.

That she recognizes her husband in the crowd, for example, is significant enough for Hawthorne to have called that chapter "The Recognition." What she apparently recognizes is his legal authority to judge and condemn her, and by that act of recognition she betrays how thoroughly, how unconsciously, she has assimilated patriarchal patterns of thought. Moreover, the priority of Chillingworth's claims on her in this scene, added to the fact that he arrives in disguise and she recognizes him anyway, suggests that Old World patriarchy has merely reconstituted itself in America under a new name, that it has gone underground. When Hester first sees him, in the chapter's opening sentence, Chillingworth is said to have "irresistibly [taken] possession of her thoughts" (1:60). The effect of that usurpation is evidenced a few pages later, when we find her "still with a fixed stare towards [him]; so fixed a gaze, that, at moments of intense absorption, all other objects in the visible world seemed to vanish, leaving only him and her" (1:63). Essentially, her frame of mind is "fixed" at the outset. She can see only two roles to be played in the world, two modes of action: to be either the oppressor—the judge, the authority—or the oppressed victim. This is the inner burden that she will carry with her until the end of the novel, and Hawthorne suggests that this story of the psychological toll exacted by patriarchy is the second story that needs to be publicized.

This initial image of Hester's conquered and divided mind prepares readers for her more visible and seemingly contradictory actions on the scaffold. Her first public action after her private recognition is to refuse to answer to the church fathers, who demand the name of her partner in adultery. Her first spoken words are "Never! . . . I will not speak!" (1:68). Hester's self-imposed silence is easily recognizable as a political strategy. She takes a stance outside the law, which demands that she "give [her] child a father" (1:68), and outside the language that has labeled her a criminal; she appears unwilling to use language against another as it has been used against her. If we are tempted to read any unqualified ethical dimension into her denunciation, however, or to read it, like the "poor culprit" Dimmesdale, as the "wondrous strength and generosity of a woman's heart" toward her fellow sufferer, we have too sympathetically judged Hester's character (1:68). Later in the book Hawthorne will describe her action in this scene thus: "She was supported by an unnatural tension of the nerves, and by all the combative energy of her character, which enabled her to convert the scene into a kind of lurid triumph" (1:78). He will also suggest that her "generosity" toward Dimmesdale had its roots "perhaps in the misanthropy of her own trouble" (1:193). The point seems to be that Hester's silence in this scene is motivated less by ethical standards than by resentment and hostility toward the sociopolitical order that has cast her out. There is even a sense that by choosing silence in this instance she is merely choosing a safer mode of self-defense against further incrimination, as she will later choose not "to pray for her enemies," to be silent again, "lest, in spite of her forgiving aspirations, the words of the blessing should stubbornly twist themselves into a curse" (1:85).

The gravest reservation we are made to feel toward her silence, then, is that it represents a double victimization: it is both culturally and self-imposed. It reveals Hester Prynne caught in a double bind, her choice of action delimited by her own either/or frame of mind. Setting herself up in polar opposition to the fathers, she necessarily reinforces her own sentence of otherness; choosing to be silent, she confines herself to the role of vengeful victim. Hester's psychological acculturation has taken hold too strongly for her to be able to break the unconscious bond between the guardian-oppressor and the oppressed, and this sense that she is constrained to play only one role or the other in these early scenes is further evidenced in her actions toward her child.

If Hester willfully and misguidedly plays the victim to those in power, she as surely plays the oppressor to the only being in her charge. Wrapped up in her own painful thoughts, she is said to have "pressed her infant to her bosom with so convulsive a force that the poor babe uttered [a] cry of pain. But the mother did not seem to hear it" (1:61). We have seen too many victims go unheard in American romantic fiction to miss Hawthorne's message here. His unique stress, though, falls on the virtual unconsciousness of Hester's act, which he emphasizes again at the end of this first scaffold scene, when he tells us, "her spirit could only shelter itself beneath a stony crest of insensibility": "The infant, during the latter portion of her ordeal, pierced the air with its wailings and screams; she strove to hush it, mechanically, but seemed scarcely to sympathize with its trouble" (1:69). Thus the inner plight of the oppressed mother is passed down to the daughter, potentially to the next generation, and thus, as the story progresses, we should not be surprised when Hester continues to pass on Chillingworth's injunction of silence—"Peace, Hester, peace!" (1:174)—and Dimmesdale's—"Hush, Hester, hush!" (1:195, 256)—to young Pearl: "Hush, Pearl, hush!" (1:107, 229); "Hold thy tongue, naughty child! . . . else I shall shut thee into the dark closet" (1:181). With this role reversal Hawthorne shows how deeply Hester has internalized "the long hereditary habit" of her culture, "which has become like nature" (1:165), and the result, as in her choice to be silent, is that we must see her as the "poor victim of her own frailty and man's hard law" (1:87).

The regrettably divided state of Hester's inner life in these opening scenes prefigures the many images of halving, doubleness, and role reversal which Hawthorne will use to delineate her character traits and flaws throughout. She will continue to be characterized, for example, by the half-and-half quality of her mind. "What she compelled herself to believe" about her personal motivations for staying in New England "was half a truth, and half a self-delusion" (1:80); later she will see herself "half maddened by the ignominy" of her status as outcast (1:167). At one point she "half doubt[s]" whether Pearl knows more of her mother's story than she lets on, and she habitually responds "half playfully" to the child, "half-smiling" (1:98, 179). This halving of her emotional response to her daughter results in an answering doubleness in Pearl's developing character. It also suggests the sad diminishment of Hester's moral force as a mother and as a member of the community, which is evidenced in yet another image of doubleness: "She stood apart from moral interests, yet close beside them, like a ghost that revisits the familiar fireside and can no longer make itself seen or felt" (1:84). Finally, Hester's unconscious role reversal in the first scaffold scene, her subtle—"mechanical"—transformation from victim to oppressive guardian, specifically foreshadows the precarious ethical dynamics of her renewed relationship with Arthur Dimmesdale in their forest interview. When she finally breaks her long silence, and ostensibly, her hated "secret bond" with Chillingworth, she becomes, in turn, Dimmesdale's guardian, binding him to her, she rationalizes, with "the iron link of mutual crime" (1:160). Such dyads are representative social units for Hawthorne, test cases, so to speak, and when Hester assumes authority over Dimmesdale's actions, whatever her good intentions, she merely recapitulates the power politics her escape strategy is meant to repudiate.

Before turning to the specifics of that scene, it is necessary to look for a moment at Dimmesdale's characterization, for it shows in similar ways the harmful effects of patriarchal "supervision" on the individual and even the best-intentioned mind. Like Hester, Dimmesdale is portrayed as being unconsciously victimized by Roger Chillingworth: "A secret enemy had been continually by his side, under the semblance of a friend and helper, and had availed himself of the opportunities thus afforded for tampering with the delicate springs of Mr. Dimmesdale's nature" (1:166). The two are, symbolically, "lodged in the same house," and thus, under Chillingworth's medical supervision, "the sufferer's conscience had been kept in an irritated state, the tendency of which was, not to cure by wholesome pain, but to disorganize and corrupt his spiritual being" (1:125, 193). What Chillingworth does is un-"wholesome" indeed. His "authorized interference" with the younger man's mind keeps Dimmesdale, like Hester, divided against himself (1:193). There is a difference between these two victims: Hester's "nature" is corrupted by her resentment—"Everything was against her. The world was hostile" (1:165); and Dimmesdale's by guilt over transgressing patriarchal law—"his mind was darkened and confused by the very remorse that harrowed it" (1:200). Hawthorne makes it very clear, however, that the effect is the same. By keeping Hester's and Arthur's dis-ease ever active, Chillingworth and the patriarchal authority he represents keep them obsessed with their individual dilemmas and thus diminished in moral effectiveness. Dimmesdale's "moral force was abased into more than childish weakness. It groveled helplessly on the ground, even while his intellectual faculties retained that pristine strength, or had perhaps acquired a morbid energy, which disease only could have given them" (1:159).

What I mean, then, by saying that Chillingworth's influence keeps Dimmesdale divided against himself is revealed in this latter image of the minister's divided inner life. Chillingworth's presence in his house, for example, has traditionally been read as the outer manifestation of Dimmesdale's overactive superego, that inner repository of cultural values that go against his "nature." Hawthorne underscores this point and this sense of inner division when, in the forest interview, he allows Hester to berate the young man, "What hast thou to do with all these iron men and their opinions? They have kept thy better part in bondage too long already!" (1:197). Hester's argument, however—or rather, Hester's presentation of this argument as an attempt to win away Dimmesdale's allegiance—also suggests that the minister's psychological predicament is analogous in many ways to that of the androgynous Roderick Usher. This literary analogy provides a useful and necessary qualification to the strictly Freudian one. That is, it helps fill in more of the details of Hawthorne's metaphorical value system: the split between Dimmesdale's conscience and his nature, between his intellectual and his moral faculties, is for Hawthorne a split along gender lines, and the "better part" is consistently imaged as feminine.

Like Roderick, whenever Dimmesdale champions, admires, or identifies with his feminine "better half," his actions are countermanded by his male guardians, who dismissively interpret his sympathetic gestures as the products of a weakened mind. In the first scaffold scene, for example, he initially opposes the Puritan fathers' injunction that he "prevail over" Hester with his ministerial authority, claiming that "it were wronging the very nature of woman" to make a public ceremony of her powerlessness. The elder Reverend Wilson here artfully persuades Dimmesdale to renounce such "oversoftness" in his nature and to become a proper guardian: "The responsibility of this woman's soul lies greatly with you" (1:65). (Hawthorne's description of Wilson is also significant in this context, for he comments that the elder man's "kind and genial spirit" had been "less carefully developed than his intellectual gifts, and was, in truth, rather a matter of shame than self-congratulation with him" [1:65]. The passage reinforces the sense that the repression of sympathetic "feminine" traits in authority figures is indeed an American tradition.) Dimmesdale gives over, apparently, to Wilson's patriarchal rationale for male dominance; but when Hester successfully opposes his authority, he openly admires her "wondrous strength," her ability to do in public what he could not. And at this point, discerning "the impracticable state of the poor culprit's mind," the elder clergyman takes control of the situation and delivers a "carefully prepared . . . discourse on sin" (1:68).

Usher's guardian-narrator would surely feel in good company with these iron men who rely on a text to restore a mind to order, as he would with Dimmesdale's other mental monitor, old Roger Chillingworth. In "The Minister's Vigil," Dimmesdale identifies with Hester to the point of mounting the scaffold and "standing where Hester Prynne had stood" (1:152), standing, in fact, with Hester and with Pearl, who is elsewhere described as the "visible . . . tie that united them" (1:206). Such identification with the feminine, however, is visible only to the minister's villainous "healer," who, like Wilson, exerts his control over the younger man's mind by using the rhetoric of masculine bonding and guardianship: "We men of study, whose heads are in our books, have need to be straitly looked after! . . . Come, good Sir and my good friend, I pray you, let me lead you home!" Regrettably, the strategy works. Dimmesdale "yield[s] himself to the physician, and [is] led away" (1:157).

By giving over to Chillingworth's influence, Dimmesdale here shows that he is finally unlike Roderick Usher, and this dissimilarity is as instructive of Hawthorne's intent as the previous similarities. In the first scaffold scene, the minister, like the early Roderick, had merely sympathized with the feminine Other and had let those sympathies be silenced—this is the first time we see him with his hand upon his heart, a gesture apparently intended to conceal his "better part." In the second scaffold scene, however, Hawthorne actively stresses the potential salvific effects of the feminine and thus shows Dimmesdale all the more damned for choosing to give up that salvation. When Dimmesdale links himself with Hester and Pearl on the scaffold, "there came what seemed a tumultuous rush of new life, other life than his own, pouring like a torrent into his heart, and hurrying through all his veins, as if the mother and the child were communicating their vital warmth to his half-torpid system" (1:153). And when the minister allows himself to be led away from this promise of new life by Chillingworth, the act foreshadows his final damnable decision to remain a spokesman, not for the outcast, as his early sympathies might have suggested, but for the dominant sociopolitical order. Thus, whereas Roderick, at the end of his story, has eyes only for Madeline and decidedly, if fearfully, meets her embrace, Dimmesdale begins his final act by refusing to look at, to recognize, Hester: "She could scarcely forgive him . . . for being able so completely to withdraw himself from their mutual world; while she groped darkly, and stretched forth her cold hands, and found him not" (1:240). His final words to her are that it is henceforth "vain to hope that we could meet hereafter, in an everlasting and pure reunion. God knows. . . . Praised be His name! His will be done!" (1:256–57). Thus he gives over to the God of his fathers and denies the vital warmth of feminine sympathy which, Hawthorne says, is the only thing that might have revived his half-torpid system.

This stress on the salvific effects of the feminine provides the key to Hawthorne's moral vision and moral criticism. He uses feminine sympathy as a metaphor for the only corrective to patriarchal legalism. This is what has been repressed out of male-dominant culture—out of Dimmesdale and too often out of Hester, and this is what must be recovered if America's half-torpid system is to be saved. There is one last qualification, and it too is imaged in the second scaffold scene. When Dimmesdale joins hands with "the mother and the child" he feels what Hawthorne has called elsewhere in the book "the softening influences of maternity" (1:95). In Hawthorne's fiction, the highest—he would probably say the most sacred—form of feminine sympathy is maternal.

The theme of redemptive maternal influence is more actively associated with male characters in Hawthorne's next novel, *The House of the Seven Gables*, but he employs it in connection with Dimmesdale in this novel, as a sign of the minister's need to be morally regenerated. Hester's accusation, for example, that "these iron men . . . have kept thy better part in bondage" looks forward to Hepzibah's description of the morally ineffective Clifford—"They persecuted his mother in him"—and to her accusation to the iron-willed Jaffrey—"You have forgotten that a woman was your mother!" (2:236). That Hawthorne intended readers to see the same moral diminishment in Dimmesdale, to see that his repressed "better part" had been initially the product of a mother's influence, is evidenced in "The Interior of a Heart." In that chapter Dimmesdale's "inward trouble" causes him to have guilty visions, among them one of "his white-bearded father, with a saint-like frown, and his mother, turning her face away as she passed by" (1:144, 145). Dimmesdale's vision of maternal estrangement is particularly significant in that it contrasts markedly with the image Hawthorne uses to suggest Hester's greater potential for moral regeneration. Before this chapter, in the first scaffold scene, we had witnessed the interior of Hester's heart and her vision of her mother's face, "with the look of heedful and anxious love which it always wore in

[Hester's] remembrance, and which, even since [the mother's] death, had so often laid the impediment of a gentle remonstrance in her daughter's pathway" (1:58). Finally, Dimmesdale's divided inner vision reveals the priority of paternal influence over maternal, which is in the process of being effaced altogether, and thus foreshadows his final and fatal determination to regain (for all eternity, it would seem) his Father's approval.

In such ways Hawthorne shows the harmful effects of patriarchal acculturation on the individual mind: moral tendencies are turned away, silenced, in favor of self-interest, self-defense, self-image. He uses similar images of division to portray these demoralizing effects on language, and Dimmesdale's case is again instructive of Hawthorne's cultural criticism. Dimmesdale's speech, for example, his ministerial Tongue of Flame, is a metaphorical mixture of the two gender-linked modes of communication we have seen previously. Like David Gamut and Roderick Usher, whose similarly divided allegiances cause them to use both words and music, Dimmesdale speaks both in the "grosser medium" of mere "words" and in the "native language" of the heart (1:243, 142). As Joel Porte has so aptly put it, "it is Dimmesdale's soul music, not his religious libretto, that signifies" his "better part."[7]

In characterization, this double-edged language reinforces the sense one gets in the first scaffold scene that Dimmesdale might swing either way; that he might become the spokesperson for other values than those held by the dominant culture. As the plot progresses, however, it soon becomes obvious that he consistently makes the wrong choice. He relies on words, as he places his hand over his heart, to conceal rather than reveal his true sympathies, his moral nature, and thus he keeps his power to do good, his "soul music," ever an undertone. Moreover, Hawthorne is particularly insistent that this duality in Dimmesdale's speech be seen as the result of his choice to uphold his public rather than his moral responsibilities. There is no doubt, for example, that "it was his genuine impulse to adore the truth," and in "The Interior of a Heart" we are told that "he longed to speak out, from his own pulpit, at the full height of his voice, and tell the people what he was. 'I, whom you behold in these black garments of the priesthood,—I, who . . . hold communion, in your behalf . . . I'" (1:143). But even in this fantasized speech, the moral impulse is repressed. The true self gets lost beneath the public one, and the truth beneath the rhetoric: there are seven "I"'s and seven public identities before the final emergence of the truth—"am utterly a pollution and a lie!"—and even that "truth" is melodramatically veiled in metaphor.

"Could there be plainer speech than this?" Dimmesdale asks rhetorically, but it is obvious that the words "have clogged the spiritual sense," and Hawthorne acknowledges that the young man is a "subtle, but remorseful hypocrite" (1:144, 243).

The worst aspect of Dimmesdale's language, however, is that it manipulates and represses other natures than his own. Reduced to clinical terms, he uses—or misuses—his "soul music" as positive reinforcement for his dishonest, self-serving words, and the result is his damnable talent for "sad, persuasive eloquence. Oftenest persuasive, but sometimes terrible! The people knew not the power that moved them thus." "The virgins of his church," for example, grow "pale around him, victims of a passion so imbued with religious sentiment that they imagine . . . it to be all religion" (1:142). The word *victims* is suggestive here and foreshadows the final scene of the Election Sermon, where the congregation is held in a hypnotic "spell" and Dimmesdale looks "down from the sacred pulpit upon an audience, whose very inmost spirits had yielded to his control" (1:248, 246–47). When the sermon is over, he wears a "ghastly . . . and strangely triumphant" look, reminiscent of Chillingworth's "ghastly rapture" at the moment he believes Dimmesdale to be completely in his power (1:252, 138). The phrasing throughout this scene suggests that Dimmesdale has committed the one unpardonable sin in Hawthorne's value system. By choosing finally to act as spokesperson for patriarchy, he has valued authority over sympathy, power over morality, and hierarchy over mutuality. He has used language, not in the service of truth, but to tamper with, to coerce, and to control other minds and other lives. Hawthorne's message is clear: the psychology engendered by patriarchy results in language that is power-conscious and thus morally depleted.

All of which brings us back to the scene of the forest interview, for it is in that scene that Hawthorne portrays Hester and Dimmesdale trying unsuccessfully to outwit patriarchy, that is, trying to free themselves of its influence and failing because they are blind to its psychological hold over them. In this scene, all previous patterns of action are reversed: Hester breaks her long silence; Dimmesdale gives up, momentarily, his role as authority figure; and Hester takes the lead in determining what they should do to escape their Puritan bonds. The importance of this scene is that it shows that such role reversal—the redistribution of power—is not enough, and thus it points to the central tenet in Hawthorne's moral schema, which will be fully delineated only at the end of the book: change must take place in the interior of a heart, or in more modern terms, in the interior of the individual mind, where patriarchy has done its secret damage.

The thematic significance of this scene is also heightened because it seems to begin with such promise. Above, for example, I said that in his last public pronouncement Dimmesdale chooses, among other things, hierarchy over mutuality. In this forest scene Hawthorne prepares us for the wrongheadedness of that choice by showing the positive benefits of mutuality. The interview opens with images of Hester and Arthur meeting as equals:

> So strangely did they meet, in the dim wood, that it was like the first en-counter, in the world beyond the grave, of two spirits who had been inti-mately connected in their former life, but now stood coldly shuddering, in mutual dread. . . . Each a ghost, and awestricken at the other ghost! . . . The soul beheld its features in the mirror of the passing moment. . . . Ar-thur Dimmesdale put forth his hand, chill as death, and touched the chill hand of Hester Prynne. The grasp, cold as it was, took away what was dreariest in the interview. They now felt themselves, at least, inhabitants of the same sphere.
> Without a word more spoken,—neither he nor she assuming the guid-ance, but with an unexpressed consent,—they . . . sat down. [1:190]

The movement from equality to unity and, most important in this pas-sage, the sense of neither acting as the other's guardian prepare the way for the redemptive effect of this new-found mutuality: there is an end to repression; they seem at last able to speak the truth to each other, to "throw open the doors of intercourse, so that their real thoughts might be led across the threshold" (1:190). A specific instance of this truth-telling occurs when Hester, with "all her sympathies . . . both softened and in-vigorated," begins to speak the truth about Chillingworth's identity (1:193).

Given the themes of guardianship and divisiveness we have seen throughout this book, there can be no doubt that Hawthorne is suggest-ing a new—at least a nonpatriarchal—form of human relationship and, by extension, a new social system in this tentative dyadic mutuality; one based on sympathy rather than a desire for power, on generosity rather than self-interest. There can also be no doubt that this system collapses almost as soon as it has begun. As long as Hester and Dimmesdale act in sympathy in this scene, they are on the right track. As soon as their thoughts turn to self-preservation and avenging their past sorrows, they turn power-conscious and thus reveal how immured they are in patriarchal patterns of thought. This is evidenced, for example, in Dimmesdale's seemingly split-second decision that he needs a guardian literally to help him think, to tell him how to counter Chillingworth's power and thenceforth how to proceed in life. Tellingly, he presses "his hand nervously against his heart,—a gesture that [has] grown involuntary with him" and demands, "Think for me, Hester! Thou art strong. Resolve for me!" (1:196). Repression and guardianship now make a sad mockery of Hester's and the minister's joined hands.

Even more regrettable is Hester's answering role reversal, which is specifically dramatized in her use of language. As soon as she assumes the guidance in this dyad, her truth-telling turns first to official-sounding imperatives—"'Thou must dwell no longer with this man,' said Hester, slowly and firmly" (1:196)—and next to artful persuasion, as she urges him to flee with her from America: "'Is the world then so narrow?' exclaimed Hester Prynne, fixing her deep eyes on the minister's, and instinctively exercising a magnetic power over a spirit so shattered and subdued, that it could hardly hold itself erect" (1:197). "Instinctively" is surely an ironic gesture on Hawthorne's part, for Hester's persuasive rhetoric reveals how unconsciously she has assumed the long hereditary habit of her culture, which has become like nature—a habit that will be seen again in Dimmesdale's final magnetic control over his audience during the Election Sermon. She uses language here, no longer in the service of truth, but to control another's mind and action. Thus it should come as no surprise at the end of this scene when she acts not only as the authority figure but also the teacher, the inculcator of patriarchal "ethics." "Give up this name of Arthur Dimmesdale," she advises him, "and make thyself another, and a high one" (1:198). A Captain Farrago would probably be proud of such self-righteous renaming, but Hawthorne's readers must suspect that Hester Prynne's seven years of silent meditation of the dynamics of political power have "taught her much amiss" (1:200). Her use of language, like her role reversal in general, merely redistributes that power; at base it recapitulates and reinstills the speech psychology of patriarchy.

Immediate evidence of this involuntary repetition is that the "new life" Hester prescribes for them so ominously parallels her earlier marriage bond with Chillingworth, a man who would also take another name to disguise his unethical power plays (1:201). That ill-fated union too had been described as "a new life . . . a new life, but feeding itself on time-worn materials" (1:58). Further evidence that Hester and the minister have entrapped themselves in time-worn—and deadly—patterns is found in their subsequent behavior. In "The New England Holiday," for example, Hester seems psychologically to be back where she started. In the first scaffold scene, "turning pale as death," she had relied on "all the combative energy of her character . . . to convert the scene into a kind of lurid triumph" (1:68, 78). Here Hawthorne's description of her combat-conscious inner life is virtually the same, and the significance of her deathlike demeanor in such instances is finally revealed. Surrounded by spectators again, she composes her face like a mask to conceal her hostility and "to convert what had so long been agony into a kind of triumph" of self-defense: her face was "like a mask; or rather, like the frozen calmness of a dead woman's features; owing this dreary resemblance to the fact that Hester was actually dead, in respect to any claim of sympathy" (1:226).

This deadly lack of sympathy prefigures Dimmesdale's actual death. Hawthorne notes that upon leaving the forest, the minister is a "lost and desperate man," struggling to subdue his new-found "sense of power" over innocent and unsuspecting souls. Dimmesdale is specifically obsessed with the power of language, as in "The Minister in a Maze," where he feels "potent to blight all the field of innocence . . . and develop all its opposite with but a word" (1:220). He approaches the Election Sermon, in which he will wield that power so hypnotically, wrapped up in his own "unsympathizing thoughts" and withdrawn from his and Hester's "mutual world," which had once, momentarily, offered a truly new life (1:240). His death belies his final "confession" for it shows that he has once and for all repressed that "better part" which had so long sustained his half-torpid system.

Dimmesdale dies, then, from lack of moral sustenance. But Hester merely disappears for a while with her daughter. Her survival and her return to America from "that unknown region" where despair had driven her testify to Hawthorne's determination to stress, metaphorically, the still redemptive potential of feminine and maternal values in American culture (1:262). Hester's assumption of guardianship, of leadership authority, in the forest scene had led to no good, to no ethical solution to the problem of patriarchal domination. At the end of the book, perhaps as a result of her at last having given her undivided attention to mothering, she rejects that power-conscious mode of authority: "As Hester Prynne had no selfish ends, nor lived in any measure for her own profit and enjoyment, people brought all their sorrows and perplexities, and besought her counsel. . . . Women, more especially,—in the continually recurring trials of wounded, wasted, wronged, misplaced, or erring and sinful passion,—

or with the dreary burden of a heart unyielded, because unvalued and unsought,—came to Hester's cottage, demanding why they were so wretched, and what the remedy! Hester comforted and counseled them, as best she might" (1:263). The passage suggests her sympathy and generosity, but the contrast suggested here between the exclamatory demand and the humble qualification—"as best she might"—points especially to her new-found humility and to the surest sign, in Hawthorne's world, of her genuine ethical stature. "Earlier in life," we are told, "Hester had vainly imagined that she herself might be the destined prophetess" of a new social order, but in contrast to Dimmesdale, who had finally deluded himself into believing "it was his mission to foretell a high and glorious destiny" for the American people (1:249), she "had long since recognized the impossibility that any mission" of leadership or guardianship should be hers (1:263). She has chosen at last not to speak the power-conscious language of authority.

This stress on the moral rehabilitation that comes of renouncing authority over other lives is more fully delineated in *The House of the Seven Gables*. Here, what remains is to look briefly at Pearl's character, for the only hope for moral regeneration rests with her. Early in the story, for example, Hester had informed the Puritan magistrates that the scarlet letter "daily teaches me . . . lessons whereof my child may be the wiser and better, albeit they can profit nothing to myself" (1:111). Hawthorne seems to have hoped that *The Scarlet Letter* might do the same for a rising generation of Americans. "The angel and apostle of the coming revelation must be a woman, indeed" (1:263), he proclaims at the end of this story, and that woman is the now grown-up Pearl, who resides in a region yet "unknown" to his readers.

Throughout the story, Pearl exhibits the same divided nature that so plagues her parents. She is often imaged, for example, in terms of doubleness and character division that make her unreal and inhuman, as in "The Child at the Brookside," where her reflected image in the water, "so nearly identical with the living Pearl, seemed to communicate somewhat of its own shadowy and intangible quality to the child herself" (1:208). Such images suggest that Pearl is as yet unsubstantial as a potential ethical force, but she is most tellingly described as "some half-fledged angel of judgment—whose mission was to punish the sins of the rising generation" (1:103). Before she can become the full-fledged angel of the coming revelation, as promised on the last page, she needs "a grief that should deeply touch her, and thus humanize and make her capable of sympathy" (1:184).

It is sympathy, not judgment—which had been her father's final choice—
that Pearl must offer as a lesson to the future, and this revelation is
glimpsed at the scene of her father's death: "Pearl kissed his lips. A spell
was broken. The great scene of grief, in which the wild infant bore a part,
had developed all her sympathies; and as her tears fell upon her father's
cheek, they were the pledge that she would grow up amid human joy and
sorrow, nor for ever do battle with the world"—as her mother had—"but
be a woman in it" (1:256).

We never see Pearl firsthand again in this book, although Hawthorne
"faithfully believes" that she is "not only alive, but married and happy, and
mindful of her mother" (1:262). She appears again, recast in his next novel
in the character of Phoebe Pyncheon, another who is "mindful of her
mother" and thus another living emblem of Hawthorne's faith in the
redemptive potential of America's maternal heritage. But that Pearl never
speaks at the end of *The Scarlet Letter* deserves final mention. Throughout
the story her conflicted inner state is consistently rendered through her
erratic use of language. She vacillates, for example, between her mother's
resentful silence and her father's false speech: "If spoken to, she [will] not
speak again" (1:94), or if she does, it is to "speak words amiss," in an
"unknown tongue" reminiscent of Dimmesdale's duplicitous Tongue of
Flame (1:112, 94). Given the ethical promise inherent in Pearl's development, it would seem that Hawthorne portends some equally promising
view of language; that with the spell of patriarchal influence broken and
all her sympathies developed, this child of speech and silence must speak
the truth at last. That promise cannot be kept; such revelation is still to
come.

That Pearl never speaks at the end of this romance implies, first, how
strongly Hawthorne believed that the truths she had to tell had not yet
been heard in America, that patriarchy and patriarchal language still controlled and limited the minds of his audience. It also suggests how constrained he felt by those same cultural limitations and by the implications
of his own "authority." We must remember that, from the beginning,
Hawthorne identified not with Pearl but with Hester, that is, with
Hester's otherness, with her victimization and her flawed psychology.
Like Hester in the forest scene, he had also chosen to authorize others'
speech and actions, and like Hester at the end, he must admit to living a
"real life" in New England (1:262), where the truthful language of a Pearl
was still "unknown," still a hopeful fiction. Finally, there is a strong sense
at the end of this book that if, like Hester, he can do no positive good in

bringing about change, at least he will do no more harm. He will not
project his authority into the future by putting words into Pearl's mouth.
He will only counsel Americans as best he might—and by personal example—about the harmful effects of patriarchal culture on individual minds
and on language.

The House of the Seven Gables is similarly colored by Hawthorne's emphasis on the flawed ethics and power-conscious language that result from
the internalization of patriarchal norms. It opens much as *The Scarlet
Letter* had, with a previously sequestered female character crossing the
threshold of narrative, her inner life made public for the first time. The
main difference between these two romances is that the second seems to
take up, thematically, at the point of suspect role reversal witnessed in the
first book's climactic forest scene. That is, *The House of the Seven Gables* is
more specifically structured around the theme of role reversal, to dramatize more clearly, apparently, the ethical dangers inherent in that frame of
mind, in believing that merely meeting patriarchy on its own terms is
good enough.

This novel provides an especially intriguing contrast to Poe's "The Fall
of the House of Usher," which had explored in similar structural and
familial terms the interior of a disordered mind. Hawthorne's house is
also likened to "a human countenance" (2:5), but this house/mind is maintained by a daughter of the family, Hepzibah Pyncheon, and it is her
androgynous brother Clifford who has been unfairly incarcerated for a
crime he did not commit. The novel opens with Hepzibah's anxious preparations for her brother's return from prison, which she anticipates with
great joy, and at one point, when her young cousin Phoebe comments that
she had heard Clifford had died, Hepzibah jokingly dismisses that rumor
in words that ironically recall Poe's earlier tale: "In old houses like this,
you know, dead people are very apt to come back again!" (2:75–76). Neither the joke nor the townspeople's rumor that "this long-buried man was
likely . . . to be summoned forth from his living tomb" (2:22) is farfetched,
for although "both his heart and fancy [had] died within him," once
Clifford returns to the house we are told that Phoebe's influence "was just
what he required, to bring him back into the breathing world" (2:140). It
is Phoebe's presence, then, and the artist Holgrave's that constitute the
greatest difference between Poe's story and Hawthorne's, for Hawthorne
peoples his house with more possibilities for survival. The life-giving

household order Phoebe Pyncheon establishes is markedly different from that which the Ushers' visitor had tried to enforce, and unlike that repressive storyteller, Holgrave is introduced as the bearer of "cheery influences," "genuine sympathy," and enthusiastic support for Hepzibah's attempt to break with tradition and make her own living, an effort he regards as both "healthy and natural" (2:43–45). Together this young couple revitalizes this family's self-consuming energies by showing how the psychological bases for action in America might be—and must be—changed.[8]

Hawthorne establishes Hepzibah's otherness at the outset of this romance with images that are by now familiar. She has not only been psychologically isolated from society, from a common humanity, "with locks, bolts, and oaken bars, on all the intervening doors" (2:30), but she is also said to be "at the drowning point," whatever good she may have to offer threatened with extinction. Hawthorne stresses the economic basis for her seclusion and oppression: "In this republican country, amid the fluctuating waves of our social life, somebody is always at the drowning-point" (2:38), and Hepzibah's "tragedy" is that, being a woman, she has almost no other economic resource than to open a cent-shop so she can redeem herself by engaging in "the business of life" (1:31). Thus Hawthorne makes her femininity, as he had Hester's, partly a metaphor for elements in American society that have been devalued and disempowered by patriarchy. And thus we are made to sympathize with her very real desperation to survive—but only up to a certain point, for there is another sad similarity between Hepzibah and Hester: both are shown to have internalized and to have imprisoned themselves in their culture's half-formed ethical standards. "Though she had her valuable and redeeming traits," Hawthorne says, Hepzibah had "grown to be a kind of lunatic, by imprisoning herself so long in one place, with no other company than a single series of ideas" (2:174).

Hepzibah's desperation, then, leads her to what is at base the same unethical, stimulus-response behavior exhibited in *The Scarlet Letter*: she shortsightedly chooses role reversal. This is imaged again in ominously familiar terms. She becomes not only a shopkeeper—reenacting the role of "an unworthy ancestor" who had originally "fitted up [the] shop" (2:34)—but also a doorkeeper, and the psychological and ethical implications of this latter role are not long in coming. At the beginning of the story, for example, Hepzibah's actions seem innocent enough, even potentially redemptive, for she takes down "the bar from the shop-door, leaving the entrance free—more than free—welcome, as if all were household friends—to every passer-by" (2:40), and, in particular, she opens her door to "the young, blooming, and very cheerful face" of Phoebe Pyncheon, "which presented itself for admittance into the gloomy old mansion" (2:68). Soon, however, we learn that Hepzibah intended all along to use her new-found economic power to establish her authority as a guardian over her brother Clifford, recently released from his own imprisonment at the hands of patriarchy. When the villainous Jaffrey Pyncheon, the agent of Hepzibah's and Clifford's oppression, tries to enter the house to gain an interview with Clifford, she issues forth, "as would appear, to defend the entrance, looking, we must needs say, amazingly like the dragon which, in fairy tales, is wont to be the guardian over an enchanted beauty. . . . She [makes] a repelling gesture with her hand, and [stands], a perfect picture of Prohibition, at full length, in the dark frame of the doorway" (2:126–27).

There can be no doubt that Hawthorne genuinely sympathizes with Hepzibah's actions in this scene, that he identifies as strongly with her desperation to deny patriarchal prerogative as he had with Hester Prynne's, and thus that he cannot entirely condemn her for her worthy intentions. But as his authorial disclaimers suggest ("as would appear," "we needs must say"), neither can he rest easy with the ethical implications of her guardianship, which he allows to flower into dark proofs in the scene of Hepzibah's second confrontation with Jaffrey. In that scene Hepzibah meets the Judge on his own terms, her words motivated by a "bitterness that she could repress no longer," and it is precisely by her use of language that Hawthorne shows the dangers inherent in her strategy of role reversal (2:227). That the two meet as equals is evidenced in the fact that Jaffrey, no more than Hepzibah, considers himself Clifford's "natural guardian" and that her seemingly involuntary outbursts echo his artful rhetoric in this brief struggle for power (2:235). "You err . . . in keeping your brother so secluded," he chides her, "Do not act like a madwoman, Hepzibah!" (2:226, 233). "It is you that are diseased in mind," she answers, in response to his threat of subjecting Clifford to a similar "confinement"; "why should you do . . . so mad a thing?" (2:236, 237). They attack each other's language, each basing his or her authority on an even higher one, as if to deny the other's right to speak once and for all. "Talk sense, Hepzibah, for Heaven's sake!" (2:237). " 'In the name of Heaven,' cried Hepzibah, . . . 'in God's name, whom you insult—and whose power I could almost question, since he hears you utter so many false words, without palsying your tongue—give over'" (2:227–28). Finally, Hepzibah shows that such power-conscious tactics have indeed become second nature to her, for in the midst of the battle she tries to impose on Jaffrey the sentence that had been imposed on her: "Forbear! Not another word!" And here Hawthorne comments begrudgingly on her "utter denial . . . of his claim to stand in the ring of human sympathies" (2:228).

I say "begrudgingly" because again Hawthorne leaves no doubt but that he sympathizes—identifies, in fact—with Hepzibah's perceptions of Jaffrey's character, her anger and her accusations, even as he feels constrained to criticize her retributive frame of mind as being ultimately unproductive of any ethical resolution. It is this personal ethical dilemma, I believe, that accounts for what critics have long recognized as the biting and often hateful tone of his irony in this book and for what seems a paradoxical ending to this scene in particular.[9] Hepzibah appears to give over—"You are stronger than I," she finally admits (2:237)—but Hawthorne appears unwilling to have her lose the battle. While she goes to bring Clifford for the dreaded interview with his persecutor, Hawthorne contrives for Jaffrey to die of "natural causes"—like Dimmesdale before him, of physical and moral deterioration.

Hawthorne has created a situation in which he can both have his cake and eat it too. By authorizing Jaffrey's death, he vicariously achieves a measure of revenge for what his prefaces show to be his own sense of victimization. He also, however, makes that death serve his ethical argument: the outward forms of patriarchy are not the biggest problem; what Americans need to recognize is the pervasive psychological effect, the inner damage, that comes of living under such domination. He maintains that argument by showing Clifford's and Hepzibah's actions after Jaffrey's death. Seemingly free at last, they try to leave the burdensome house and all its deadly contents behind, only to find that they still carry the psychic burden. Hepzibah finds, for example, that the "old house was everywhere! It transported its great, lumbering bulk . . . and set itself down on whatever spot she glanced at" (2:258). A closer look at the brother's and sister's interactions will show how undeniably they have become "strangely enfranchised prisoners" of their psychological acculturation (2:256).

Their first response, even before leaving the house, is to reverse their previous roles. The formerly passive Clifford begins to give orders "in a tone of brief decision, most unlike what was usual to him," and Hepzibah "yield[s] without a question, and on the instant, to the will which Clifford express[es]" (2:250–51). The reference to Clifford's speech is especially

significant, for though Hawthorne dramatizes in Clifford all the regrettable traits of guardianship mentality, the worst of these is the usurpation of
language. Once the pair has boarded the train, for example, Clifford is
said to have "made himself the purse-bearer" (2:259), but his newly assumed authority is most often witnessed in his "strange aptitude of
words" (2:266). "At home, [Hepzibah] was his guardian," Hawthorne
tells us; "here, Clifford had become hers, and seemed to comprehend
whatever belonged to their new position, with a singular rapidity of intelligence. He had been startled into manhood" (2:258)—or, as Clifford himself puts it, "For the first time in thirty years, my thoughts gush up and
find words ready for them. I must talk, and I will!" (2:262). Throughout
this chapter ("The Flight of Two Owls"), he uses language to assert his
authority. He contradicts other passengers' use of language; he arrogates
the power of naming to himself—"These murderers, as you phrase it," are
but "unfortunate individuals" (2:265); and he silences his sister—"Be
quiet. . . . I must talk" (2:262). Such power-conscious language signals
what Hawthorne consistently shows to be the outcome of such benighted
"flights" from patriarchy: the redistribution of power merely assures endless rounds of role reversal. At the end of this chapter, Clifford and
Hepzibah can still see no other alternative—"You must take the lead now,
Hepzibah" (2:266)—and they must return to the House of the Seven
Gables, a house/mind they never really left.

The solution to the problem of patriarchy, then, lies not in an exchange
of power but in a change of mind, and Hawthorne offers this solution, as
he had in *The Scarlet Letter*, in the person of a young female character who
represents the softening influences of maternity in a rigidly masculine
world. There is a strong sense, as I suggested earlier, that Phoebe Pyncheon functions as a reincarnation or second draft of Pearl. She is three times
identified as "Arthur's only child," for example (2:104, 105, 117)—Arthur,
who had "died early, and in poor circumstances" (2:24). But she is more
obviously her mother's child. Hepzibah recognizes at once that "Phoebe
is no Pyncheon. She takes everything from her mother" (2:79). Phoebe's
talents for putting the house back in order, the older woman tells her,
"must have come to you with your mother's blood" (2:77), and the young
woman admits to "an odd kind of motherly sentiment" toward Hepzibah
and Clifford (2:216). Phoebe is also imaged as an angel of redemption,
having "a spirit that was capable of Heaven" (2:168). When she is about to
leave the house for a while, the wise Uncle Venner reminds her that the
aging pair "can never do without you now—never, Phoebe, never!—no

more than if one of God's angels had been living with them, and making their dismal house pleasant, and comfortable" (2:221). Here, however, the comparison between Phoebe and Pearl ends, or rather, here Phoebe's originality as a character begins, for she responds, "I'm no angel. . . . But I suppose people never feel so much like angels as when they are doing what little good they may. So I shall certainly come back!" (2:221). Unlike Pearl, Phoebe does come back in the end—to establish a new household and a new psychology—because in this story Hawthorne is determined to make her moral influence "real!" She represents "the Actual," he tells us (2:140), but she seems more obviously to represent Hawthorne's greater insistence in this second novel that there is actual possibility of changing the American mind, of reinstilling forgotten values and redeveloping its moral sense: "A nature like Phoebe's has invariably its due influence, but is seldom regarded with due honor" (2:137).[10]

That Hawthorne honors her maternal/moral influence, especially as it revitalizes minds damaged by patriarchy, is seen throughout this romance, but most tellingly in his characterization of the artist Holgrave, who, as others have observed, seems a fictional version of Hawthorne himself.[11] Holgrave, too, is an angry young man, certainly as angry as the author who feels compelled to kill off a Jaffrey Pyncheon. Like Hawthorne, apparently, Holgrave dwells in the House of the Seven Gables that he "may know the better how to hate it" (2:184), but like him also, the young American has a "sense, or inward prophecy . . . that we are not doomed to creep on forever in the old, bad way, but that, this very now, there are the harbingers abroad of a golden era, to be accomplished in his own lifetime" (2:179). Phoebe is, for both, the harbinger of that better life, but of the two artists, only Holgrave is finally able to experience, to realize, the change of mind that will let him begin anew. There is, finally, a difference between the two artists, and this is first dramatized in Holgrave's repudiation of his own artistic authority. After reading Phoebe his story "Alice Pyncheon," he seems to recognize that his tale of victimization has taken hold of the young girl's mind and left her in a "curious psychological condition," which to the reader is the familiar mental state that Hawthorne finds so dangerous: "A veil was beginning to be muffled about her, in which she could behold only him, and live only in his thoughts and emotions" (2:211). "There is no temptation so great as the opportunity of acquiring empire over the human spirit," Hawthorne admits. "Let us, therefore . . . concede to the Daguerreotypist the rare and high quality of reverence for another's individuality" (2:212). Holgrave releases Phoebe from his spell and by this ethical choice prepares the way for *The House of the Seven Gables'* dual ending.

In that ending it is obvious that Hawthorne remains divided against himself. On one hand, he tries to tie up the ends of his ethical argument, showing that a change of mind, or of the interior of a heart, as he had phrased it in *The Scarlet Letter*, can lead to a new life. Holgrave's final statement about the houses he had formerly hated is the capstone of that argument. He and Phoebe leave the House of the Seven Gables to live in a country house previously owned by the villainous Pyncheon patriarch, suggesting that he has reconciled himself to his legacy of Americanness: he cannot change the past, and he will no longer expend his energies trying to get even for past grievances. More revealing is his criticism of the Judge's method of building a house. He wonders out loud that the man "should not have felt the propriety of embodying so excellent a piece of domestic architecture in stone, rather than in wood. Then, every genera-tion of the family might have altered the interior . . . while the exterior, through the lapse of years, might have been adding venerableness to its original beauty, and thus giving that impression of permanence, which I consider essential to the happiness of any one moment" (2:314–15). With this statement Hawthorne shows that Holgrave has learned the valuable moral lesson that so many of his other characters have not: that to give any "permanence" to American life, the "interior," the inner life, must be changed. Holgrave's imaginative reconstruction of a house/mind, how-ever, is something that Hawthorne himself seems finally unable to do, and this is evidenced in the fact that the new "family" leaves the House of the Seven Gables, but Hawthorne returns to it. In the last paragraph, he turns his eye away from the future that he has tried to envision for them and back to the house/mind that has been his obsession throughout. By so doing, he suggests once again that for all his insight into the damaging psychological effects of American patriarchal culture, he is still one of its victims. He has yet to put his house/mind in order.

Margaret Fuller, one of Hawthorne's contemporaries and one of his acquaintances, wrote of "the mind of the age" that it "still . . . struggles confusedly with [its] problems, better discerning as yet the ill it can no longer bear, than the good by which it may supersede it."[12] Hawthorne seems a case in point. His attempts to repudiate the ills perpetrated by patriarchal language ever turn back on themselves to reveal an author who uses language the way he criticizes his characters for using it: to "autho-rize" others' lives and deaths and to further his own self-interest, which is to say, to express deep resentment over his societal and cultural grievances. His struggles with his own "authority" do not in any way negate his complex insights into the damaging effects of patriarchal culture, however; rather, they seem to reinforce the truth of his claims. In particular, his use of "femininity" and "masculinity" as mutually exclusive metaphors for "good" and "bad" psychological traits stands in marked contrast to Cooper's and Poe's more flexible metaphorical experiments with androgyny and shows finally how deeply Hawthorne was himself immured in the cultural either/or mentality he meant to expose and disavow in his "second stories."

7

Telling the Whole Story: Melville's *Pierre*

The question most asked of Melville's *Pierre* is how to account for its troublesome form. The novel has been called, among other things, a tragedy, a Hawthornian romance, a sentimental romance, and a self-reflexive parody, and though all of these readings are individually useful and persuasive, the coexistence of such a variety of formal labels without contradicting one another suggests that Henry A. Murray was right when he called Melville's novel "a literary monster, . . . whose appearance is marred by a variety of freakish features. . . . It is a compound of incongruities and inconsistencies that is shocking to a nicely regulated intellect."[1] Equally shocking is that Melville took such pains to show cause for what readers have judged to be formal oddities. *Pierre* may be a literary monster, but it is also a self-explanatory text, for it reveals the many ways an author's best intentions may be undermined by factors beyond his control. In this bleak book about a young author's search for a narrative form that will tell the truth at last, all texts, including his own, become malformed as a result of publishing practices, misreadings, and their authors' psychosocial conditioning, and the greatest threat to textual form, for a male author, is his socialized, or "inherited," responses to women.

The plot of *Pierre* is structured around this latter issue. At the outset, Pierre's life is imaged as a "sweetly-writ manuscript," but its form is incomplete, marred by "one hiatus": "A sister had been omitted from the text."[2] The textual omission is the fault of the father who authored this young man's life and whose illegitimate daughter has not been named in the family history. Pierre's task, once he has discovered his unacknowledged sister, is to author a new "manuscript" that will reveal the "miserably neglected Truth to the world" (7:283), and to do so, he must create a narrative form that will do justice to the lost sister and reinstate her in the text. Instead—and unfortunately, for all concerned, the young author uses the language that is his paternal legacy to delegitimize his sister a second time. Unwilling to sully his dead father's reputation or to expose his sister's real identity by acknowledging her as his social equal, he rewrites her role as that of dependent "wife." Furthermore, it soon becomes clear that his conscious desire to protect her masks an unconscious desire to possess her sexually, a truth he momentarily realizes but immediately tries to conceal from himself and others. By such self-serving fictions and omissions, he authors merely another life text that fails to tell the whole story, and the last image of this life text, just before the despairing young man brings it to a premature close, shows that he has indeed authored a "literary monster": "Here, then," Pierre berates himself, "is the untimely, timely end;—Life's last chapter well stitched into the middle!" (7:360).

Recent criticism has tended to read Melville's uncharacteristic use of women in this novel as evidence of his criticisms of the feminization of authorship and thus authority in contemporary America. More specifically, feminist criticism has read *Pierre* as a debunking attack on the popular form of domestic romance, written by women novelists and preferred over Melville's own metaphysical adventure novels by the era's large audience of women readers.[3] Neo-Freudian criticism has read it as an ill-fated search for an absent father authority, angrily and parodically set in "a society extraordinarily feminized."[4] My argument here is that Melville introduces female characters into this work to dramatize the imaginative limits of any male-authored literary form and of the half-truthful language that is a male author's only lasting paternal legacy in America. Melville's attacks on contemporary publishing practices, readers, and the socialization processes and societal obligations that limit a male author's imaginative freedom are shown to be real but nevertheless "gnat-like torments" compared to this greater limitation (7:340): language that is exclusively patriarchal, androcentric, and thus incapable of telling both sides of the American story—in this case, the sister's as well as the brother's.

The last question that must be asked is whether Melville believed his own ability to tell the truth to be as limited, and thus his own text as malformed, as Pierre's. Despite the many similarities between the two authors' lives and literary careers, there is both textual and biographical evidence to suggest that Melville felt he had succeeded where Pierre had failed. As he emphasized to his publisher, for example, Melville conceived of his novel as a "*new book*," and in it, he accomplishes what Pierre's tradition-bound text could not: *Pierre* tells the whole story, incorporating the sister's and the brother's separate stories into one interconnected narrative.[5] This novel is new in other ways as well. It includes two "sister"-artists, Pierre's Aunt Dorothea and his sister Isabel, and the otherness of their art suggests potential alternatives and correctives to the exclusive androcentric tradition from which the young male artist is trying to free himself. Moreover, in narrative form and in language, *Pierre* is much more similar to these sisters' stories than to the brother's—and, in fact, so different from the other literary productions of its time that one of its first reviewers speculated that "Mr. Melville may have constructed his story upon some new theory of art to a knowledge of which we have not yet transcended."[6] That response, and so many others like it, suggests that its author had indeed written a new book. It also suggests that if *Pierre* continues to be judged a literary monster, it is because Melville's irregular artistry still transcends the imaginative limits of readers whose overly regulated intellects prevent them from seeing the whole story.

Texts come in all shapes and sizes in *Pierre*—letters, manuscripts, proof sheets, pamphlets; but the one characteristic they all have in common is their vulnerability to unforeseen formal changes once the written word has been committed to paper. The paper itself may be so poorly manufactured that it evokes a negative response from prospective readers, who view the text as little more than "waste paper." Such is the case with the "Chronometricals and Horologicals" pamphlet Pierre finds in the city: "It was a thin, tattered, dried-fish-like thing; printed with blurred ink upon mean, sleazy paper" (7:206), and it is the decrepit form of this text as much as its unprepossessing title which "did almost tempt him to pitch it out of the window" (7:207). Ink is another factor capable of undermining the formal integrity of a text and thus an especially ungovernable determinant of reader response. The fateful letter that first informs Pierre that he has an illegitimate sister is "stained . . . with spots of tears, which chemically acted upon by the ink, assumed a strange and reddish hue—as if blood and not tears had dropped upon the sheet" (7:64–65). The author, Isabel, had assumed that "the tears would dry upon the page, and all be fair again," but she was mistaken, and Pierre's response is determined more by the ink's chemical properties than by her carefully chosen words: "Thy tears dried not fair, but dried red, almost like blood; and nothing so much moved my inmost soul as that tragic sight" (7:159).

Melville's wry criticisms of the commercial materials that dictate the perceived form of a text make up only a small part of his attack on the "business" of publishing.[7] As a young author, for example, Pierre is wooed by businessmen who would change the physical appearance of his works by binding them in leather—"printer's and binder's bills on the day of publication" (7:247)—and by interpolating illustrations—"cash down on delivery" (7:248). Such services are financially tempting, "inasmuch as the placard of the title-page indubitably must assist the publisher in his sales" (7:250), but they are also symbolic of the ways an author's own conceptions of his work—his imaginative freedom—may be co-opted. Melville knew from his experience in writing *Moby-Dick* the tribulation Pierre eventually suffers in this novel: the first chapters of his book having been sent to the printer, "the printed pages now dictated to the following manuscript. . . . Therefore, was his book already limited, bound over, and committed to imperfection, even before it had come to any confirmed form or conclusion at all" (7:338).[8]

If the economic practices of the publishing business undermine the formal integrity of texts, the reading public is no less a threat. In *Pierre* readers devalue texts or value them for the wrong reason; they are careless of them or actively resist what a text has to tell them; and they willfully deny authorial intent and attack authors, twisting their words into another meaning. And all of these acts of misreading are imaged in terms of readers' tampering with textual form, creating all on their own "literary monsters." When Pierre finds the Plinlimmon pamphlet, it has not only been left accidentally on the seat of a public coach, but its pages have been crumpled and its conclusion torn off so that it "came to a most untidy termination" (7:215). In contrast to this careless or hostile treatment, but no less destructive, is the fanatical behavior of one of Pierre's own literary groupies, who, "finding a small fragment of the original manuscript [of "The Tear"] containing a dot (*tear*), over an *i* (*eye*), esteemed the significant event providential" and turned what was already a partial text into a brooch (7:263).

As a reader Pierre is equally to blame for altering texts. As a young author, he makes "allumettes of his sonnets when published" to light his cigars (7:263). But he also takes great liberties with other authors' "letters," especially those that shake his complacency and cause him to question his own actions and motives. When he first receives Isabel's mysterious letter, he hopes to read in it a dinner invitation, requiring only a "stereotyped reply." As his "interior monitions" about the letter's significance change (7:62), however, and he begins to intuit that "in some dark way the reading of it would irretrievably entangle his fate," he indulges in a "selfish destruction of the note" (7:63), so that the text he finally dares to read is "completely torn in two by Pierre's own hand" (7:65). Such actions

symbolize the preconceptions and psychological defenses readers bring to
their task and show all too well the resulting transformation of the text.
Even the course of action Pierre eventually chooses, to renounce family
and friends and make a new life with Isabel, results from his having
attributed to the letter a meaning its author did not consciously intend,
for as Isabel later explains to him, "Thou dost not know what planned and
winnowed motive I did have in writing thee; nor does poor Bell know
that; for poor Bell was too delirious to have planned and winnowed motives then" (7:159).

Both of these symbolic patterns of reader behavior are shown to be
characteristic of Pierre, who alters the form of other authors' texts either
by psychological resistance or by using a text for his own purposes in a
way its author never foresaw. Once his complacency has been shattered by
Isabel's letter, for example, he turns to the texts he had formerly enjoyed as
"an admiring reader," when "neither his age nor his mental experience . . .
had qualified him" to be "touched" by them (7:169). Now he sees each as a
"too true volume" and resists their truths (7:168). "Dante had taught him
that he had bitter cause of quarrel; *Hamlet* taunted him with faltering in
the fight." Thus "torn into a hundred shreds the printed pages of *Hell* and
Hamlet lay at his feet, which trampled them, while [to his eyes] their
vacant covers mocked him" (7:170). At the end of the novel he will turn
that self-defensive violence against authors themselves. Denying Glen
Stanly's and Fred Tartan's accusation that he is a liar who has dishonored
their cherished Lucy, he (mis)reads their letter as a "lie" (7:359), and wad-
ding his pistol with a torn-off portion of it among the bullets, he sends it
back at them in deadly form. The repercussions of such a willful misreading kill his cousin Glen, who, as an author of a now malformed text,
was surely Pierre's "own kindred" (7:360).

Pierre's failings as a reader spring from the same source as his failings as
a writer: this young author is fettered by "the infinite entanglements of all
social things" (7:191), which invariably predetermine the initial form his
texts will take. This is evidenced once Pierre has moved to the city, where
his financial responsibilities as male head of a household with female
dependents are imaged in his having to turn his attention from his self-
exploratory writing to the "business" of getting his work published:
"Every evening, after his day's writing was done, the proofs of the beginning of his work came home for correction. . . . They were replete with
errors; but preoccupied by the thronging, and undiluted, pure imaginings
of things, he became impatient of such minute, gnat-like torments; he

randomly corrected the worst, and let the rest go; jeering with himself at the rich harvest thus furnished to the entomological critics." As a "most unwilling states-prisoner of letters" and of societal obligations, Pierre thus participates—as businessman, reader, and author—in the malformation of his own text (7:340).

Finally, although Melville depicts a variety of disruptive psychosocial entanglements in *Pierre*, the greatest threat to the formal integrity of a male author's text lies in his association with women. The intrusion of a woman into a man's life makes him false to other men and even to himself, for the more men harbor "a secret and poignant feeling [for a woman], the higher they pile the belying surfaces" (7:224). The results in literary terms are false "letters" to male readers. The boyhood letters between Pierre and his cousin Glen had been formal testimonials to their "boy-love" (7:216). They had been passionately and spontaneously written, "naturally frank" (7:219); they had communicated true feelings. Maturity, however, and the socialization process that turns carefree boys into so-cially experienced men had resulted in "departing spontaneities" and de-parting truthfulness (7:218). The literary effects of Glen's social entangle-ments become evident when, returning from a trip abroad, the newly "Europeanized" Glen sends Pierre "a letter all sudden suavity," and in a second, "now half-business letter (of which mixed sort nearly all the sub-sequent ones were)," he revises the salutation to a lesser endearment than before (7:219). Such stylistic revisions prefigure the even greater formal artifice to come, for "the eventual love for the other sex forever dis-miss[es] the preliminary love-friendship of boys" (7:217), and once Pierre becomes engaged to Lucy, the jealous Glen composes a masterpiece of deception to hide his true feelings: "Glen culled all his Parisian portfolios for his rosiest sheet, and with scented ink, and a pen of gold, indited a most burnished and redolent letter, which, after invoking all the blessings of Apollo and Venus, and the Nine Muses, and the Cardinal Virtues upon the coming event; concluded at last with a really magnificent testimonial to his [cousinly] love" (7:220).

The distance between this carefully controlled piece of artifice and Glen's earlier, authentic testimonials seems a sad measure of male matu-rity, but it dramatizes a theory of language and literary form that Freud, writing later in the century, would have found roughly compatible with his own view of (male) personality development as a process of socializa-tion. Glen's determination to falsify his text can be traced back to his jealous desire to possess another man's woman and his obligation as a mature, socialized man to deny and conceal such antisocial feelings, which Pierre will later call the "not-to-be-named things" (7:313). Moreover, Glen's use of archaic literary conventions—his reference to Apollo and Venus, the Nine Muses, and the Cardinal Virtues—reveals the historical link between the linguistic dilemma and the contemporary literary one. Male authors have been taught that just as there are certain civilized standards of male behavior, so are there standard forms of literary expression when the subject is women or men's feelings for women. By transforming his true feelings for Lucy into idealized prose in this instance, Glen merely reveals his unconscious indoctrination into a long-standing literary tradition established by such forefathers as Dante and Shakespeare—a tradition his cousin-author Pierre will try to reject. Unfortunately, however, the growing dishonesty in Glen's letters prefigures in miniature the fate that will befall Pierre's life text and the new book he would give to the world because Pierre has unconsciously assimilated the same behavioral, linguistic, and literary models.[9]

The unconscious nature of Pierre's psychosocial conditioning and the subsequent effect on his use of language are made apparent in the opening scene of the novel, in which Pierre seeks out his fiancée, Lucy. Calling up to her in her bedroom window, he fancies her an "angel" looking down from heaven and swears that she belongs "to the regions of an infinite day!" When she asks him why young men "always swear" such things when they are in love, he answers her with another pretty conceit:

> "Because in us love is profane, since it mortally reaches toward the heaven in ye!"
> "There thou fly'st again, Pierre; thou art always circumventing me so. Tell me, why should ye youths ever show so sweet an expertness in turning all trifles of ours into trophies of yours?"
> "I know not how that is, but ever was it our fashion to do." And shaking [a] casement shrub, he dislodged [a] flower, and conspicuously fastened it in his bosom.—"I must away now, Lucy; see! under these colors I march."
> "Bravissimo! oh, my only recruit!" [7:4]

The exchange allows a number of insights into Pierre's psychic makeup. First, he is unconsciously following a fashion of language use that is characteristic of men. That fashion is to falsify or, as Lucy realizes, to circumvent the truth when the subject is women, and the truth, as Pierre's reference to profane love suggests, is the desire for sexual possession, which must be masked by renaming, idealizing—and thus, fictionalizing. Elsewhere we are shown that Pierre can articulate his desire to possess Lucy only "to himself inwardly," and even then he must mask it in classical literary terms: "I am Pluto stealing Proserpine; and every accepted lover is" (7:59). More often in these introductory scenes, Melville shows him renaming his baser desire in the terms of military guardianship and possession that, like his linguistic fashion in general, he has inherited from his fathers. He woos her in a phaeton "fit for a vast General," carrying her far out of range of their snoopy neighbors, whom he envisions as "sharpshooters behind every clap-board" (7:31, 23). Even his courting rhetoric is framed in military metaphor, for he not only marches under her colors but also claims "the unchallenged possession" of her for his "inalienable fief" (7:36).

The desire to possess, to dominate, to have power over, is finally the key to Pierre's psychology and his use of language, and Melville lays the blame for such behavior on the patriarchal socialization process that has sanctioned the "power over" mentality and placed white, educated, monied men at the top of the social hierarchy because it has prevented the young man from imagining any other way of relating to his world. Thus underlying the youthful playfulness of the opening dialogue is a very unflattering view of this young American author's paternal legacy, which has prescribed the fashion of his behavior. Melville soon undercuts the status of Pierre's revolutionary descent by showing how the family's nationalistic pride expresses itself in pride of ownership, not only of the land, which "seemed as sanctified through [its] very long uninterrupted possession by his race" (7:8), but even of stolen souvenirs of battle, which become icons of patriarchal power: "an old tattered British banner or two, . . . captured by his grandfather, the general, in fair fight," and "a British kettle-drum also captured by his grandfather in fair fight" (7:12). He also points out what revisionist historians have begun to stress in the last twenty years or so, that the same patriots who fought so fiercely for freedom from one group—in "fair fight"—were at the same time appropriating the lands and personal rights of others.[10] The Indian-fighting, slaveowning Glendinning patriarchs acquired and maintained their privileged status as landed gentry through acts of racial domination, which are carried on, in spirit, in young Pierre's acts of class and sexual domination. He exercises a patriarchal prerogative repeatedly in the opening chapters of the novel, but especially in respect to the family servant, upon whom he tellingly confers the subordinate title of "Sergeant Dates" and from whom he expects "automaton obedience" (7:17); and the young working-class women of the community, whose sewing circle he condescends to visit and whom, as his mother reminds him, he "shall one day be lord of the manor of" (7:45).

Finally, to return to the issue of patriarchal language, Pierre's unconscious acceptance of such behavioral models only points that much more clearly to his unconscious acceptance of linguistic and authorial ones. He may use language playfully, cavalierly, to mask an underlying desire to have power over all he surveys, but his speech acts prove to be merely another way of enacting that desire, for they show him repeatedly assuming the power of naming, or more specifically, renaming. At the beginning of the novel, he labels his mother with the "fictitious title" of "sister" (7:7), just as he will later rename his sister "wife." Similarly, his labeling Lucy an "angel" in the opening scene foreshadows his renaming her his "cousin," when he allows her to join him and his fictitious "wife" in the city, or before that, when he knows not what role to assign her, his replacing her name with an empty cipher: "Like an algebraist, for the real Lucy, he, in his scheming thoughts, had substituted but a sign—some empty X" (7:181). Pierre unconsciously assumes the right to assign and deny roles to others according to what he wants or needs from them. His use of language is thus ever self-centered and, as his renaming of women shows in particular, androcentric: their titles merely signify the relationship he chooses to enact with them.

On a larger scale, Melville also equates renaming with the act of storytelling, for as a young author, Pierre has apparently learned his craft in a storied world in which all stories refer back to, and thus reinforce, the power and privilege conferred on him by his forefathers. The entire countryside that surrounds Pierre's hereditary estate had been conquered and renamed so that it would thereafter ever recall "the proudest patriotic and family associations" (7:5), but it is also "storied with the great deeds of the Glendinnings" (7:92). Pierre's mother, Mary Glendinning, is "the most storied beauty of all the country round" (7:97), but even these stories, ostensibly about the woman herself, are curiously androcentric, for her social status and visibility have been conferred by marriage, and the honor afforded by such stories accrues to the Glendinning name and not her own. In keeping with this idea, Melville repeatedly emphasizes her role as power-proud dowager, brandishing the old General's baton, which she cherishes as the symbol of her son's inheritance, his "command," and acting in all ways as the agent of Pierre's father, the man from whom her own power is derived: "Always think of him and you can never err; yes, always think of your dear perfect father, Pierre" (7:19).

At the beginning of the novel, Pierre is portrayed as having grown up in a world of false language and fictions that assure his inherited authority by denying it to others, and Melville first images this false legacy of androcentric entitlement in terms of Pierre's life being a "sweetly-writ manuscript" with one significant "hiatus": "A sister had been omitted from the text." The androcentric bias implicit in this phrasing, which suggests that Pierre can only imagine a sister's life as subordinate to his own, sets the scene for the main challenge to Pierre's life text and to his abilities as an author. While growing up he had lived in the world, as in the Glendinning mansion, in the "repose of a wide story, tenanted only by himself" (7:84), but as the novel opens, his repose is about to be shattered by the knowledge that he has a sister; that she has gone unnamed in the family history (his-story); and, in particular, that she has her own story to tell—a second story that requires a form and finally a language different from any he has been trained to imagine.

Melville leads up to the "Story of Isabel" with three incidents that reveal the extreme otherness of gynocentric stories in Pierre's world. By *gyno-centric* I mean narratives either in which a woman is the main character or in which all action is caused by and thus refers back to a woman. The first incident is introduced during Pierre and Lucy's first outing, when Lucy asks him to tell her again "the story of the face" (7:37). On a visit to the village sewing circle with his mother, Pierre had been strangely moved by the face of a young woman who had shrieked and fainted at the mention of his name and whose later veiled glances at him had caused him to lose "conscious possession of himself" (7:47). His sexual and intellectual attraction to her had been so great that he is thereafter unable to put her out of his mind, but the greater significance of the incident is that he manfully tries to put her out of his language; that is, he dutifully tries not to talk about her or his various responses to her.

I say "manfully" because his dilemma is presented literally as a challenge to his manhood: the young woman's powerful effect on him, he thinks to himself, "almost unmans me with its wonderfulness" (7:49). His first act after leaving the gathering is to speak excitedly of the girl to his mother, but, ever the jealous agent of patriarchal strictures, she is aghast at the passionate nature of his outburst and reminds him of his contractual obligation to Lucy. He dutifully retracts his expression of interest, claiming he meant "nothing—nothing" (7:48), and acts and speaks once again as a young man should. The irony is that to act as a young man should means to suppress the true "story" of his attraction and thus to become a "falsifyer" in his speech (7:51). The outing scene with Lucy reveals that he had apparently tried to tell her "the story of the face" as well, but when Lucy here asks him to tell it again, he recants once more, citing as his creed the masculine ideology that determines the fashion of manly speech in this novel: "Never should I have told thee the story of that face, Lucy. I have bared myself too much to thee. Oh, never should Love know all!" (7:37).

The implications of such denials are of course foreboding, for in his first test as an aspiring young author, Pierre has unwittingly omitted his sister's story from the text of his life. On a theoretical level, the incident suggests both the cause and the effect of androcentric thinking. First, it would appear that men try to suppress stories that reveal their lack of control over the world and over their own actions, stories that would put a woman at the center as the source of power. In his attempts to exorcise the girl from his mind, for example, we are told that Pierre likes to think that he has "a power over the comings and the goings of the face," but he realizes that this is not so "on all occasions" (7:53) and thus must struggle repeatedly to maintain his "power over" such otherness. Again, however, Melville's criticism falls on the socialization process that has shaped Pierre's thought patterns. That is, though the cause of such exclusionary thinking may be a man's inherent desire to place himself at the center of all stories, the greater evil, according to Melville, is that generations of fathers have sanctioned that tendency above all others and encoded it in a language that is exclusively androcentric. As a result, Pierre has inherited a language that has no words, no "names," with which to tell a gynocentric story, even if he were to try to break out of his own self-centeredness. In reliving the experience of the face in his mind, he can only refer to its "nameless beauty" and "nameless fascination" (7:49, 51). He is equally at a loss for words to describe his sudden lack of self-control: he searches for "some possible homely explication of all this nonsense—so he would momentarily denominate it" and elsewhere calls it a "sort of unhealthiness . . . for, in his then ignorance, he could find no better term" (7:52, 53).

The second incident, his receipt of Isabel's letter, informing him she is his illegitimate sister, continues this theme, for that text begins: "The name at the end of this letter will be wholly strange to thee. Hitherto my existence has been utterly unknown to thee" (7:63). It is also suggested, in a foreshadowing of something we will learn in her later, lengthier story, that the language Isabel must use to communicate with Pierre is foreign to her as well. "I knew not how to write to thee," she admits, "nor what to say," and indeed, to have committed the daring act of presenting herself, a woman, as storyteller and namer, she has had to break into a language that has previously excluded her: "Yes, Pierre, Isabel calls thee her brother— her brother! oh, sweetest of words, which so often I have thought to myself, and almost deemed it profanity for an outcast like me to speak or think" (7:63–64). The new element here, however, is that to reinforce the idea of the otherness of Isabel's letter and of the literary as well as social codes that she must break to write such a letter, Melville stresses the "irregular" form of the sister's text, which is inscribed in an "irregular hand, and in some places almost illegible, plainly attesting the state of the mind which had dictated it;—stained, too, here and there, with spots of tears, which chemically acted upon by the ink, assumed a strange and reddish hue—as if blood and not tears had dropped upon the sheet;—and so completely torn in two by Pierre's own hand, that it indeed seemed the fit scroll of a torn, as well as bleeding heart" (7:64–65). The passage suggests, in general, the ways any author's text becomes transformed once it has been committed to paper—and ink—and is read by even one other person. More important, it suggests that the initial form of any text or "story" is determined by its author's state of mind; that an author's state of mind is determined and delimited by his or her relationship to language; and therefore, that when a woman authors a text, its initial form will be irregular because her relationship to language is that of outcast. Isabel's illegitimate status in relation to Pierre thus serves as a metaphor for her illegitimate status as storyteller in a world that has reserved that privilege for men only, and it is the form as much as the content of her letter that challenges his exclusive birthright.[11]

Pierre's first intimations of the otherness of Isabel's letter cause him to tear it in two even before he reads it, an act Melville describes as "selfish" (7:63)—self-centered, self-defensive. The image of halving the threatening text also has more specific connotations, for it signifies the sexist double standard in which Pierre has been indoctrinated and the subsequent halving of his capacity to credit any gynocentric story that threatens his patriarchal world view; thus, before the appointed hour of his interview with Isabel, he will be portrayed as "half wishful that the hour would come; half shuddering that every moment it still came nearer" (7:109). In context, the image of the halved text sets the scene for the third incident involving a half-credited gynocentric story, which Melville presents in flashback. After finally daring to read his sister's letter, Pierre is reminded of his father's dying words, "My daughter! my daughter!" Melville describes them as the product of "unmentionable thoughts," which, at the moment of death, seemed "to acknowledge no human jurisdiction." Even as a young child, however, and certainly as a dutiful son, Pierre had supplied the psychosocial "jurisdiction" necessary to keep his father's image sacrosanct: he had mentally replaced the threatening intimation of illegitimacy with "sweeter remembrances . . . , and covered it up" (7:71). The act of reading Isabel's letter leads to the uncovering of that memory and finally to the recovery of another "sister's" story, which has similarly been half-tucked away in some dark closet of his mind.

As a child, Pierre had once asked his father's sister to explain to him why the image of his father in a portrait she owned looked so different from that in a portrait his mother proudly displayed in the Glendinning mansion. His Aunt Dorothea had then told him the story of his father's rumored romantic involvement with a beautiful, though socially unacceptable, young foreigner, a refugee from the French Revolution, during his bachelor days. Their cousin Ralph, an artist whose subjects—all men—always wore "their best expressions to him" (7:75), had slyly contrived to capture the more spontaneous expression on the elder Pierre's face after his daily visits with the young woman, as he sat in a chair in the artist's studio "self-forgetful," still thinking of her. Once the elder Pierre had realized that Ralph had been "stealing his portrait" (7:77) and thus depicting an image of himself he preferred to keep hidden, he had demanded that the artist not "show it to any one, keep it out of sight." Cousin Ralph had then secretly placed the portrait in Dorothea's keeping, knowing how much she loved her brother, whatever his true nature, but he had also, dutifully, imposed a prohibition against any display of his too-true art, making her "solemnly promise never to expose it." Thus it was only after her brother's death that Dorothea had dared to hang the painting in her chambers or finally to tell young Pierre "the story of the chair-portrait" (7:78).

This story incident carries multiple significance. The actions of cousin Ralph, for example, suggest that even though male artists are capable of producing art that tells the truth about human nature—for example, that women are capable of wielding great power over men's minds and that men are capable of forgetting themselves and all notions of social propriety in their desire to possess women sexually—nevertheless they are constrained by male bonding to suppress such art. They are only allowed to image men wearing their "best expressions." As a woman artist, or storyteller, Dorothea fares little better, for though she eventually tells the story her brother would have preferred to keep hidden, as sisters are wont to do in *Pierre*, she is long constrained by male prohibitions against doing so, and she breaks her long silence only at the repeated demands of the latest male heir to the family history, who dictates the pace of her story and interrupts and criticizes it at will: "Tell me. . . . Don't tell me. . . . I don't understand. . . . Don't talk that way. . . . Do go on" (7:74–77).

Finally, as in the case of Isabel's letter, it is the form as much as the content of Aunt Dorothea's story that makes it "a very strange one" to the young Pierre (7:78). That Ralph uses paint and Dorothea uses words to tell essentially the same story suggests that men and women produce different forms of art, but the form of this sister's story is also especially characterized by its irregularity. Her narrative of events fails to follow the linear order Pierre expects, and her voice, like Isabel's handwriting, becomes "very strange," in this case "hoarse": "Don't talk that way," her young listener objects, "you frighten me so, aunt" (7:75, 76). The main difference between the male and the female artists' versions of the same story is also revealing. Whereas Ralph's painting had shown only the effects of the young Frenchwoman on the elder Pierre, only implied her centrality in the man's life, Dorothea brings her into the narrative proper, as a powerful presence in her own right, even though she apparently does not know the woman's name and must admit that "no one on this side of the water certainly knew her history." To tell the story of a woman is thus to tell of unnamed otherness, of a poor outcast "emigrant" who has previously found no home in androcentric stories and whose fate yet remains a mystery: her story is "not in any little book," and as to her destiny, "there is no telling" (7:74, 76).

Pierre's revived memory of his aunt's story prepares him at last to hear Isabel's and even, once the fateful interview is under way, "to sit passively and receive its marvelous droppings into his soul, however long the pauses" (7:119). The latter phrasing refers to the by now familiar irregularity of this sister's gynocentric story, which is told in fits and starts and fraught with passionate "offshootings" and speculations that cause her "continually to go aside from the straight line of her narration" (7:121, 136). For the newly attentive and sympathetic Pierre, the erratic delivery of Isabel's narrative testifies to her highly emotional state, her lack of sophistication, and her otherworldliness; and the mysterious chronology of unnamed places and people that makes up her story seems to fill in the last pieces of the family puzzle. "Did not this," he detects in her "first recall-able recollection" of "a strange, French-like country," "surprisingly corre-spond with certain natural inferences to be drawn from his Aunt Doro-thea's account of the disappearance of the French young lady," after her liaison with his father (7: 137)? As in the previous story incidents, however, Pierre fails to perceive the larger significance of his sister's narrative or his own unwitting complicity in the history that has excluded her story.

"The Story of Isabel," as Melville so dignifies it in his chapter titles, marshals all of the suggestions and partial evidence introduced in the three previous story-incidents into an extended allegory that reveals, once and for all, the outcast status of woman in relation to patriarchal language. Isabel's earliest recollections, for example, are of a childhood virtually bereft of language, a lack that rendered her functionally invisible and inaudible. The unnamed strangers who had charge of her "seldom or never spoke" to the child, and "no name; no scrawled or written thing; no book, was in the house" to inform her of "its past history" or her own (7:115). Having no paternal name is thus equated with having no identity, no rightful place in the human family.[12] It was a long time indeed, Isabel recalls, before she became "sensible" of herself as "something human" (7: 122), and that task is imaged both in terms of having to travel from one country to another—from her mother's to her father's—and of having to learn to speak the father's language: "I have, I know not what sort of vague remembrances of at one time . . . chattering in two different . . . languages; one of which waned in me as the other and latter grew. . . . gradually displacing the former" (7:116–17). The first result of these vari-ous displacements seems to have been something close to madness, per-haps schizophrenia, for she tells of being incarcerated in a house full of "strangely demented people," where "hand-clappings, shrieks, howls, laughter, blessings, prayers, oaths, hymns, and all audible confusions is-su[ed] from all the chambers." The loss of self-control implicit in such linguistic chaos—the loss of the ability to control one's identity, one's story—is further emphasized by Melville's use of a second-story meta-phor: Isabel had been "lodged up-stairs in a little room" with the "door . . . locked" (7:120).

Having had no proper or common names for her experience, Isabel cannot in her present narrative explain her incarceration or her retrieval from the madhouse, which was but an early way station in her allegorical quest for a socially acceptable, that is, paternally sanctioned, identity. That she was retrieved by "strangers" (7:121) (instead of, for example, initiating her own escape) establishes and foreshadows the outcast daughter's dependent status in her father's country, her various roles as visitor and observer (7:122), foster child (7:122–24), and hired girl (7:125) during her "unavoidable displacements and migrations from one house to another" as she grew older (7:153). The beginning of the end of her quest came when she discovered her father's name, "the talismanic word—Glendinning," and the power encoded in it (7:147). Melville here heightens the allegorical nature of Isabel's story by making her discovery and decoding of her father's name a dark parody of female language acquisition in patriarchal culture. Isabel had been given a handkerchief accidentally left by her father during one of his occasional visits to her foster family after he had learned of her whereabouts. Unknown to her foster mother, who had been paid to keep such knowledge from the child, it had been embroidered in one corner with the name *Glendinning*, in "small . . . faded" letters. After her father's death, Isabel had ironed the handkerchief into a small book shape, with the contraband name, her only paternal legacy, "invisibly buried in the heart of it." It was "like opening a book and turning over many blank leaves," the sister tells the brother who had inherited their "father's fastidiously picked and decorous library" (7:6), "before I came to the mysterious writing, which I knew should be one day read by me, without direct help from any one. Now I resolved to learn my letters, and learn to read, in order that of myself I might learn the meaning of those faded characters. No other purpose . . . did I have in learning then to read. . . . I soon mastered the alphabet, and went on to spelling, and by-and-by to reading, and at last to the complete deciphering of the talismanic word—Glendinning" (7:146–47).

Thus Isabel is portrayed as having to acquire, on the sly, a language that is not considered rightfully hers so she can establish her identity and finally tell her story in words that will be heard.[13] Melville is equally insistent, however, on the idea that what he presents as the father's "faded" language is inadequate to express all the "truths" a woman has to tell. Proper names—nouns—do not seem to suit Isabel's purpose, for example, for she undoes the unique or proper meanings of many words, substituting for common nouns subjective paraphrases: "four-footed creatures" instead of any specific names of animals (7:114); "tree-like things" for what appear to have been ship masts (7:117); "dumb-like men" and "ignorant-looking men" for those who might otherwise have been called attendants or overseers in the madhouse (7:119–20). At first glance, Melville's attention to such stylistic details might seem merely the result of his intent to depict Isabel as a nonnative speaker whose knowledge of the common English names for things is still limited. Later in her story, however, he makes it clear that in her presocialized state, that is, before she understood the power conferred by the talismanic word *Glendinning*, the young woman had had no innate desire to know her father by a unique name: "I did not ask the name of my father; for I could have had no motive to hear him named, except to individualize the person who was so peculiarly kind to me; and individualized in that way he already was, since he was generally called [by her foster family] *the gentleman*, and sometimes *my father*" (7:145).

Isabel's initial lack of interest in proper names suggests that the difference between her innate and her socialized views of language is much greater than between, say, French and English. Even in her present narrative, she still chafes at certain words, names, nouns that would delimit or objectify the subjectivity she insists upon, as when she prohibits Pierre from using the word *madhouse*: "Thou must, ere this, have suspected what manner of place this . . . was. . . . But do not speak the word to me. That word has never passed my lips. . . . The word is wholly unendurable to me" (7:121). More often, she subverts the prescribed order of patriarchal language to express more adequately, apparently, her own perceptions of reality. She creates verb-nouns—*unknowingness* (7:117); *smilingness, whirlingness, bewilderingness* (7:122); adjective compounds—*sparkling-gay* (7:117), *submerged-freighted* (7:159); and a variety of other irregular grammatical combinations—*life-thoughts* (7:114); *a heart friend* (7:125); *soul-composed, bodily-wandering* (7:120); *up-pointed cloud-shapes* (7:118); the *out-lookings of his eyes* (7:124).[14]

Stylistic irregularities such as these implicitly challenge the dominant forms of discursive order, but they also foreshadow the "other" language Isabel ultimately uses to tell the sequel to her story. Although the outcast daughter has had to learn the father's language so as to obtain an audience, she has also eventually recovered what she proudly insists is her mother's language, a nonverbal—or antiverbal—mode of communication that, like Cooper, Poe, and Hawthorne before him, Melville images as "music." In the course of her narrative, Isabel tells of acquiring a guitar that resonates to her own low "singings and . . . murmurings" and that communicates a realm of meaning "beyond all telling" (7:125): "Not in words can it be spoken" (7:126). The source of this other language, Isabel would have her brother understand, is "the word *Isabel*," which she finds engraved in the interior of the guitar and which she "instinctively" knows to be the name of her mother. The guitar with the mother's name in its "hidden heart" (7:148) thus symbolizes a very different linguistic system than that symbolized by the handkerchief-book with the father's name "invisibly buried in the heart of it," and the daughter does indeed speak in two languages, gynocentric and androcentric.

Small wonder, then, that Pierre's responses during the various stages of Isabel's story—and his actions thereafter—confirm the impossibility of her whole story ever being made public. The receipt of Isabel's letter, which precipitates his encounter with a series of stories told by and about outcast women (Aunt Dorothea's story about Isabel's mother, Isabel's story about herself and her sequel about her mother, and Isabel's story about Delly Ulver, the seduced-and-abandoned farm girl Isabel has befriended), seems to Pierre to have been a "great life-revolution" (7:225). Reading the letter had first caused him to reject outright the patriarchal ordering of his world views: "His whole previous moral being was overturned, and . . . for him the fair structure of the world must . . . be entirely rebuilded again, from the lowermost corner stone up" (7:87). Later, after hearing the first installment of Isabel's story and being moved, for the first time in his life, to gynocentric thinking—"Now all his ponderings, however excursive, wheeled round Isabel as their center" (7:140)—the young author had similarly rejected one-sided male-authored fictions, novels and dramas, whose "false, inverted attempts at systematizing" life, he now believed, had no longer any power over him (7:141). After hearing the whole of his sister's story and pledging to acknowledge her as his equal in the eyes of the world, he even inspires Isabel to "take no terms from the common world, but . . . make terms to it, and grind [her] fierce rights out of it!" The latter phrasing would imply that Pierre has finally seen to the heart of the problem and is ready to reject not only androcentric social and literary forms but even the androcentric language by which such forms maintain their cultural dominance. That revolutionary phrasing is Isabel's, however, not Pierre's: he swears to "crush the disdainful world" if it will not acknowledge her as his equal, and she interprets his oath to mean that she shall be free from the androcentric "terms" that have delegitimized her solely on the grounds of her sex (7:160). The point of this exchange is that Isabel can imagine an end to androcentric language, or at least the possibility of another form of public discourse, but that Pierre cannot, for by the time this dialogue occurs, Pierre has repeatedly failed to imagine new terms and thus, any new narrative form, and for the remainder of the novel those foreshadowings are substantiated.

It is significant, for example, that after reading Isabel's letter and while waiting for his meeting with her, Pierre had tried "to imagine to himself the scene which was destined to ensue. But imagination utterly failed him here" (7:111). Having lived so long in "the repose of a wide story, tenanted only by himself," he cannot imagine a second story, and even when he hears it and is at least partially moved by it, he still tries to translate it into his own terms, to make it conform to more traditional literary models: "He strove to condense her mysterious haze into some definite and comprehensible shape" (7:136). The "clew-defying mysteriousness of Isabel's narration . . . put[s] on a repelling aspect to our Pierre," and to make the otherness of her story less repellant, he even goes so far as to rename certain of her experiences. "Isabel had . . . vague impressions of herself crossing the sea;—*re*-crossing, emphatically thought Pierre" (7:137), referring to his assumption that she had been conceived in America, had been carried to France *in utero*, and had later returned to her father's country. (In this instance, he negotiates between Aunt Dorothea's story and Isabel's, thus formulating his own.)

Given these foreshadowings, it comes as no surprise that Pierre's final solution to the problem of how to include his sister in his life text is by the "nominal conversion of a sister into a wife" (7:177), that is, by acknowledging her identity, not on her own terms, as a sister, but in terms the common world will find acceptable. Neither is it surprising that he cannot finally tell a story that will do justice to his sister, that will bring her "new, or at least miserably neglected Truth to the world." The book he tries to write tells not her story but his, "directly plagiarized from his own experiences" (7:302), and that it is only a partial rendering of the human story is suggested by its fragmentation (7:302–3); it comes to no "confirmed form or conclusion at all" (7:338). Thus, although Pierre has consciously rejected all inherited literary models—novels and dramas, the *Inferno* and *Hamlet*—he unconsciously replicates them because he can imagine no new literary form to take their place: "Like knavish cards, the leaves of all great books were covertly packed. He was but packing one set the more; and that a very poor jaded set and pack indeed" (7:339).

What Pierre himself believes to be his "life-revolution," then, is never more than half effected, and the halving imagery Melville uses throughout the novel is especially useful in explaining the source of Pierre's imaginative failure. The shock of reading Isabel's letter, for example, had left the young man "half-lifeless" (7:65). During her narrative, when she had moved from the part of the story that dealt with their father to the part that dealt with her mother, Pierre's face had saddened into "a look of half-regret" and "a half-smile" (7:147), and what he perceived as the incomprehensible otherness of Isabel's sequel had caused him to halve her story, just as he had halved her letter: striving "to dispel the mystic feeling" and "to beat away all thoughts," he had postponed hearing the remainder of her narrative until the following evening (7:128–29). Such phrasings are reminiscent of Poe's depictions of men with "half-formed" thoughts, who are incapable of perceiving "but one meaning," but there are even closer correspondences to be found in Hawthorne's portrayal of Arthur Dimmesdale's divided mind. In *The Scarlet Letter*, acknowledging the outcast woman and the illegitimate daughter would bring new life to the young man's "half-torpid system," but Dimmesdale is never more than half-convinced that he should make that acknowledgment because to do so, he would have to reveal the falseness of the public image of the sacrosanct (church) father. Thus his moral capacity—his better half—is held captive by what Hawthorne sees as the "long hereditary habit" of patriarchal loyalty, a situation which Hester Prynne sees all too clearly. "What has thou to do with all these iron men and their opinions?" she berates him during the forest interview. "They have kept thy better part in bondage too long already!"

Pierre's moral dilemma is analogous, although Melville's emphasis falls more directly on the effects of such a long hereditary habit on the male author's creative faculties. "I will no more have a father" (7:87), Pierre swears after first learning that he has an illegitimate sister, but "the idea of his father tyrannized over his imagination" (7:104). The receipt of Isabel's letter overturns a number of Pierre's complacencies and gives him new insights into his world. In each instance, however, he suppresses the newfound private truth with a public fiction. He understands at last why the two portraits of his father convey such different expressions, but his loyalty to his dead father's pristine public image leads him first to turn the chair-portrait to the wall and finally to burn it, just as he will fabricate a fictitious marriage rather than publicize Isabel's shameful paternity. By such actions, he symbolically replicates the aesthetic choices of his cousin-artist Ralph, who had suppressed his own too-true art according to the strictures of male bonding. Pierre also comes to understand that his mother will never accept Isabel or her story because that lady had been "bred . . . under the sole influence of hereditary forms and world-usages" (7:89). Consequently, he convinces himself that his "fictitious alliance" with Isabel (7:175), although it will turn his mother against him, will at least preserve her "blessed memory" of his father (7:92), and he indulges in what he believes to be a "charity of cruelty" toward her (7:183). If the oxymoron recalls Franklin's artful renaming of manly "virtues," there is good reason. The public fiction Pierre authors in deference to his father's memory participates in the long-standing literary tradition handed down by America's first literary fathers: "Would'st thou," he asks, when he reveals his plan to Isabel, "be willing for thee and me to piously deceive others, for both their and our united good?" (7:189).

There is yet another reason for Pierre's failure to author a life text that will tell the whole truth at last, although it is related to the idea of his father's tyrannical hold over his imagination because it results from the fashion of manly thinking that is Pierre's hidden legacy. Pierre's decision to champion Isabel, to protect her, is partly motivated by his physical attraction to her and his unconscious desire to possess her sexually. After his first interview with her, for example, he "felt that never, never would he be able to embrace Isabel with the mere brotherly embrace; while the thought of any other caress, which took hold of any domesticness, was entirely vacant from his uncontaminated soul, for it had never consciously intruded there"(7:142). Although for the remainder of the novel Pierre has moments of "self-revelation" as to his true feelings (7:192), he repeatedly represses such self-knowledge to preserve a more honorable self-image, just as his father had suppressed the sensual image of himself in favor of the portrait that revealed only his "best expression." By his nominal conversion of a sister into a wife, then, Pierre acts consciously in his father's best interest and unconsciously—or at most, half-consciously—in his own: he secures the right to live with Isabel, to embrace her openly, under cover of "terms" the common world will condone.

Pierre's incest with Isabel is never certainly revealed in this novel, but his possession of her by his fiction-making, to do with as he desires, is established by Melville's recurring use of jailing imagery. Leaving the "old home of his fathers" with Isabel and Delly Ulver in tow and intending to make a new life for them all, Pierre believes he has created a new role for himself as champion and protector of outcast women (7:3). His first act upon arriving in the city, however, is to place them in jail—which he renames as an "office" to make it appear more hospitable (7:235)—while

he searches for better lodgings. Later, in the small apartment he has chosen for them, he houses them in separate rooms, with a locked door
between his and theirs (7:297), and when Lucy arrives to share their lodg-
ing, herself already imprisoned in an ideal love for Pierre and pursued by
two other would-be "champions" (7:325), her brother and Glen Stanly,
Pierre fights for possession of her as well and locks her, symbolically, in
the same room with Isabel and Delly (7:326)—for their combined "protection." Such acts of physical confinement are the external manifestation of
Pierre's androcentric thinking. He determines the physical and conceptual
space "his" women shall have, and Isabel does indeed become just another
of his possessions, imprisoned alike with the lady and the farm girl in
Pierre's limited and limiting concept of "woman."

The result of what Pierre believes to be his "life-revolution" thus turns
out to be merely an unconscious reenactment of the same "power over"
mentality he had inherited from his fathers, and the effect of such immutable thought processes is, for Isabel, exactly the reverse of what Pierre had
consciously intended. "All words are thine, Isabel," he promises her,
"words and worlds with all their containings, shall be slaves to thee"
(7:313). Once she is saddled with the fictitious name of "Mrs. Pierre Glendinning," however, Isabel becomes little more than a slave. As a dependent
wife, she is no longer free to earn her own living, and the meager earnings
of her "husband" provide her with only the barest necessities. Denied a
socially useful livelihood and deprived of the large and varied community
that had been hers in the country village, Isabel must devote all her energy
to attending to Pierre's wants, and even in this she is limited, for her
offerings are usually rebuffed. Finally, as a storyteller herself, Isabel fares
no better than she does as a "wife." Her continued life as "Mrs. Pierre
Glendinning" is conditional on her never making her story public—his
story takes precedence—and Pierre even denies her the status of coauthor
of his book. When both Isabel and Lucy offer to be his "amanuenses;—
not in mere copying, but in the original writing," he rejects their assistance in the same manly fashion of combative metaphor that had characterized his speech in the opening pages of this novel: "Impossible! I fight
a duel in which all seconds are forbid" (7:349).

The suggestion of male and female coauthorship, however brief, is a
provocative addition to a novel depicting a male author's search for a
narrative form that will give the sister's story equal status with the brother's, and Pierre is shown to be all the more damned for rejecting that
solution and continuing to author, instead, mere one-sided fictions.

Rather than give up his sole authority and participate in the creation of a new book that would indeed contain "original writing," he blindly continues in the tradition of his fathers and becomes a plagiarist, recreating prior fictions only to place himself at their center. By renaming Isabel his wife, for example, he merely replicates the family his-story authorized by his father, a life text from which the sister has been omitted. He even plagiarizes from the sister's own story, for the fictitious life he creates for Isabel stands as a dark parody of her previous narrative psychodrama, with Pierre now as author, producer, director, and star. Isabel's new life in the city parallels her earlier migration to her father's country and her attempts to decipher the social and linguistic codes authorized by patriarchy. The madhouse and the linguistic chaos she experienced there are recast as the jailhouse in which Pierre himself incarcerates her and in which she is assaulted by a "combined babel of persons and voices" (7:240). He retrieves her, but only to reenact the various supporting and subordinate roles she has already rehearsed, and just as she once had to decipher the father's language from the little handkerchief-book so as to be able to translate her story into his words, so now she must spend her time "mastering the chirographical incoherencies of [Pierre's] manuscripts, with a view to eventually copying them out in a legible hand for the printer" (7:282). In such ways, a gynocentric story is transformed into an androcentric one, and the transformation parodies the literary reform that authentic coauthorship would have effected.

By the end of Melville's novel, Pierre's unconscious social conditioning has invaded and poisoned his conscious, everyday life as surely as the actual poison that he uses to kill himself. He has consistently failed to communicate any but half-truths to the various readers of his life text and his book. As a result, all of his earlier good intentions regarding his sister have come to nothing, and his book, which remains unfinished, has already been rejected by his publishers as a "blasphemous" plagiarism, "filched" from his literary forefathers (7:356). Confronted with his many failures and yet still unwilling to accept his own culpability, Pierre repeatedly turns his anger outward in a frenzy of self-defense. He turns against Isabel, for example, and even his Aunt Dorothea, now rejecting both—all—sisters' stories on the traditional grounds that they were "anything but legitimately conclusive" and had seduced him from his true calling (7:353). By this point in his "mental confusions" (7:354), though, the young author is equally alienated from male-authored story forms—in this case, Fred Tartan's and Glen Stanly's letter accusing him of deceiving their cherished Lucy. Pierre can go neither forward nor backward in his search for a literary form that will tell the truth at last, because in Melville's novel, truth is finally equated with self-revelation. In the last pages, Pierre chooses to kill his cousin Glen and then himself rather than admit to his various deceptions. What he sees as the ultimate self-defense Melville depicts as the inevitable self-destruction that comes of androcentric thinking: the young male author's narcissistic proliferation of self-centered, self-serving fictions attests to the sterility of his literary imagination and results at last in personal and professional suicide.

The jail cell that provides the setting for the novel's last scene substantiates the many foreshadowing images of confinement that have come before and reveals, once and for all, the real culprit—or culprits—in this American tale. As Pierre had once momentarily realized, "men are jailers; jailers of themselves; and in Opinion's world ignorantly hold their noblest part a captive to their vilest" (7:91). The jail cell is an image of Pierre's limited and limiting imagination, constrained to exclusive androcentric thinking by generations of "men" who have politicized all language, all stories, in their own behalf. It is also the place where Pierre, Isabel, and Lucy—and all hope for the broken family that is America—must die, for the psychological limitations that constrain Pierre militate against any equitable social or literary reform. By the end of this novel, the American brother still insists on the precedence of his story over any other, and the result of such monstrous narcissism is a life text that, in suppressing half of the American story, must come to a false and precipitate conclusion: "Here, then, is the untimely, timely end," Pierre berates himself, moments before his suicide, "Life's last chapter well stitched into the middle!" Thus for all his halfhearted attempts to find a narrative form that will bring the "new, or at least miserably neglected Truth to the world," Pierre finally capitulates to his father's tyrannical hold over his imagination and authors just one more in a long history of literary monsters.

Presented with such final images of failure and devastation, readers must of course wonder to what extent Melville intended this novel to be self-revelatory, how closely he identified with his young author-hero, and whether he felt *Pierre* to be as limited and malformed as Pierre's own book. Scholars have long recognized the similarities between Melville's life and Pierre's—the genteel family backgrounds, the early literary successes, and the falls from popularity and severely reduced circumstances attendant on both authors' narrative quests after the everlasting elusiveness of Truth.[15] Neither can there be any doubt that this novel's repeated satiric attacks on contemporary publishing practices, shortsighted readers, and restrictive psychosocial entanglements, ostensibly on Pierre's behalf, come from an author who had frequently expressed his own anger at being "so pulled hither & thither by circumstances." "Dollars damn me," Melville had written to Hawthorne in June of 1851, while working on *Moby-Dick.* "What I feel most moved to write, that is banned,—it will not pay. Yet, altogether, write the *other* way I cannot. So the product is a final hash, and all my books are botches."[16]

Taken by itself, this last statement would seem an especially tempting bit of evidence for arguing that, in the book that followed, Melville did indeed identify with Pierre and with the young man's literary failure. There is further biographical evidence, however, to suggest that between the close of *Moby-Dick* and the beginning of *Pierre*, Melville became optimistic about his capacity as an author to grow, to change, and to write books that were not botches. Five months after the above letter to Hawthorne, for example, he would write his friend again, jubilantly predicting that "Leviathan is not the biggest fish;—I have heard of Krakens": "Lord, when shall we be done growing? As long as we have anything more to do, we have done nothing. . . . The very fingers that now guide this pen are not precisely the same that just took it up and put it on this paper. Lord, when shall we be done changing?"[17] Despite his recurring periods of despair in the years to come, despite the poor reception of *Pierre* from its publication up to the present day, and despite Melville's obvious plagiarism from many of his own past experiences in writing the novel, the Melville who created Pierre clearly did not identify with him. Or perhaps it would be more accurate to say that he no longer identified with him, that Pierre represented a former self, one whom Melville felt he had surpassed in self-knowledge and in literary skill, and whose failings could thus be delineated with greater objectivity and candor. The persona he uses to narrate his character's most private thoughts, for example, frequently reveals "things that [Pierre] knew not" (7:107), and the distinction between narrator and character is repeatedly stressed: "The thoughts we here indite as Pierre's are to be very carefully discriminated from those we indite concerning him" (7:167). "Easy for me to slyly hide . . . things, and always put him before the eye as immaculate," the narrator says, but "I am more frank with Pierre than the best men are with themselves . . . therefore you see his weakness" (7:108).

Pierre's main weakness, his inability to break the hold of old hereditary forms on his imagination and thus to author a truly new book, is also one that Melville specifically and emphatically disclaimed as soon as he had finished writing this novel. Discussing publication plans with Richard Bentley, in a letter dated April 16, 1852, Melville used the word *new* five times, claiming that *Pierre* was not only a *"new book,"* but that with it he was embarking on an entirely "new field of productions." Granted, that letter was intended to reassure his publisher (and probably himself, partly) that if "nothing has been made on the old books, may not something be made out of the new?"[18] Nevertheless, having just written such a detailed indictment against the harmful social and psychological effects of "old books," his insistence on newness here suggests that he had in mind far larger issues than mere self-promotion. It is especially intriguing to note that having just attributed Pierre's personal and professional suicide to his inability to write any but androcentric stories, Melville hoped to begin his own new field of productions by writing a story with a woman as its central character.

On July 6, 1852, he wrote to Hawthorne about a conversation he had had with the lawyer John Clifford. The conversation had begun with their talking about "the great patience, & endurance, & resignedness" of sailors' wives, whose husbands were away for such long periods of time, and had led to Clifford's telling him the true story of one such deserted wife, Agatha Hatch Robertson.[19] Between July and October, Melville wrote to Hawthorne several times concerning his "very great interest" in "the story of Agatha," first suggesting a possible treatment of the material and urging his friend to write the woman's story ("this thing lies very much in a vein, with which you are peculiarly familiar") and eventually deciding to write it himself and asking for Hawthorne's suggestions.[20] James R. Mellow has speculated that Melville was hoping for a collaboration, and given Melville's flirtation with the image of the coauthored text in *Pierre*, the speculation makes a good deal of sense: the new production would have been coauthored, if not by a man and a woman, at least by specialists in man-centered and woman-centered stories, and it would thus overcome the problem of one-sidedness that had plagued authors like Pierre.[21]

If Melville ever actually completed the story of Agatha, the manuscript has not survived.[22] His eventual literary successes or failures following *Pierre*, however, are not my province here. His letters show that in planning *Pierre* and in the months immediately following its publication, Melville felt that he had surpassed his previous productions and outgrown the

former self on whom Pierre Glendinning seems modeled. The question
that remains, then, is in what ways, if any, does Melville's book differ from
Pierre's, and one set of evidence suggests that Melville's narrative is different in the same ways that Isabel's is different. That is, the formal elements
of this novel are much closer to those of the sister's truly unconventional
story than to any of the brother's tradition-bound fictions.

One noticeable similarity is that Melville's narrative, like Isabel's (and
like Aunt Dorothea's), follows no traditional or strictly logical order. Not
only is it nonlinear, but nonlinearity and irregularity are self-consciously
stressed as principles of composition. "I shall follow the endless, winding
way" among Pierre's innermost thoughts, the narrator tells us early on,
"careless whither I be led, reckless where I land." The task is presented as
one of letting the subject dictate the narrative form, rather than the other
way around; of revealing Pierre's character as fully and truthfully as possible, flaws and all, rather than making it conform to social and literary
ideals. Later, introducing a digression on the subject of "Young America
in Literature" and a flashback titled "Pierre, as a Juvenile Author, Reconsidered," the narrator again stresses how little he cares for conventional or
predictable narrative forms. He prefaces the first of these digressions with
a brief description of the two major "modes of writing history," one of
which sets down "all contemporaneous circumstances, facts, and events
. . . contemporaneously," and the other, which includes only those phenomena that the preconceived "stream of the narrative shall dictate." But,
he insists, "I elect neither of these; I am careless of either" (7:244). Thus,
as has been clear from the novel's early pages, this "history goes forward
and backward, as occasion calls" (7:54), and the resulting narrative form
accomplishes what the sister's had accomplished and the brother's had
not.

In Pierre's book, for example, Melville presents a parody of patriarchal
"history": his-story, with the emphasis on "his." Pierre fails to author a
new book because he cannot free himself from the psychosocial conditioning that has trained him to see reality through the narrow filter of exclusive self-interest. Thus his book has only one character, the hero Vivia,
and the lack of genuine fellow-feeling, of human interconnectedness, results in a narrative form that is no form at all but merely fragments of
isolated soliloquies (7:302–3). "The Story of Isabel," though told in emotional fits and starts that cause her "continually to go aside from the
straight line of her narration," nevertheless is much more interconnected.
Despite her many experiences of displacement, she insists on giving her

story a social context, going forward and backward as occasion calls and memory allows, and surrounding herself with the many characters and "families" who helped shape her life. Melville does the same in *Pierre*, going back and forth in time so as to connect the story of his young hero with other stories—his grandfather's, father's, mother's, sister's; his cousin Glen's, Aunt Dorothea's, and cousin Ralph's; Lucy's, her Aunt Tartan's, and her brother Fred's; the Reverend Falsgrave's and the Miss Pennies'; Dates's and Delly Ulver's; and in the city, those of his childhood friend Charlie Millthorpe and the inscrutable Plotinus Plinlimmon. Like Isabel's story, then, *Pierre* is an unorthodox "family" history, and unlike Pierre, Melville omits virtually no one from the text. On a more symbolic level, the novel's new narrative form, with its emphasis on extended family, rewrites American history—and reforms American society—so as to legitimize the many characters excluded by patriarchal paradigms: the illegitimate, the unmarried, the poor, the workers, the failed or unknown artists, and especially, the "sisters," who are the lowest common denominator in all of these categories.

It is not surprising, then, that *Pierre*'s first reviewers objected to the novel most heatedly because of its unorthodox form, which one writer accurately and angrily perceived to be an attack on "the very foundations of society."[23] In their objections, however, they showed themselves to be just the sort of tradition-bound, complacent, self-defensive readers Melville was criticizing. "Mr. Melville may have constructed his story upon some new theory of art to a knowledge of which we have not yet transcended," the reviewer for the *Literary World* complained. He "evidently has not constructed it according to the established principles of the only theory accepted by us until assured of a better."[24] In particular, such reviewers showed themselves to be very like Pierre, who "strove to condense [Isabel's] mysterious haze into some definite and comprehensible shape" and who liked to believe that the irregularity of her narrative was "entirely unintended" (7:136)—that is, if she had been more familiar with or more skilled in literary conventions, she would have told a better, more immediately comprehensible story. "What the book means, we know not," another reviewer wrote of *Pierre*, and in his attempt to assign it meaning, he too tried to condense it into some definite "shape": "To save it from almost utter worthlessness, it must be called a prose poem, and even then, it might be supposed to emanate from a lunatic hospital." The charge of madness here provides yet another link between the perceived otherness of Isabel's story and of Melville's. Just as the former had been judged "an imaginative delirium" (7:354), a confused jumble of "wild idiosyncrasies" (7:136), so the latter was judged to be the "craziest fiction extant," its style "disfigured," "nonsensical and ungrammatical," marred by "incoherencies of thought, infelicities of language"—in sum, "a very mad book."[25]

The final similarity between Melville's narrative and Isabel's has to do with their shared "infelicities of language." Like the woman storyteller, *Pierre*'s narrator frequently subverts the traditional order of grammar and syntax.[26] He turns verbs into nouns—*outgushing* (7:65), *protectingness* (7:140), *unthinkingness* (7:136); adjectives into nouns—*unidentifiableness* (7:89), *impassionedments* (7:142), *unstimulatedness* (7:227); and nouns into adjectives—*fresh-foliaged* (7:68), *poniarded* (7:70), *unsistered* (7:142). He turns old nouns into new ones—*diamondness* (7:4), *gladiatorianism* (7:226) —and he creates altogether new combinational word forms: *thought-veins* (7:14), *music-moan* (7:136), *death-milk* (7:360), *daughter-proud* (7:26), *eye-expanded* (7:68), *infamy-engendering* (7:179), *soul-shivering* (7:305), *hate-shod* (7:357), *leapingly-acknowledging* (7:66), *not-yet-repressed* (7:236). Again, the novel's first reviewers recognized Melville's attempt at newness, but again, they condemned him for it. The *American Whig Review* complained that he had "torn our poor language into tatters," and *Godey's Lady's Book* went so far as to offer a clever "imitation of his style": "We have listened to its outbreathing of sweet-swarming sounds, and their melodious, mournful, wonderful, and unintelligible melodiousness has 'dropped like pendulous, glittering icicles,' with soft-ringing silveriness, upon our never-to-be-delighted-sufficiently organs of hearing; and, in the insignificant significancies of that deftly-stealing and wonderfully-serpentining melodiousness, we have found an infinite, unbounded, inexpressible mysteriousness of nothingness."[27]

What these early and seemingly astute readers failed to recognize is the symbolic significance of such linguistic otherness. Isabel had had to make up words to tell a story that had never been told before, and her story thus stands as an implicit criticism of the androcentric language of her father's country, the language that is always self-referential for brothers but that renders sisters invisible and inaudible. Melville's foreign-sounding words serve the same critical function, in a greater variety of ways. They too lay bare America's family secrets, not just the sisters' suppressed stories but the mother's secret pain over her husband's youthful philandering—her "hate-grief unrelenting"—and the father's secret remorse over disowning his daughter—his "sin-grief irreparable" (7:287). They also reveal the larger problem, the extent to which thought and behavior in the father's country are dictated by patriarchal paradigms, bequeathed by a succession of cultural fathers. Often, for example, Melville transforms the proper names of literary forefathers into adjectives that demonstrate those men's qualifying and restrictive influence on subsequent generations. Early on, Pierre had hoped to escape the fate of modern "man," who had been "bleached and beaten in Baconian fulling-mills" (7:198). Once embarked on his "new" life in the city, however, he finds such escape impossible. His confreres at the Church of the Apostles, whose "immemorial popular name" has been "transferred to the dwellers therein" (7:268), have allowed themselves to become physically and psychologically malnourished by "Shellian dietings" (7:299) and "Kantian Categories" (7:300), and Pierre himself finally capitulates to past influences and becomes, in the tradition of Shakespeare, a plagiarist of dead men's writings. As the narrator had pointed out earlier, *Hamlet* "is but Egyptian Memnon, Montaignized . . . for . . . Shak[e]speare had his fathers too" (7:135).

Since his main task in the novel is to reveal the inner life of Pierre and the cultural influences that shaped his thought processes, Melville's most frequent invention of new words occurs when the narrator must describe the young man's responses to the new situation in which he finds himself. At times, for example, it would appear that new words are needed to describe the effect of the sister's otherness on the brother who has no names for her "nameless fascination." After hearing the first part of her story, he sits "motionless and bending over, as a tree-transformed and mystery-laden visitant, caught and fast bound in some necromancer's garden" (7:128). Tellingly, he tries to dispel "that night's never-to-be-forgotten scene" from his mind, tries to drive off "all intrudings of thoughtfulness" regarding his "new-found sister," and burdened with a new feeling of "life-weariness," he wishes her back into "the wonder-world from which she had so slidingly emerged" (7:129). The source of Pierre's problem is, of course, that as a young man, he has been conditioned to act out of self-interest, and Melville exposes this behavioral paradigm in the narrator's repeated use of "self-" constructions during scenes of Pierre's intense but ever-limited introspection: *self-concealment* (7:105) and *self-interest* (7:106) before his first meeting with Isabel; *self-conceit* (7:136), *self-sacrificing*, *self-disdainful* (7:137), *self-insinuated* (7:138) between the two interviews; *self-renunciation* (7:176), *self-complacent* (7:177), *self-suggested* (7:178), and *self-upbraiding* (7:181) to describe the thought processes that led to his resolve to leave Saddle Meadows.

The many formal similarities between Melville's novel and Isabel's story thus suggest that Melville intended to write the new book that Pierre's psychosocial conditioning had prevented him from writing. One last issue that needs to be addressed, however, concerns Melville's portrayal of his women characters. Again, he seems to have intended not only to represent women in a new way but especially to expose the way in which traditional—male-authored—literary forms have misrepresented them. As we have seen, the idea that men are trained to use set forms of discourse when the subject is women is broached in the novel's opening scene, in which Pierre explains that he calls Lucy an angel because it was ever the manly fashion to do so. In the second chapter, however, Melville's narrative persona shows himself to be at odds with that fashion.

He begins by trying to describe Lucy on her picnic outing with Pierre, but his prose rapidly becomes inflated with preposterous superlatives and classical allusions—"her hair was Danae's, spangled with Jove's shower" (7:24). He eventually compares her not only to angels but to goddesses, empresses, queens—until he begins to realize that he has been led into a "rather irregular sort of writing." "We began by talking of a certain young lady that went out riding with a certain youth; and yet find ourselves," according to "immemorial usage," conducted "among mighty Queens, and all other creatures of high degree." The points of his argument—and the newness of his own representation—soon become clear. First, "immemorial usage" demands that male authors give a certain predetermined and highly artificial form to their texts when writing about women, and the word *irregular* suggests that such malformed texts are mere parodies of the genuinely irregular (*un*conventional) forms that women would use if they were to tell their own stories. We are told, for example, that Lucy herself "would . . . shrink from all this noise and clatter! She is bragged of, but not brags." Next, we are shown that this storyteller is not as unthinking in these matters as Pierre, who has already shown himself to be a complacent slave to hereditary forms. Once the narrator realizes that he has allowed his imagination to be "bound" by literary conventions, he struggles against them—"Never shall I get down the vile inventory!"— and finally decides to "martyrize" himself, as an author, by revealing not just "the angelical part of Lucy" but also the more mundane and not always flattering "details" of her life (7:25). He reveals her likes and dislikes, her family's strengths and weaknesses, and especially her embarrassment at having a "purse-proud" mother who is also a manipulating "match-maker" (7:27). The reader is even treated to a "germ of suspicion as to Lucy's collusion" in her mother's scheme to seduce Pierre into proposing marriage and made to witness her all too human "vexation" at her mother's blatant tactics (7:28).

The narrator's self-conscious struggle with literary conventions in this scene foregrounds Melville's criticisms of traditional narrative forms that fail to represent women as they really are, and the narrator's victory over such conventions, his choice to include details about Lucy's life that would normally have been omitted, foreshadows the novel's subsequent acts of recovery. Melville's choice to tell Isabel's story, which her father had tried to suppress, and Aunt Dorothea's, which father and male artist both had conspired to suppress, are further indications of his intent to break with what he portrays as a falsifying and inequitable literary tradition. This is not to say, however, that Melville comes across as an uncritical champion of "real" women. Rather, like Hawthorne, he seems to have had a second motive, to reveal finally the ways in which women too are held in psychological bondage in patriarchal culture. Like Pierre, for example, who is consistently portrayed as patriarchy's unwitting "victim" (7:302), the women in this novel are socialized to accept a "power over" mentality and thus unwittingly become willing participants in a sociopolitical system that ever relegates them to second-class—and second-story—status. Invariably, their highest goal is to attach themselves to a man, to live through him, to obtain his patronage and, vicariously, his power. This idea is introduced very early, in a scene in which Pierre's power-proud mother happily fantasizes about the influence she wields over her son, all the while flexing, absent-mindedly, her father's military baton (7:20). Isabel's and Lucy's competition for Pierre's attention and (ironically) protection shows them to be equally imprisoned in such ultimately self-defeating delusions of power, but the degree to which they have internalized America's man-centered value system is revealed even more suggestively in the eventual transformation and co-optation of their art. Isabel, as we have seen, forgoes her own unique style and subject and becomes a mere amanuensis, literally and figuratively a slave to man-made stories. Lucy's art is similarly denaturalized. Early in the novel the legs of her painter's easel symbolically serve as a trellis for growing vines (7:39); later, to join Pierre in the city, she must apparently sever her art from its natural sources, for the vines are cut and the artist willingly reduces herself to painting nothing but the portraits of men (7:318, 330–32). The jail imagery at the novel's end is thus as significant of these "sisters'" psychic bondage as of the brother's. At the center of the book, Pierre had placed Lucy and Isabel in jail to serve his own purposes, but in the closing scene they choose to join him there and by that choice confine themselves once and for all to social and cultural nonexistence.

In such ways *Pierre* stands as a cautionary tale, addressed to America's brothers and sisters alike. Like the narrative re-visions and reformations of Cooper, Poe, and Hawthorne, however, it also represents a more positive endeavor. By including the sisters' stories side by side with the brother's and by imagining and assuming Isabel's prelapsarian irregularities of style and subject matter, Melville demonstrated that it was still possible for American authors to deny their cultural fathers, to write new books—and to tell the whole story.

Notes

Introduction to Part I

1. Hannah Arendt, *On Revolution* (New York: Viking Press, 1965), p. 21.
2. Michael Davitt Bell, *The Development of American Romance: The Sacrifice of Relation* (Chicago: University of Chicago Press, 1980), p. 3. Two excellent reassessments of the literature of this period are Robert A. Ferguson, *Law and Letters in American Culture* (Cambridge, Mass.: Harvard University Press, 1984), and Cathy N. Davidson, *Revolution and The Word: The Rise of the Novel in America* (New York: Oxford University Press, 1986).
3. *The Writings of Thomas Jefferson*, ed. Andrew A. Lipscomb and Albert E. Bergh, 20 vols. (Washington, D.C.: Thomas Jefferson Memorial Association, 1907), 13:339–40.
4. William S. Cardell, "Circular Letter from the Secretary of the American Academy of Language and Belles Lettres," *Port Folio*, 5th ser., 11 (June 1821): 398, quoted in Dennis E. Baron, *Grammar and Good Taste: Reforming the American Language* (New Haven: Yale University Press, 1982), p. 101.
5. American Academy of Language and Belles Lettres, *Circular No. III* (New York, 1822), p. 10, quoted in Baron, *Grammar and Good Taste*, pp. 109–10.
6. For discussions of such proposals and debates, see David P. Simpson, *The Politics of American English, 1776–1850* (New York: Oxford University Press, 1986), pp. 3–121, and Baron, *Grammar and Good Taste*, pp. 7–118.
7. Noah Webster, *Dissertations on the English Language* (Boston, 1789), pp. 19–20.
8. Noah Webster, *A Compendious Dictionary of the English Language, in which Five Thousand Words are added to the number found in the best English Compends* (New Haven: Sidney's Press, 1806), p. xxii.
9. Noah Webster, "Memorial to the Legislature of New York," January 18, 1783, in *The Letters of Noah Webster*, ed. Harry R. Warfel (New York: Library Publishers, 1953), p. 6. See Richard M. Rollins, *The Long Journey of Noah Webster* (Philadelphia: University of Pennsylvania Press, 1980), pp. 34–37.
10. Noah Webster to J. Pemberton, March 15, 1790, Historical Society of Pennsylvania Archives, Philadelphia, quoted in Rollins, *Long Journey of Noah Webster*, p. 127; see ibid., pp. 131–38.
11. For a representative selection of such treatments, see Linda Kerber, *Federalists in Dissent: Imagery and Ideology in Jeffersonian America* (Ithaca, N.Y.: Cornell University Press, 1970), pp. 194, 197–99; John P. Diggins, *The Lost Soul of American Politics: Virtue, Self-Interest, and the Foundations of Liberalism* (New York: Basic

Books, 1984), esp. pp. 18–47; Albert Furtwangler, *The Authority of Publius: A Reading of the Federalist Papers* (Ithaca, N.Y.: Cornell University Press, 1984), esp. pp. 62–64; Joyce Appleby, *Capitalism and a New Social Order: The Republican Vision of the 1790's* (New York: New York University Press, 1984), pp. 14–16; and Jay Fliegelman, *Prodigals and Pilgrims: The American Revolution against Patriarchal Authority, 1750–1800* (Cambridge: Cambridge University Press, 1982), pp. 208–12.

12. Douglass G. Adair, "Experience Must Be Our Only Guide: History, Democratic Theory, and the United States Constitution," in *The Reinterpretation of Early American History: Essays in Honor of John Edwin Pomfret*, ed. Ray Allen Billington (San Marino, Calif.: Huntington Library, 1966), p. 132.

13. Martin Diamond, "Democracy and the *Federalist*: A Reconsideration of the Framers' Intents," *American Political Science Review* 53 (March 1959): 63.

14. Daniel Boorstin, *The Americans: The National Experience* (New York: Random House, 1965), p. 280. See, for example, John Pickering, *A Vocabulary, or Collection of Words and Phrases which have been supposed to be peculiar to the United States of America, to which is prefixed an Essay on the Present State of the English Language in the United States* (Boston, 1816). See also Baron, *Grammar and Good Taste*, pp. 7–40.

15. Diggins, *Lost Soul of American Politics*, p. 361; Gordon S. Wood, *The Creation of the American Republic, 1776–1787* (Chapel Hill: University of North Carolina Press, 1969), p. viii.

16. See, for example, Arthur O. Lovejoy, *Reflections on Human Nature* (Baltimore: Johns Hopkins University Press, 1961), pp. 37–65.

17. *Federalist* No. 37, in *The Federalist Papers*, ed. Clinton Rossiter (New York: New American Library, 1961), pp. 228–31. All further citations are to this edition.

18. *Federalist* No. 1, p. 36.

19. Arendt, *On Revolution*, p. 40.

20. Joseph Fauchet to the French commissioner of foreign relations, October 31, 1794, quoted in Jackson Turner Main, *The Anti-Federalists: Critics of the Constitution, 1781–1788* (New York: Norton, 1974), p. ix.

21. *Federalist* No. 37, pp. 230–31.

22. *Federalist* No. 10, p. 83.

23. Thomas Paine, *The American Crisis*, No. 1, December 23, 1776, in *The Complete Writings of Thomas Paine*, ed. Philip S. Foner, 2 vols. (New York: Citadel Press, 1945), 1:50; *Rights of Man*, Part Second, February 1792, ibid., 1:359, 354.

24. *Writings of Thomas Jefferson*, ed. Lipscomb and Bergh, 15:40, 7:459.

25. Benjamin Franklin, *The Autobiography of Benjamin Franklin*, ed. Leonard W. Labaree et al. (New Haven: Yale University Press, 1964), pp. 190–91.

26. *The Political Thought of Benjamin Franklin*, ed. Ralph Ketcham (New York: Bobbs-Merrill, 1965), pp. 400–402, 415–16.

27. For excellent analyses of the ways the Framers of the Constitution used language to turn "a necessarily ambiguous text into an effective tool of ideological conformity within a divided world," see Ferguson, *Law and Letters*, pp. 59–64, and "Ideology and the Framing of the Constitution," *Early American Literature* 22 (1987): 157–65.

28. *Federalist* No. 53, p. 331; Bernard Bailyn, *The Ideological Origins of the Ameri-*

can Revolution (Cambridge, Mass.: Harvard University Press, 1967), pp. 190 (Hamilton, quoted p. 188), 176, 182–83, 181.

29. Bailyn, *Ideological Origins*, p. 184.

30. *Federalist* No. 25, p. 187; *Federalist* No. 73, p. 442; *Federalist* No. 48, pp. 308–13; Bailyn, *Ideological Origins*, p. 181.

31. *Federalist* No. 78, pp. 465, 467; Ferguson, *Law and Letters*, pp. 62, 22 (Ferguson argues that the doctrine of judicial review, which became national policy in *Marbury* v. *Madison* in 1803, had been argued by John Adams as early as 1765 and that its validity had been generally assumed by the late 1780s and 1790s, see pp. 20–24); Arendt, *On Revolution*, pp. 200–201 (the quotation from Hamilton, also cited in Arendt, appears in *Federalist* No. 78, p. 465); John P. Roche, "The Founding Fathers: A Reform Caucus in Action," *American Political Science Review* 55 (December 1961): 815.

32. Stanley Fish, *Is There a Text in This Class? The Authority of Interpretive Communities* (Cambridge, Mass.: Harvard University Press, 1980), p. 14.

33. Lynn Hunt, *Politics, Culture, and Class in the French Revolution* (Berkeley and Los Angeles: University of California Press, 1984), p. 24.

34. Ibid., pp. 21, 26.

35. Arendt, *On Revolution*, p. 221; Bailyn, *Ideological Origins*, pp. 23–25.

36. Charles S. Sydnor, *American Revolutionaries in the Making: Political Practices in Washington's Virginia* (New York: Free Press, 1965), p. 62, quoting *Memoirs of the Life and Peregrinations of the Florentine Philip Mazzei, 1730–1816*, trans. Howard R. Marraro (New York: Columbia University Press, 1942), p. 213.

37. Thomas Jefferson, *Notes on the State of Virginia*, ed. William Peden (Chapel Hill: University of North Carolina Press, 1955), pp. 146, 148, 147.

38. Excerpted in Hugh Henry Brackenridge, *Incidents of the Insurrection*, ed. Daniel Marder (New Haven: College and University Press, 1972), pp. 66–67.

39. Jefferson, *Notes on the State of Virginia*, p. 140; *Writings of Thomas Jefferson*, ed. Lipscomb and Bergh, 19:213. Michael Paul Rogin has pointed out that Jefferson "placed talent above birth in theory, but in practice found most men of talent among the members of the old leading families." See *Fathers and Children: Andrew Jackson and the Subjugation of the American Indian* (New York: Knopf, 1975), p. 21. Wood makes the same point in *Creation of the American Republic*, pp. 213, 237.

40. See, for example, Daniel Boorstin, *The Lost World of Thomas Jefferson* (Boston: Beacon Press, 1948), pp. 224–25. For a discussion of Rush's views on female education, see Linda Kerber, *Women of the Republic: Intellect and Ideology in Revolutionary America* (Chapel Hill: University of North Carolina Press, 1980), pp. 210–13, 227–30, quote on 191–92.

41. Edmund S. Morgan, *The Birth of the Republic, 1763–1789* (Chicago: University of Chicago Press, 1956), p. 100; see Daniel Marder, *Hugh Henry Brackenridge* (New York: Twayne, 1967), pp. 105–15.

42. Edwin G. Burrows and Michael Wallace, "The American Revolution: The Ideology and Psychology of National Liberation," *Perspectives in American History* 6 (1972): 182, 180, 176, 261, 262.

43. Thomas Paine, *Common Sense*, in *Complete Writings of Thomas Paine*, ed. Foner, 1:25; see, for example, Michael T. Gilmore, "Eulogy as Symbolic Biography:

The Iconography of Revolutionary Leadership, 1776–1826," *Harvard English Studies* 8 (1978): 131–54.

44. Winthrop D. Jordan, "Familial Politics: Thomas Paine and the Killing of the King, 1776," *Journal of American History* 60 (1973): 308; Fliegelman, *Prodigals and Pilgrims*, p. 200; Gilmore, "Eulogy as Symbolic Biography," pp. 143, 146–47; George B. Forgie, *Patricide in the House Divided: A Psychological Interpretation of Lincoln and His Age* (New York: Norton, 1979), p. 8 and n. 12.

45. Gilmore, "Eulogy as Symbolic Biography," p. 146; Forgie, *Patricide in the House Divided*, p. 28.

46. Fliegelman, *Prodigals and Pilgrims*, pp. 197–200.

47. Ibid., p. 199, see pp. 197–226; *Federalist* No. 10, p. 82; *Federalist* No. 49, p. 316; *Federalist* No. 63, p. 384.

48. *Federalist* No. 49, p. 317; *Federalist* No. 23, p. 153.

49. Franklin, *Autobiography*, pp. 135–36. In discussing Franklin's intentions, I am following the lead of the editors of this edition, who point out that although neither Vaughan's letter nor Abel James's is in the manuscript, once Franklin began to think of publication, he either included them himself or left instructions for them to be included. See ibid., p. 133, n. 1.

50. Hugh Henry Brackenridge, *Modern Chivalry*, ed. Claude M. Newlin (New York: American Book Company, 1937), pp. 5, 77, 602, 492.

51. Jacques Ehrmann, "On Articulation," *Yale French Studies* 39 (1967): 19.

52. Between 1787 and 1792, Brown was a member of the Belles Lettres Club in Philadelphia, a group of young men who met to improve their writing and speaking skills and who occasionally held their meetings at Franklin's house. See Donald A. Ringe, *Charles Brockden Brown* (New York: Twayne, 1966), pp. 11, 18. That Brown held the elder man in particular esteem is evidenced in his having twice come before the public in defense of Franklin, once in 1789 with a eulogistic poem "closely modelled after a widely known attack upon Franklin which circulated in Philadelphia and elsewhere during the American Revolution," and again in 1806 in an essay entitled "Character of Dr. Franklin," a "highly complimentary" piece apparently written in response to another attack. See A. Owen Aldridge, "Charles Brockden Brown's Poem on Benjamin Franklin," *American Literature* 38 (May 1966): 230, 234, n. 11.

53. Franklin, *Autobiography*, p. 143.

Chapter 1

1. Benjamin Franklin, *The Autobiography of Benjamin Franklin*, ed. Leonard W. Labaree et al. (New Haven: Yale University Press, 1964), pp. 47–48. All further references to this Yale edition will appear parenthetically in the text.

2. For discussions of how Franklin's ambivalence toward Josiah may be traced in the *Autobiography*, see Michael T. Gilmore, *The Middle Way: Puritanism and Ideology in American Romantic Fiction* (New Brunswick, N.J.: Rutgers University Press, 1977), pp. 48–55; Hugh J. Dawson, "Fathers and Sons: Franklin's 'Memoirs' as Myth and Metaphor," *Early American Literature* 14 (1979–80): 269–92; and

Jesse Bier, "Benjamin Franklin: Guilt and Transformation," *Pennsylvania Magazine of History and Biography* 106 (January 1982): 89–97.

3. Although Franklin's addressing his narrative to William has commonly been taken as an empty rhetorical gesture, Dawson has shown that late in his life Franklin stressed that he had indeed intended the work for his son. See "Fathers and Sons," p. 286, n. 2.

4. There is external evidence to suggest that Uncle Benjamin's fondness for texts provided the initial impetus for the *Autobiography*. Dawson points out, for example, that "on July 11, 1771, Franklin had by chance purchased some old pamphlets once owned by his namesake and favorite uncle. These seem to have turned his mind to the family's past just prior to his stay at Twyford," where he began writing. See "Fathers and Sons," p. 287, n. 6.

5. These anonymous articles were the Silence Dogood Papers, published in the *New-England Courant* in 1722.

6. I am borrowing Dawson's terms, although he uses them only in regard to Parts One and Two. That is, he argues that starting with the "Art of Virtue" section and throughout the remainder of the work, Franklin "makes no explicit postcolonial political statement." See "Fathers and Sons," pp. 274, 284. See also A. Owen Aldridge, "Form and Substance in Franklin's *Autobiography*," in *Essays on American Literature in Honor of Jay B. Hubbell*, ed. Clarence Gohdes (Durham: Duke University Press, 1967), pp. 47–62. Aldridge argues that Parts Two through Four were intended to "emphasize moral concepts rather than family reminiscences" and thus, starting in 1784, Franklin wrote "for publication instead of for an intimate circle" (p. 51).

7. Edward W. Said, *Beginnings* (New York: Basic Books, 1975), p. 22.

8. In light of this theme, it is interesting that Franklin apparently intended to include in his text two of Uncle Benjamin's poems which also emphasize names. In the first, "Sent to My Name upon a Report of his Inclination to Martial affaires," the uncle aphoristically admonishes his namesake against the "Dangerous Trade" of the sword, which "Makes Many poor few Rich and fewer Wise." It is the second, however, which, if included, would have provided a specific contrast to Peter Folger's bald statement of his proper name, for it is an acrostic that artfully incorporates the name "Benjamin Franklin" into a framework of behavioral precepts:

Sent to B. F. in N. E. 15 July 1710
B e to thy parents an Obedient Son
E ach Day let Duty constantly be Done
N ever give Way to sloth or lust or pride
I f free you'd be from Thousand Ills beside
A bove all Ills be sure Avoide the shelfe
M ans Danger lyes in Satan sin and selfe
I n vertue Learning Wisdome progress Make
N ere shrink at Suffering for thy saviours sake
F raud and all Falshood in thy Dealings Flee
R eligious Always in thy station be

A dore the Maker of thy Inward part
N ow's the Accepted time, Give him thy Heart
K eep a Good Conscince 'tis a constant Frind
L ike Judge and Witness This Thy Acts Attend
I n Heart with bended knee Alone Adore
N one but the Three in One Forevermore.

See J. A. Leo Lemay and P. M. Zall, *The Autobiography of Benjamin Franklin: A Genetic Text* (Knoxville: University of Tennessee Press, 1981), Appendix 2: Uncle Benjamin Franklin's Poems, pp. 177–79.

9. My argument regarding Franklin's eventual assumption, and thus validation, of his father's mode of authority is very similar to that of Christopher Looby, in "'The Affairs of the Revolution Occasion'd the Interruption': Writing, Revolution, Deferral, and Conciliation in Franklin's *Autobiography*," *American Quarterly* 38 (Spring 1986): 72–96. Whereas I maintain that Franklin's increasing promotion of paternalistic verbal strategies in the years following the Revolution is representative of his generation, however, Looby argues that Franklin's use of such strategies was exceptional and reflected merely his personal resolution of Oedipal conflict.

10. Dawson, "Fathers and Sons," p. 275.

11. See Gilmore, *Middle Way*, pp. 62–64.

12. See John S. Martin, "Rhetoric, Society and Literature in the Age of Jefferson," *Midcontinental American Studies Journal* 9 (Spring 1968): 78.

13. John F. Lynen gives a similar description of Franklin's (and his contemporaries') belief in the provisional nature of any authoritative guidelines, although he attributes such a belief to an essentially comic view of the human condition. According to Lynen, the *Autobiography* demonstrates that a "man must live by rules, general concepts, formulas, and the like, yet his understanding is so imperfect that he cannot get his principles straight or even understand what they mean. There is always some discrepancy . . . between what we think we mean by a given statement and the meaning our statement would have if we could see all its implications, yet man's rules would not be rules if they did not pretend to universal validity; they mean to be the actual principles of reality, though in fact they are but inferences from a partial view of things. The self is thus placed in the comic position of having to act upon its generalizations as if they were certain truths while, at the same time, remaining aware of their provisional character" (*The Design of the Present: Essays on Time and Form in American Literature* [New Haven: Yale University Press, 1969], p. 136).

14. Hannah Arendt, *On Revolution* (New York: Viking Press, 1965), pp. 201, 203.

15. Whether the *Autobiography* demonstrates any artistic unity is a matter of long debate. For a representative range of interpretations, see Robert F. Sayre, *The Examined Self: Benjamin Franklin, Henry Adams, Henry James* (Princeton: Princeton University Press, 1964); Dawson, "Fathers and Sons"; and A. B. England, "Some Thematic Patterns in Franklin's *Autobiography*," *Eighteenth-Century Studies* 5 (1972): 421–30. Sayre, for example, argues that the work is as "shapeless" as Franklin is "protean" (pp. 12–13); Dawson, that the first two sections, those of 1771

and 1784, possess "the only rounded unity" (p. 269); and England, that the whole is unified by "the consistency with which images of confusion are juxtaposed with images of order" (p. 424).

16. See Lewis P. Simpson, "The Printer as a Man of Letters: Franklin and the Symbolism of the Third Realm" in *Benjamin Franklin: A Collection of Critical Essays*, ed. Brian M. Barbour (Englewood Cliffs, N.J.: Prentice-Hall, 1979), p. 45. Simpson defines "the politics of literacy" as "a politics based not on the idea of conquest of illiteracy—of the achievement of a universal literacy by means of a gross diffusion of elementary reading and writing skills—but on the concept of achieving a universal freedom of the educated secular mind. . . . This would be accomplished through the larger association of men of letters in a worldwide community created by a diffusion of pamphlets, magazines, and books and through an increase of the influence of men of letters."

17. Sayre, *Examined Self*, pp. 12–13, describes Franklin's general principle of "self-teaching" in the *Autobiography* in similar terms: "For him self-teaching did not mean conclusions but repeated new beginnings."

18. *Federalist* No. 37, p. 226. See also Madison's comment, in *Federalist* No. 43, "That useful alterations will be suggested by experience could not but be foreseen" (p. 278), and Hamilton's, in *Federalist* No. 14, that the "leaders of the Revolution" had "formed the design of a great Confederacy, which it is incumbent on their successors to improve and perpetuate" (p. 105).

19. Franklin's sense of what an "improved education" for women might be is revealing, once again, of his belief that *men* should be instructed in language skills. Women, according to Franklin, should be instructed not in letters, but in numbers—in "the Knowledge of Accompts," thus enabling them, "in Case of Widowhood . . . to continue perhaps a profitable mercantile House . . . till a Son is grown up fit to undertake and go on with it" (pp. 166–67). For discussions of women's limited education and limited literacy during the postrevolutionary period, see Linda Kerber, *Women of the Republic: Intellect and Ideology in Revolutionary America* (Chapel Hill: University of North Carolina Press, 1980), pp. 189–231; and Joan Hoff Wilson, "The Illusion of Change: Women and the American Revolution," in *The American Revolution: Explorations in the History of American Radicalism*, ed. Alfred F. Young (DeKalb: Northern Illinois University Press, 1976), esp. pp. 410–14.

20. The "Advertisement" with the accompanying letter was not included in the manuscript autobiography, but Franklin left instructions that it should be inserted. See *Autobiography*, p. 217, n. 5.

21. Tzvetan Todorov, "How to Read?" in *The Poetics of Prose*, trans. Richard Howard (Ithaca, N.Y.: Cornell University Press, 1977), p. 238.

22. Aldridge, "Form and Substance," p. 59.

23. Sayre, *Examined Self*, p. 18.

24. D. H. Lawrence, *Studies in Classic American Literature*, in *The Shock of Recognition*, ed. Edmund Wilson (New York: Random House, 1943), pp. 921, 926, 915, 916, 924.

25. Gilmore, *Middle Way*, pp. 61–62.

26. Malini Schueller has applied Mikhail Bakhtin's terms *monologic* and *dialogic*

to Franklin's mode of discourse in the *Autobiography* and arrived at a similar conclusion. "Instead of merely refuting other ideologies," Schueller argues, Franklin's "authoritative voice for a while apparently accepts them, and when the acceptance seems almost complete, the monologic voice co-opts them and reasserts itself." Thus "potential dialogism is coerced into monologism by his not allowing other voices to participate fully in the text." See Schueller, "Authorial Discourse and Pseudo-Dialogue in Franklin's *Autobiography*," *Early American Literature* 22 (1987): 94–107.

27. Jay Fliegelman, *Prodigals and Pilgrims: The American Revolution against Patriarchal Authority, 1750–1800* (Cambridge: Cambridge University Press, 1982), p. 197.

Chapter 2

1. Hugh Henry Brackenridge, *Modern Chivalry*, ed. Claude M. Newlin (New York: American Book Company, 1937), p. 24. All further references to the Newlin edition will appear in parentheses in the text.

2. Lewis Leary has pointed out that Brackenridge was forced to withdraw from politics for a time starting in 1786 because he allegedly remarked that "he could vote as he pleased and then write a piece for his paper [the *Pittsburgh Gazette*] to appease the people, for the people were fools." Although the report was never verified, public opinion turned violently against him. See Leary, Introduction to *Modern Chivalry* (New Haven: College and University Press, 1965), p. 11. For detailed accounts of Brackenridge's experiences as a public figure in an era increasingly suspicious of leadership, see Daniel Marder, *Hugh Henry Brackenridge* (New York: Twayne, 1967); and Claude M. Newlin, *The Life and Writings of Hugh Henry Brackenridge* (Princeton: Princeton University Press, 1932). For an excellent overview of conflicting views of leadership and of the language of leadership in the Federalist era, see Linda Kerber, *Federalists in Dissent: Imagery and Ideology in Jeffersonian America* (Ithaca, N.Y.: Cornell University Press, 1970), esp. pp. 173–215.

3. Newlin's Introduction to *Modern Chivalry* includes a discussion of Brackenridge's political beliefs (pp. xxviii–xxxv), which focuses mainly on the classical influences on his thought and isolates as his chief themes "the ambition of unqualified persons to rise to high position," "the lack of intelligent discrimination on the part of voters," and "the excesses of democracy" (p. xxviii). Newlin stresses the critical function of the work rather than its function as a future-oriented model of instruction. More recently, Michael T. Gilmore has emphasized this latter function in "Eighteenth-Century Oppositional Ideology and Hugh Henry Brackenridge's *Modern Chivalry*," *Early American Literature* 8 (1973): 181–92. Gilmore also addresses the theme of language, but his argument differs from mine in that he sees Brackenridge's chief concern to be the decay of language in America; for example, "Brackenridge associates the corruption of language in the new republic with the rage for self-advancement" (p. 188).

4. Wendy Martin offers a similar view of Farrago as a thankless hero, although

she sees Teague as the con man in this work and the Captain's verbal artistry merely as the "rational man's" attempts to thwart his servant's self-interest. See "The Rogue and the Rational Man: Hugh Henry Brackenridge's Study of a Con Man in *Modern Chivalry*," *Early American Literature* 8 (1973): 179–92. For an opposing view, see Emory Elliott, *Revolutionary Writers: Literature and Authority in the New Republic, 1725–1810* (New York: Oxford University Press, 1982), pp. 171–217. Elliott reads the Captain as a self-serving "member of the declining aristocracy in America," who has "no desire to contribute to society or to the education and advancement of men like his servant" (p. 185). Thus, he claims, the narrator-author is the true hero of *Modern Chivalry*, one of his main functions being to expose and satirize the shallow pretensions of Farrago (e.g., pp. 183–88). I would agree here that the Captain does occasionally appear to be the object of satire—as in the case of his laughable "simplicity" in the opening pages, when he tries to reason with an unreasonable mob, or in subsequent scenes in which he channels Teague's actions with nonsensical arguments, when sense will not do. I would argue, however, that Brackenridge's satire always has a larger, more sophisticated dimension, which posits scorn not on Farrago, but on the ignorant, irrational populace, who force the well-intentioned man into laughable rhetorical contortions in the interest of the public good.

5. Most critics attribute the formal deterioration of *Modern Chivalry*'s second half to Brackenridge's dwindling artistic powers, but they also acknowledge that he became increasingly critical of and disillusioned with national politics. See Newlin, in *Modern Chivalry*, pp. xxvii–xxviii; and Daniel Marder, *The Hugh Henry Brackenridge Reader* (Pittsburgh: University of Pittsburgh Press, 1970), pp. 43–45.

6. In discussing Brackenridge's use of *Don Quixote* as a literary model, Joseph H. Harkey makes the same point in support of his argument that Brackenridge "Americanized" his materials. See Harkey, "The *Don Quixote* of the Frontier: Brackenridge's *Modern Chivalry*," *Early American Literature* 8 (1973): 198.

7. Lucille M. Schultz has attributed Brackenridge's distrust of the uncorrected imagination to his education in Scottish Common Sense philosophy, in "Uncovering the Significance of the Animal Imagery in *Modern Chivalry*: An Application of Scottish Common Sense Realism," *Early American Literature* 14 (1979–80): 306–11. For a detailed study of this Enlightenment school of thought and its influence on early American literature, see Terence Martin, *The Instructed Vision: Scottish Common Sense Philosophy and the Origins of American Fiction* (Bloomington: Indiana University Press, 1961).

8. Leary, "A Note on the Text," *Modern Chivalry*, p. 21. For detailed discussion of the changes in tone in the second half of the novel, see Elliott, *Revolutionary Writers*, pp. 202–17.

9. For discussions of madness as a recurring theme in this novel, see Amberys R. Whittle, "*Modern Chivalry*: The Frontier as Crucible," *Early American Literature* 6 (1971–72): 263–70; and Harkey, "The *Don Quixote* of the Frontier," esp. p. 194. Both of these authors see Farrago as the only sane inhabitant of a mad world.

10. Wendy Martin has viewed Brackenridge as "the first American novelist to focus on the theme of the alienated artist in a democracy," although she argues that

he also presents the American artist as finding a solution "by developing a sense of self based on reflective habits rather than social rituals" ("The Rogue and The Rational Man," pp. 189–90).

11. Most treatments of Brackenridge's use of satire stress his respect for and reliance on classical and neoclassical authors—Horace, Juvenal, Swift, Cervantes. See, for example, Newlin, in *Modern Chivalry*, pp. xxxvi–xl; Harkey, "The *Don Quixote* of the Frontier"; and Whittle, "*Modern Chivalry*," esp. p. 264.

12. Northrup Frye, *Anatomy of Criticism* (Princeton: Princeton University Press, 1957), p. 229.

Chapter 3

1. Fred Lewis Pattee, Introduction, *Wieland, Or The Transformation, Together with Memoirs of Carwin the Biloquist*, by Charles Brockden Brown (New York: Harcourt, Brace and World, 1926), p. xliii; Paul Witherington, "Charles Brockden Brown: A Bibliographical Essay," *Early American Literature* 9 (Fall 1974): 180. For an opposing view of the extent and the effects of Brown's haste in composition, see Sydney J. Krause, "*Ormond*: How Rapidly and How Well 'Composed, Arranged and Delivered,'" *Early American Literature* 13 (Winter 1978–79): 238–49.

2. Larzer Ziff, "A Reading of *Wieland*," *PMLA* 77 (March 1962): 53; Witherington, "Charles Brockden Brown," p. 181, quoting Joseph Katz, "Analytic Bibliography and Literary History: The Writing and Printing of *Wieland*," *Proof* 1 (1971): 8–34.

3. Michael Davitt Bell, "The Double-Tongued Deceiver: Sincerity and Duplicity in the Novels of Charles Brockden Brown," *Early American Literature* 9 (Fall 1974): 148; Mark Seltzer, "Saying Makes It So: Language and Event in Brown's *Wieland*," *Early American Literature* 13 (Spring 1978): 85; Terence Martin, *The Instructed Vision: Scottish Common Sense Philosophy and the Origins of American Fiction* (Bloomington: Indiana University Press, 1961), p. 135. Important reassessments of Brown's artistry include Norman S. Grabo, *The Coincidental Art of Charles Brockden Brown* (Chapel Hill: University of North Carolina Press, 1981), and Arthur G. Kimball, *Rational Fictions: A Study of Charles Brockden Brown* (McMinnville, Ore.: Linfield Research Institute, 1968); of *Wieland* in particular, James Russo, "'The Chimeras of the Brain': Clara's Narrative in *Wieland*," *Early American Literature* 16 (1981): 60–88; Michael T. Gilmore, "Calvinism and Gothicism: The Example of Brown's *Wieland*," *Studies in the Novel* 9 (Summer 1977): 107–18; Wayne Franklin, "Tragedy and Comedy in Brown's *Wieland*," *Novel* 8 (Winter 1975): 214–25; and Nina Baym, "A Minority Reading of *Wieland*," in *Critical Essays on Charles Brockden Brown*, ed. Bernard Rosenthal (Boston: G. K. Hall, 1981), pp. 87–103. I find the latter essay especially intriguing, for although Baym finds this novel to be seriously flawed, she attributes its failings to Brown's unsuccessful attempts to juggle two story lines at once: "The flaw in Brown's *Wieland* is basic and central: there is a continuous sacrifice of story line and character—hence, long-term coherence—for the sake of immediate effect. As the

narrative progresses, indeed, a second plot, designed to maximize the opportunities for such effects, overtakes and ultimately obliterates the main story" (p. 88).

4. Leslie Fiedler, *Love and Death in the American Novel*, rev. ed. (New York: Stein and Day, 1966), p. 155.

5. Quoted by Frank Kermode, *The Sense of an Ending: Studies in the Theory of Fiction* (New York: Oxford University Press, 1966), p. 174.

6. Charles Brockden Brown, *Edgar Huntly, or Memoirs of a Sleepwalker*, vol. 4 of *The Novels and Related Works of Charles Brockden Brown*, CEAA-CSE Bicentennial Edition, ed. Sydney K. Krause et al. (Kent, Ohio: Kent State University Press, 1984), p. 293. All further references to the Bicentennial Edition of Brown's novels will appear in parentheses in the text.

7. Bell has pointed out this pun in "Double-Tongued Deceiver," p. 156.

8. See J. Hillis Miller, "The Problematic of Ending in Narrative," *Nineteenth-Century Fiction* 33 (June 1978): 3–7. Miller argues the possibility of interpreting any given narrative ending as either a closure or a denouement; Brown's novels seem to argue the impossibility of a narrative's achieving either.

9. Kermode, *Sense of an Ending*, p. 17.

10. See Bell, "Double-Tongued Deceiver," pp. 146–47.

11. Arthur G. Kimball, "Savages and Savagism: Brockden Brown's Dramatic Irony," *Studies in Romanticism* 6 (1967): 221.

12. See *OED* entry for "Demon."

13. Bell, "Double-Tongued Deceiver," p. 146.

14. Brown states, in his "Advertisement," that some of the incidents related in *Wieland* "approach as nearly to the nature of miracles as can be done by that which is not truly miraculous" (1:3), but I believe this to be an authorial disclaimer as inconclusive as others found throughout the novel. For example, I find it highly suggestive that in this book full of authors of fictions, God is twice identified as an "author" (1:74, 166).

15. Kimball, "Savages and Savagism," p. 216.

16. That Brown's self-professedly virtuous characters are capable of murder is demonstrated in the later *Ormond*: "the violence of Ormond had been repulsed by equal violence" on the part of Constantia Dudley, who chooses to kill rather than to lose her "virtue" (2:291). James R. Russo provides detailed evidence of the moral inconstancy of Constantia, in "The Tangled Web of Deception and Imposture in Charles Brockden Brown's *Ormond*," *Early American Literature* 14 (1979): 205–27; and see Kenneth Bernard, "*Edgar Huntly*: Charles Brockden Brown's Unsolved Murder," *Library Chronicle* 33 (Winter 1967), 30–53, in which Bernard argues that Huntly, the narrator, "is in fact guilty of Waldegrave's murder, and his internal drama of guilt is played out with Clithero as alter-ego." The latter is cited in Witherington, "Charles Brockden Brown," p. 182.

17. Gilmore, "Calvinism and Gothicism," p. 112.

18. Clara's need to believe in stories that ostensibly tie up loose ends helps to account for her inclusion of the Conway-Maxwell story in her sequel. Ziff, "Reading of *Wieland*," sees this story as evidence of Brown's poor planning, his need, because he had lost control of Carwin's characterization, to invent a new seducer

to enact the crimes for which the biloquist had originally been slotted; and Katz, "Analytic Bibliography," sees it as proof that Brown had insufficient time to revise. The new story fulfills important thematic functions, however. By recounting a con man's seduction and destruction of a family, Clara is more able to justify her own unlikely story and to reinforce her belief in authoritative conclusions: "The evils of which Carwin and Maxwell were the authors owed their existence to"—and she gives four plausible explanations. Moreover, the story serves as an ironic parallel to Clara's own in ways she does not perceive and perhaps as a final paradigm for all stories, for though Clara attributes the central villainy—the murder—to Maxwell, she admits that "the author of this treason could not certainly be discovered," and the story ends with the unsettling comment that Maxwell "disappeared from this scene" (1:244). Such details reinforce the suspicion that all stories originate to explain away—for a time—the inexplicable.

19. The poem, first printed in the *American Register* in 1794, is called "Devotion. An Epistle" and is partially reprinted in Pattee's Introduction, p. xv.

20. A strikingly literal example of such a literary transformation occurs in *Jane Talbot*, in a letter from Jane to her lover, Henry Colden: "I should certainly bestow upon thee a hearty—*kiss* or two. My blundering pen! I recall the word. I meant *cuff*, but my saucy pen, pretending to know more of my mind that I did myself, turned . . . her *cuff* into a *kiss*" (5:278).

21. Reprinted in Charles Brockden Brown, *The Rhapsodist and Other Uncollected Writings*, ed. Harry R. Warfel (New York: Scholars' Facsimiles and Reprints, 1943), p. 43.

22. For an overview of such readings and a recent reevaluation, see Fritz Fleischmann, "Charles Brockden Brown: Feminism in Fiction," in *American Novelists Reconsidered: Essays in Feminist Criticism*, ed. Fritz Fleischmann (Boston: G. K. Hall, 1982), pp. 6–41.

Introduction to Part II

1. Alexis de Tocqueville, *Democracy in America*, ed. Phillips Bradley, 2 vols. (1835, 1840; rpt., New York: Knopf, 1945), 2:70–71.

2. Ralph Waldo Emerson, *Nature*, in *Nature, Addresses, and Lectures*, vol. 1 of *The Collected Works of Ralph Waldo Emerson*, ed. Robert E. Spiller and Alfred R. Ferguson (Cambridge, Mass.: Harvard University Press, 1971), p. 20.

3. Ibid. Traditionally, critics have tended to read Emerson's and his contemporaries' statements about language solely as measures of their epistemological concerns. Two of the most recent and most persuasive studies in this vein are John T. Irwin, *American Hieroglyphics: The Symbol of the Egyptian Hieroglyphics in the American Renaissance* (New Haven: Yale University Press, 1980); and Philip F. Gura, *The Wisdom of Words: Language, Theology, and Literature in the New England Renaissance* (Middletown, Conn.: Wesleyan University Press, 1981). My own study of the political content and implications of these authors' representations of language falls more in line with David Simpson, *The Politics of American English, 1776–1850* (New York: Oxford University Press, 1986); and Eric Cheyfitz, *The Trans-Parent:*

Sexual Politics in the Language of Emerson (Baltimore: Johns Hopkins University Press, 1981).

4. James Fenimore Cooper, *The Last of the Mohicans*, in *The Leatherstocking Tales*, 2 vols. (New York: Library of America, 1985), 1:575; Cooper, *The Prairie*, in ibid., 1:1199.

5. Cooper, *The Last of the Mohicans*, 1:820.

6. See, for example, Marie Bonaparte, *The Life and Works of Edgar Allan Poe: A Psycho-Analytic Interpretation*, trans. John Rodker (London: Imago, 1949); Frederick C. Crews, *The Sins of the Fathers: Hawthorne's Psychological Themes* (New York: Oxford University Press, 1966); and Michael Paul Rogin, *Subversive Genealogy: The Politics and Art of Herman Melville* (New York: Knopf, 1983).

7. Stephen Railton, *Fenimore Cooper: A Study of His Life and Imagination* (Princeton: Princeton University Press, 1978), p. 92.

8. See Daniel Boorstin, *The Americans: The National Experience* (New York: Random House, 1965), pp. 337–56.

9. For a more detailed analysis of these novels, see H. Daniel Peck, *A World by Itself: The Pastoral Moment in Cooper's Fiction* (New Haven: Yale University Press, 1977), pp. 96–108. For a discussion of Cooper's ambivalence toward the American Revolution, see John P. McWilliams, Jr., *Political Justice in a Republic: James Fenimore Cooper's America* (Berkeley and Los Angeles: University of California Press, 1972), esp. pp. 32–99.

10. George B. Forgie, *Patricide in the House Divided: A Psychological Interpretation of Lincoln and His Age* (New York: Norton, 1979), p. 114. Forgie is here expanding on Roy Harvey Pearce's reading of this story in "Hawthorne and the Sense of the Past or, The Immortality of Major Molineux," *ELH* 21 (1954): 327–49.

11. Michael T. Gilmore, *The Middle Way: Puritanism and Ideology in American Romantic Fiction* (New Brunswick, N.J.: Rutgers University Press, 1977), p. 66.

12. Herman Melville, *Israel Potter: His Fifty Years of Exile*, vol. 8 in *The Writings of Herman Melville* (Chicago: Northwestern University Press and the Newberry Library, 1982), p. 53. For similar assessments of Melville's portrayal of Franklin in this novel, see Gilmore, *Middle Way*, pp. 154–56; and Michael Davitt Bell, *The Development of American Romance: The Sacrifice of Relation* (Chicago: University of Chicago Press, 1980), pp. 215–16.

13. J. A. Leo Lemay, "Poe's 'The Business Man': Its Contexts and Satire of Franklin's *Autobiography*," *Poe Studies* 15 (December 1982): 29, 35. Although Lemay feels that "the real Franklin and the actual *Autobiography* are not Poe's primary objects of attack" in this complex satire, he concludes that "the *Autobiography* is satirized throughout the story" (p. 34). He also points out that elsewhere Poe criticized Thomas Jefferson's views on religion, which he considered merely one of Jefferson's "iniquities," and that he may have attacked Franklin's lack of spirituality in an earlier satire, "King Pest." See ibid., p. 37, n. 61.

14. Gerda Lerner, "The Lady and the Mill-Girl: Changes in the Status of Women in the Age of Jackson," *Mid-Continent American Studies Journal* 10 (1969): 7. See also Barbara Welter, "The Cult of True Womanhood, 1820–1860," *American Quarterly* 18 (1966): 151–74; Nancy F. Cott, *The Bonds of Womanhood: 'Woman's Sphere' in New England, 1780–1835* (New Haven: Yale University Press, 1977); Mi-

chael Paul Rogin, *Fathers and Children: Andrew Jackson and the Subjugation of the American Indian* (New York: Knopf, 1975); David Brion Davis, *The Problem of Slavery in the Age of Revolution, 1770–1823* (Ithaca, N.Y.: Cornell University Press, 1975); and John W. Blassingame, *The Slave Community: Plantation Life in the Ante-Bellum South* (New York: Oxford University Press, 1972).

15. Emerson, "The American Scholar," in *Nature, Addresses, and Lectures*, vol. 1 of *Collected Works*, ed. Spiller and Ferguson, p. 67. See also Nina Baym, *Novels, Readers, and Reviewers: Responses to Fiction in Antebellum America* (Ithaca, N.Y.: Cornell University Press, 1984), esp. pp. 26–43.

16. Nina Baym, *Woman's Fiction: A Guide to Novels by and about Women in America, 1820–1870* (Ithaca, N.Y.: Cornell University Press, 1978), pp. 11, 17. See also Mary Kelley, *Private Woman, Public Stage: Literary Domesticity in Nineteenth-Century America* (New York: Oxford University Press, 1984).

17. Frederick Douglass, *Narrative of the Life of Frederick Douglass, an American Slave, Written by Himself*, ed. Benjamin Quarles (Cambridge: Belknap Press of Harvard University Press, 1960), p. 21.

18. Margaret Fuller, *Woman in the Nineteenth Century*, intro. Bernard Rosenthal (1855; rpt., New York: Norton, 1971), pp. 25–26.

19. Michael T. Gilmore makes a similar argument, linking the American romancers with their female contemporaries on the basis of both groups' awareness of the tastes and demographic makeup of their audience. See *American Romanticism and the Marketplace* (Chicago: University of Chicago Press, 1985), p. 12. For an opposing view, see Ann Douglas, *The Feminization of American Culture* (New York: Knopf, 1977), p. 4. Douglas argues that major American authors of the Victorian period—Thoreau, Cooper, Melville, Whitman—wrote primarily to men about men and men's "economically and ecologically significant activities."

20. Bell discusses the socially deviant nature of the American romancer's endeavor at length in *Development of American Romance*, esp. pp. 29–36.

21. Simone de Beauvoir, *The Second Sex* (New York: Knopf, 1952), pp. xix-xx; xix, n. 3, quoting E. Levinas, *Temps et l'autre*, p. xxvii. I am slightly bending Beauvoir's argument here—or at least selecting out one of her subpoints—to support my claim that these authors used femininity symbolically as the lowest common denominator of otherness. The point of her book is to show that although the justifications for imposing otherness are always the same, women's response to that imposition has been unique.

22. I borrow my terminology from Sandra M. Gilbert and Susan Gubar, "Sexual Linguistics: Gender, Language, Sexuality," *New Literary History* 16 (Spring 1985): 515–43. One of their findings in this excellent essay, that twentieth-century women's writings show an increasing interest in fantasy languages as a way of validating and empowering female and feminine otherness, suggests that Cooper, Poe, Hawthorne, and Melville were ahead of their time.

Chapter 4

1. James Fenimore Cooper, Preface to *The Last of the Mohicans*, in *The Leatherstocking Tales*, 2 vols. (New York: Library of America, 1985), 1:470. Subsequent references to the Library of America edition of these novels will appear parenthetically in the text.

2. For a Freudian explanation of Natty's depiction as a father figure, see Stephen Railton, *Fenimore Cooper: A Study of His Life and Imagination* (Princeton: Princeton University Press, 1978), p. 92. Railton argues that Cooper's "unconscious need to resist his father was responsible for the creation of the Leatherstocking," who thus represents "a psychic alternative to Cooper's father."

3. There is no critical consensus as to whether this novel, or any of the Leatherstocking series, has any political content. Cooper's conservative political views in his later years, his seemingly obsessive literary treatments of class distinctions and a rigid social order, and even his many cantankerous lawsuits have all been used as evidence to argue that his "white" novels are just that much more patriarchal propaganda. See, for example, Marvin Meyers, *The Jacksonian Persuasion: Politics and Belief* (Stanford: Stanford University Press, 1957), pp. 42–75; and Eric Sundquist, *Home as Found: Authority and Genealogy in Nineteenth-Century American Literature* (Baltimore: Johns Hopkins University Press, 1979), pp. 1–40. Many studies have followed D. H. Lawrence's lead in arguing that in the Leatherstocking Tales, Cooper was able to free his imagination from the constraints of political realities and indulge instead in "wish-fulfillment." See D. H. Lawrence, *Studies in Classic American Literature*, in *The Shock of Recognition*, ed. Edmund Wilson (New York: Random House, 1943), p. 950; James Grossman, *James Fenimore Cooper* (New York: William Sloane, 1949), p. 45; and H. Daniel Peck, *A World by Itself: The Pastoral Moment in Cooper's Fiction* (New Haven: Yale University Press, 1977), pp. 86–88. Still another group of studies has argued for the political content of one or more of the Leatherstocking Tales. Joel Porte, for example, has found evidence of an antipatriarchal ethos in *The Prairie*; Annette Kolodny has found underlying patriarchal assumptions in all of the tales; and Nina Baym's reading, which concludes that Cooper was ambivalent on such sociopolitical issues, falls somewhere between the two. See Porte, *The Romance in America: Studies in Cooper, Poe, Hawthorne, Melville, and James* (Middletown, Conn.: Wesleyan University Press, 1969), p. 47; Kolodny, *The Lay of the Land: Metaphor as Experience and History in American Life and Letters* (Chapel Hill: University of North Carolina Press, 1975), pp. 89–115; and Baym, "The Women of Cooper's Leatherstocking Tales," in *Images of Women in Fiction: Feminist Perspectives*, ed. Susan Koppelman Cornillon (Bowling Green, Ohio: Bowling Green University Popular Press, 1972), pp. 135–54, rpt. from *American Quarterly* 23 (1971): 648–709.

4. Critics have also debated whether Natty Bumppo fulfills the role of the hero in this novel and have claimed variously that he does, that Uncas is the true hero, and that the traditional heroic function is shared by three "protagonists," Natty, Uncas, and Heyward. See, respectively, Arvid Schulenberger, *Cooper's Theory of Fiction: His Prefaces and Their Relation to His Novels* (Lawrence: University of Kansas Press, 1955), pp. 75–76; Donald Darnell, "Uncas as Hero: The *Ubi Sunt*

Formula in *The Last of the Mohicans,*" *American Literature* 37 (November 1965): 259–66; and Terence Martin, "From the Ruins of History: *The Last of the Mohicans,*" *Novel* 2 (Spring 1969): 226. My own reading is closer to that of Thomas Philbrick, who argues that though Natty may be "a principle of action" in this work, he is not "a repository of value." See Philbrick, "*The Last of the Mohicans* and the Sounds of Discord," *American Literature* 43 (March 1971): 39.

5. Lawrence, *Studies in Classic American Literature,* p. 952.

6. For an excellent analysis of the various sorts of doubling that occur in this novel, see Peck, *A World by Itself,* esp. pp. 134–41.

7. See Philbrick, "*The Last of the Mohicans* and the Sounds of Discord," pp. 36–39, for a similar discussion of Gamut as a failed artist, "baffled and helpless before a world which will not yield to his art."

8. Consider Emerson's advice, in "The American Scholar," that "books are for the scholar's idle times"; Melville's comment, in *Moby-Dick,* that "though of real knowledge there be little, yet of books there be a-plenty"; and his earlier depiction of the impoverished Redburn, whose father gives him a guidebook of Liverpool, now sadly out of date.

9. Both Railton, *Fenimore Cooper,* and Sundquist, *Home as Found,* have provided extensive biographical and psychoanalytic evidence of Cooper's Oedipal ambivalence toward such paternalistic authorities. See also Warren Motley, *The American Abraham: James Fenimore Cooper and the Frontier Patriarch* (Cambridge: Cambridge University Press, 1987).

10. Philbrick offers a very different, though intriguing, view of why this book is, in his words, "profoundly different in nature from Cooper's other fiction." He argues that there is "some reason to conjecture that the writer's ill health" during its composition "significantly influenced the texture and tendency of the book as a whole" ("*The Last of the Mohicans* and the Sounds of Discord," pp. 25–28).

11. For an opposing view, see David P. Simpson, *The Politics of American English, 1776–1850* (New York: Oxford University Press, 1986), pp. 164–70. Simpson argues, for example, that Cooper strongly identifies with Natty and that Natty thus speaks with "authorial approval and conviction" (p. 168).

12. See Steven Blakemore, "Strange Tongues: Cooper's Fiction of Language in *The Last of the Mohicans,*" *Early American Literature* 19 (1984): 21–41; and Simpson, *Politics of American English,* pp. 202–29.

13. See Peck, *A World by Itself,* pp. 87–88. In discussing Cooper's descriptions of dreamlike landscapes, Peck makes an intriguing comment on his narrative style in general: "To dream our own magic woods, we require a text which does not describe the space of nature in too much detail. We do not want to know the *names* of the flora and fauna . . . but only to be presented with a beautiful outline. . . . Cooper's works answer this need perfectly, for his descriptions are diffuse, inexact, generalized. They present . . . a porous quality requiring the reader to fill in gaps in the prose." Although I would not argue sustained conscious intent on Cooper's part, I find it suggestive that an author so aware and so critical of the power of naming would tend toward a paraphrastic style rather than be a "namer" himself.

14. Philbrick, "*The Last of the Mohicans* and the Sounds of Discord," p. 25. Philbrick concludes that there is no coherent ideology in this novel, that it repre-

sents Cooper's lack of confidence in his own ability as an artist to resolve the chaotic elements in American experience into one coherent value system.

15. For a different reading of the symbolic status of white women in this novel, see Baym, "The Women of Cooper's Leatherstocking Tales," pp. 145–47. Baym argues that in *The Last of the Mohicans* Cooper more or less endorses "the idea that there can be no civilization without the repression and control of 'female sexuality'; i.e., the capacity of the female to arouse the male" (p. 147).

16. See Peck, *A World by Itself*, p. 126. Peck cites John Heckewelder's account of the Lenni Lenapes' myths, first published in 1819, which Cooper refers to in the Preface to this novel.

17. See Railton, *Fenimore Cooper*, pp. 64–68.

18. See Porte, *Romance in America*, p. 47. Porte argues that the "great theme" of *The Prairie* is "the shift from a patriarchal to a matriarchal society."

19. The critical consensus regarding the second half of this novel is that it represents a dreamlike or nightmarish quest through a mythic realm. For a representative selection of such readings, see Leslie Fiedler, *Love and Death in the American Novel*, rev. ed. (New York: Stein and Day, 1966), p. 201; Darnell, "Uncas as Hero," p. 262; Philbrick, "*The Last of the Mohicans* and the Sounds of Discord," pp. 32–35; and Peck, *A World by Itself*, pp. 120–45.

20. For a Freudian reading of the various "orifices" of the Glenn's Falls cavern scene, see Kolodny, *Lay of the Land*, p. 97. Kolodny does not discuss the second cavern scene.

21. John McAleer sees Gamut as an overzealous representative of Christianity, too rigidly interpreting events in terms of biblical analogy ("Biblical Analogy in the Leatherstocking Tales," *Nineteenth-Century Fiction* 17 [December 1962]: 223–25).

22. Railton equates this dramatic turnabout with the second phase of Oedipal conflict in which the son can be satisfied only with complete submission to the father. He argues that during the last dozen years of Cooper's life, the author's psychic stance toward his father and toward paternalistic authority in general was determined by this need for approval (*Fenimore Cooper*, p. 223).

Chapter 5

1. David Halliburton, *Edgar Allan Poe: A Phenomenological View* (Princeton: Princeton University Press, 1973), p. 175. I have to admit that I am using Halliburton's terms for my own ends. He interprets the stories I am about to discuss very differently than I do; see, for example, my note 7, below.

2. Hamilton Wright Mabie, for example, argued that Poe's "creative work baffles all attempts to relate it historically to antecedent conditions; that it detached itself almost completely from the time and place in which it made its appearance, and sprang suddenly and mysteriously from a soil which had never borne its like before" ("Poe's Place in American Literature," in *The Complete Works of Edgar Allan Poe*, ed. James A. Harrison, 17 vols. [New York: Crowell, 1902], 2:xiv). Similarly, F. O. Matthiessen omitted Poe from his definitive grouping of American

Renaissance authors (Emerson, Thoreau, Hawthorne, Melville, and Whitman) on the grounds that Poe's work "relates at very few points to the main assumptions about literature that were held by any of my group" (*American Renaissance: Art and Expression in the Age of Emerson and Whitman* [New York: Oxford University Press, 1941], p. xii, n. 3). Significant recent readings of Poe as a bona fide American romancer include Joel Porte, *The Romance in America: Studies in Cooper, Poe, Hawthorne, Melville, and James* (Middletown, Conn.: Wesleyan University Press, 1969), pp. 53–94; Michael Davitt Bell, *The Development of American Romance: The Sacrifice of Relation* (Chicago: University of Chicago Press, 1980), pp. 86–125; and John T. Irwin, *American Hieroglyphics: The Symbol of the Egyptian Hieroglyphics in the American Renaissance* (New Haven: Yale University Press, 1980), pp. 43–235.

3. I refer specifically to Poe's crime metaphor, implicit in the early tales about women and highlighted as the controlling metaphor in the Dupin tales. For a comparison of Poe's and Hawthorne's treatments of criminally silenced women, see my article "Poe's Re-Vision: The Recovery of the Second Story," *American Literature* 59 (March 1987): 1–19.

4. Edgar Allan Poe, "Ligeia," in *Collected Works of Edgar Allan Poe*, ed. Thomas Ollive Mabbott, 3 vols. to date (Cambridge, Mass.: The Belknap Press of Harvard University Press, 1969–), 2:330. References to this collection will be cited throughout the text with volume and page numbers in parentheses.

5. For other readings of Poe's narrators' murderous intents in the early tales about women, see Terence J. Matheson, "The Multiple Murder in 'Ligeia': A New Look at Poe's Narrator," *Canadian Review of American Studies* 13 (1982): 279–89; and Bell, *Development of American Romance*, pp. 101, 112–17. See also, James W. Gargano, "The Question of Poe's Narrators," in *Poe: A Collection of Critical Essays*, ed. Robert Regan (Englewood Cliffs, N.J.: Prentice-Hall, 1967), pp. 164–71. Gargano argues, and I agree, that in "The Tell-Tale Heart," "William Wilson," "The Cask of Amontillado," and "The Black Cat," Poe is "conscious of the abnormalities of his narrators and does not condone the intellectual ruses through which they strive . . . to justify themselves."

6. I am going on the generally accepted assumption that if Poe did not actually originate the detective fiction genre, he at least should be credited with popularizing it. See Mabbott's Introduction to "The Murders in the Rue Morgue," 2:251: "It may not be the first detective story, but it is the first story deliberately written as such to attain world-wide popularity."

7. Roland Kuhn, "The Attempted Murder of a Prostitute," trans. Ernest Angel, in *Existence: A New Dimension in Psychiatry and Psychology*, ed. Rollo May et al. (New York: Basic Books, 1958), p. 125, quoted in Halliburton, *Edgar Allan Poe*, p. 203. Halliburton refers to this statement in his discussion of "Berenice," in which he sees forgetting and killing played off against remembering and saving. "In 'Berenice' there is a movement in both directions," he claims, arguing that this is evidence of Egaeus's both wanting and not wanting to confront his attraction to his cousin. I would argue that in this story, as in "Ligeia," the emphasis falls on the extreme selectivity of what is forgotten and what is remembered and thus reveals the narrator's mind caught in a willful act of repression.

8. Daniel Hoffman's reading of the narrator's mental block over Ligeia's name

tends to corroborate my main argument about the suppression of feminine/ maternal authority: "Ligeia is both her husband's Muse and Sacred Mother. Now it is clear why Husband has never dared to ask her or remind himself of her 'paternal name'; for if he did, he would have to face up to its being the same as his mother's" (*Poe Poe Poe Poe Poe Poe Poe* [New York: Avon Books, 1972], p. 246).

9. A number of critics have commented on Poe's use of rooms, houses, and the like to represent the mind, but most see Rowena's bridal chamber as the main such image in "Ligeia," whereas I read it as but another version of the original "closed study." See, for example, Hoffman, *Poe*, p. 251; and Bell, *Development of American Romance*, p. 107.

10. Braddy Haldeen suggests that Poe consciously manipulated his own style and particularly his point of view along gender lines so that his prose narratives more consistently portray masculine perspectives, his poetry, feminine ("Edgar Allan Poe's Princess of Long Ago," *Laurel Review* 9 [Fall 1969]: 23–31).

11. Porte, *Romance in America*, p. 73.

12. Margaret Homans has demonstrated how this structural device—subordinating a woman's speech to the language of masculine texts—functions as a criticism of patriarchal authority in *The Mill on the Floss*. At the beginning of that novel, Maggie Tulliver, like Ligeia, invents her own stories and imaginatively rewrites the male-authored texts that come her way. But as the book progresses, Homans argues, her "adult self [becomes] a battle ground for conflicting texts; when she takes up a pen or opens her mouth, the words that come forth as if they were her own are not hers" ("Eliot, Wordsworth, and the Scenes of the Sisters' Instruction," *Critical Inquiry* 8 [Winter 1981]: 228).

13. Critics have long argued over what actually happens in the second death scene. Some have read Ligeia's return as a triumph of the supernatural in a world in which the narrator tries unsuccessfully to maintain rational control. See, for example, Halliburton, *Edgar Allan Poe*, pp. 212–15; and James Schroeter, "A Misreading of Poe's 'Ligeia,'" *PMLA* 76 (September 1961): 397–406. Others maintain that the narrator, now insanely grieving over the loss of his first wife, kills Rowena and fantasizes Ligeia's return. See Porte, *Romance in America*, pp. 74–75; Roy P. Basler, *Sex, Symbolism and Psychology in Literature* (New Brunswick, N.J.: Rutgers University Press, 1948), pp. 143–59; and James W. Gargano, "Poe's 'Ligeia': Dream and Destruction," *College English* 23 (February 1962): 337–42. Matheson's article "The Multiple Murder in 'Ligeia'" is the only work I have found that argues that the narrator is responsible for both women's deaths.

14. Despite the many liberties he took with Poe's text, Hollywood director Roger Corman captured this sense of sisterhood by having the same actress play both Ligeia and Rowena in his film adaptation, *The Tomb of Ligeia*, with Vincent Price and Elizabeth Shepherd, American-International Pictures, 1964.

15. For a slightly different reading of the significance of this act of naming, see Bell, *Development of American Romance*, p. 115. Bell argues that the narrator's "incantatory repetition" of Ligeia's name is meant primarily to summon her, to test the power of words, and that the narrator's "horror at his success" shows that he "prefers her name, her verbal sign, to the reality it signifies."

16. J. O. Bailey, "What Happens in 'The Fall of the House of Usher'?" *American*

Literature 35 (1964): 445–66; Maurice Beebe, "The Universe of Roderick Usher," in *Poe*, ed. Regan, pp. 129–30; and Hoffman, *Poe*, pp. 310–11.

17. See, for example, Charles Feidelson, Jr., *Symbolism and American Literature* (Chicago: University of Chicago Press, 1953), p. 35; Porte, *Romance in America*, p. 62; and Stefano Tani, *The Doomed Detective: The Contribution of the Detective Novel to Postmodern American and Italian Fiction* (Carbondale: Southern Illinois University Press, 1984), p. 12.

18. D. H. Lawrence, *Studies in Classic American Literature*, in *The Shock of Recognition*, ed. Edmund Wilson (New York: Random House, 1943), p. 979.

19. See Judith Fetterley, *The Resisting Reader: A Feminist Approach to American Fiction* (Bloomington: Indiana University Press, 1978). I will refer to Fetterley's description of the imaginative act performed by the "resisting reader" in my conclusion.

20. Adrienne Rich, "When We Dead Awaken: Writing as Re-Vision," in *On Lies, Secrets, and Silence: Selected Prose, 1966–1978* (New York: Norton, 1979), p. 35. I will give Rich's full definition of "re-vision" later in the text.

21. G. R. Thompson has also argued the unreliability of this narrator but for different reasons. He claims that the narrator gradually comes to accept Roderick's mad interpretations and that the scene of Madeline's return is thus a dual hallucination. See *Poe's Fiction: Romantic Irony in the Gothic Tales* (Madison: University of Wisconsin Press, 1973), pp. 68–104, and "Poe and the Paradox of Terror: Structures of Heightened Consciousness in 'The Fall of the House of Usher,'" in *Ruined Eden of the Present: Hawthorne, Melville, and Poe*, ed. G. R. Thompson and Virgil L. Lokke (West Lafayette, Ind.: Purdue University Press, 1981), pp. 313–40.

22. See Tani, *Doomed Detective*, p. 4. Tani likens Dupin to Roderick Usher on the grounds that each is a poet-figure suffering from a "diseased" imagination. For other readings of Dupin as a poet-figure, see Leslie Fiedler, *Love and Death in the American Novel*, rev. ed. (New York: Stein and Day, 1966), p. 497; and Hoffman, *Poe*, pp. 114–22.

23. J. A. Leo Lemay, "The Psychology of 'The Murders in the Rue Morgue,'" *American Literature* 54 (1982): 177, 178, 187.

24. Rich, "When We Dead Awaken," p. 35.

25. Fetterley, *Resisting Reader*, pp. xx, xiv.

26. The only exception I have found is Ashby Bland Crowder, "Poe's Criticism of Women Writers," *University of Mississippi Studies in English* 3 (1982): 102–19. Crowder argues that despite Poe's professed belief that a gentleman should be silent if he had nothing complimentary to say of a woman, in critical practice he applied the same literary standards to male and female authors alike. For opposing views on this point, see Robert D. Jacobs, *Poe: Journalist and Critic* (Baton Rouge: Louisiana State University Press, 1969), p. 105; and Richard Cary, "Poe and the Literary Ladies," *Texas Studies in Language and Literature* 9 (1967): 91, 92, 94, 100.

27. See, for example, Sandra M. Gilbert and Susan Gubar, *The Madwoman in the Attic: The Woman Writer and the Nineteenth-Century Literary Imagination* (New Haven: Yale University Press, 1979), p. 25. The quotation can be found in *The Complete Poems and Stories of Edgar Allan Poe, with Selections from his Critical Writings*, ed. A. H. Quinn, 2 vols. (New York: Knopf, 1951), 2:982.

28. Nina Baym, "Hawthorne's Women: The Tyranny of Social Myths," *Centennial Review* 15 (1971): 250–51. See also Baym, "Thwarted Nature: Nathaniel Hawthorne as Feminist," in *American Novelists Revisited: Essays in Feminist Criticism*, ed. Fritz Fleischmann (Boston: G. K. Hall, 1982), pp. 58–77.

Chapter 6

1. Sigmund Freud, *A General Introduction to Psychoanalysis*, trans. Joan Riviere (New York: Washington Square Press, 1964), pp. 305–6.

2. Nathaniel Hawthorne, *The Scarlet Letter*, vol. 1 of *The Centenary Edition of the Works of Nathaniel Hawthorne*, ed. William Charvat et al. (Columbus: Ohio State University Press, 1962), p. 48. All further references to the *Centenary Edition* of Hawthorne's novels will be given in parentheses in the text.

3. See Richard H. Brodhead, *Hawthorne, Melville, and the Novel* (Chicago: University of Chicago Press, 1976), p. 77. Brodhead discusses the similar "threshold" openings of the two books but sees little similarity between Hester and Hepzibah. He attributes the melodramatic opening of *The House of the Seven Gables* to Hawthorne's ironic intent to highlight the commonplace tragedy of Hepzibah's situation, in contrast to the high tragedy of Hester's.

4. F. O. Matthiessen, *American Renaissance: Art and Expression in the Age of Emerson and Whitman* (New York: Oxford University Press, 1941), p. 219.

5. I am greatly indebted to Nina Baym's feminist reading of Hawthorne's evolving sense of his role as an American artist, in *The Shape of Hawthorne's Career* (Ithaca, N.Y.: Cornell University Press, 1976).

6. William H. Shurr, "Eve's Bower: Hawthorne's Transition from Public Doctrines to Private Truths," in *Ruined Eden of the Present: Hawthorne, Melville, and Poe*, ed. G. R. Thompson and Virgil L. Lokke (West Lafayette, Ind.: Purdue University Press, 1981), pp. 143–69.

7. Joel Porte, *The Romance in America: Studies in Cooper, Poe, Hawthorne, Melville, and James* (Middletown, Conn.: Wesleyan University Press, 1969), p. 110.

8. Brodhead gives a similar reading of this novel's main conflicts. He sees the "mutual victimization of Pyncheon and Maule" as "a model of class warfare" and as "a story of internal psychic conflict," and he sees Phoebe's and Holgrave's sympathetic bonding as something that "releases them from the pattern of domination and psychic revenge that the tale illustrates." See Brodhead, *Hawthorne, Melville, and the Novel*, pp. 78–79, 85.

9. Frederick C. Crews, for example, has argued that at this point in the book, "filial obsession . . . is beginning to destroy objective characterization and moral interest" (*The Sins of the Fathers: Hawthorne's Psychological Themes* [New York: Oxford University Press, 1966], p. 177). See also Michael T. Gilmore, *American Romanticism and the Marketplace* (Chicago: University of Chicago Press, 1985), p. 102: "The passages describing [the Judge] are remarkable in Hawthorne's writing for their unrelieved hostility and exaggerated irony." Gilmore argues that Hawthorne's irony in such instances derives from his extreme ambivalence about the artist's role in capitalist society and his extreme hatred of Jaffrey, the capitalist par excellence.

10. "Phoebe" was also one of Hawthorne's favorite nicknames for his wife, Sophia. For a discussion of how Hawthorne's new-found happiness in marriage influenced Phoebe Pyncheon's characterization, see Michael Davitt Bell, *The Development of American Romance: The Sacrifice of Relation* (Chicago: University of Chicago Press, 1980), p. 183.

11. See, for example, Gilmore, *American Romanticism and the Marketplace*, pp. 104–6. He discusses similarities between the author and the character but feels finally that "it would be a mistake to exaggerate their similarities." In particular, he attributes their differing perspectives at the end—Holgrave's repudiation of art— to the fact that the "author of *The House of the Seven Gables* had too much need of money to identify completely with Holgrave's indifference to popularity."

12. Margaret Fuller, *Woman in the Nineteenth Century*, intro. Bernard Rosenthal (1855; rpt. New York: Norton, 1971), pp. 76–77.

Chapter 7

1. Henry A. Murray, Introduction to *Pierre; or The Ambiguities*, by Herman Melville (New York: Hendricks House, 1949), p. xciii. The previous formal labels are found, respectively, in F. O. Matthiessen, *American Renaissance: Art and Expression in the Age of Emerson and Whitman* (New York: Oxford University Press, 1941), p. 467; Joel Porte, *The Romance in America: Studies in Cooper, Poe, Hawthorne, Melville, and James* (Middletown, Conn.: Wesleyan University Press, 1969), p. 170; Richard H. Brodhead, *Hawthorne, Melville, and the Novel* (Chicago: University of Chicago Press, 1976), p. 164; and Eric Sundquist, *Home as Found: Authority and Genealogy in Nineteenth-Century American Literature* (Baltimore: Johns Hopkins University Press, 1979), p. 146.

2. Herman Melville, *Pierre; or The Ambiguities*, vol. 7 of *The Writings of Herman Melville*, ed. Harrison Hayford, Hershel Parker, and G. Thomas Tanselle (Evanston and Chicago: Northwestern University Press and the Newberry Library, 1971). All further references to this edition will appear in parentheses in the text.

3. See, for example, Ann Douglas, *The Feminization of American Culture* (New York: Knopf, 1977), pp. 349–95.

4. Sundquist, *Home as Found*, p. 166.

5. Melville to Richard Bentley, April 16, 1852, in *The Melville Log: A Documentary Life of Herman Melville, 1819–1891*, ed. Jay Leyda, 2 vols. (New York: Gordian Press, 1969), 1:450.

6. Review of *Pierre*, *Literary World*, August 21, 1852, excerpted in *Melville Log*, ed. Leyda, 1:457.

7. Michael T. Gilmore has examined Melville's ambivalence toward business or "marketplace" values and their effect on American literature in *Moby-Dick* and "Bartleby, the Scrivener." See *American Romanticism and the Marketplace* (Chicago: University of Chicago Press, 1985), chaps. 6 and 7.

8. At the beginning of June 1851 Melville had written to Hawthorne: "In a week or so, I go to New York, to bury myself . . . and work & slave on my 'Whale' while it is driving thro' the press. *That* is the only way I can finish it now,—I am so pulled hither & thither by circumstances" (*Melville Log*, ed. Leyda, 1:414).

9. See Brodhead, *Hawthorne, Melville, and the Novel*, pp. 171–75. Brodhead argues that Melville's quarrel with the idealization of women is that it separates "sex and sentiment" and that "the way in which sentiment is exaggerated by the suppression of sexual awareness . . . is the essence of Pierre's predicament."

10. See, for example, Francis Jennings, "The Indians' Revolution," in *The American Revolution: Explorations in the History of American Radicalism*, ed. Alfred F. Young (DeKalb: Northern Illinois University Press, 1976), pp. 321–48; and David Brion Davis, *The Problem of Slavery in the Age of Revolution, 1770–1823* (Ithaca, N.Y.: Cornell University Press, 1975).

11. Sandra M. Gilbert and Susan Gubar trace the history of the idea and the image of woman as illegitimate storyteller in *The Madwoman in the Attic: The Woman Writer and the Nineteenth-Century Literary Imagination* (New Haven: Yale University Press, 1979), esp. chaps. 1 and 2.

12. For further discussion of this idea, see Dale Spender, *Man-Made Language*, 2d ed. (London: Routledge & Kegan Paul, 1985), pp. 24–28. Spender argues that one "direct result of this practice of only taking cognizance of the male name has been to facilitate the development of history as the story of the male line, because it becomes almost impossible to trace the ancestry of women—particularly if they do not come into the male-defined categories of importance."

13. See ibid., p. 81: "When the meanings of women are consigned to nonexistence, when the registers for discourse are male decreed and controlled, women who wish to express themselves must translate their experience into the male code." See also Adrienne Rich, *On Lies, Secrets and Silence: Selected Prose, 1966–78* (New York: Norton, 1979), p. 208: "In denying the validity of women's experience, in pretending to stand for the 'human,' masculine subjectivity tries to force us to name our truths in an alien language."

14. Cf. Luce Irigaray's speculative description of a distinct "female language," which would not only "undo the unique meaning, the proper meaning of words" but would have "nothing to do with the syntax which we have used for centuries, namely, that constructed according to the following organization: subject, predicate, or subject, verb, object": "This 'other' language . . . is radically non-unitary, does not obey the laws of consistency and object-ivity and will admit of no meta-discourse. It poses a challenge to dominant forms of discursive order to such an extent that it may be seen as the unconscious of those forms. That is, this [female] language is not simply *oppressed*, not allowed, it is radically *repressed*, impossible where current forms are possible" ("Women's Exile," trans. Couze Venn, *Ideology and Consciousness* 1 [May 1977]: 62–76).

15. See, for example, Raymond M. Weaver, *Herman Melville: Mariner and Mystic* (New York: George H. Doran, 1921), pp. 341–44; Raymond J. Nelson, "The Art of Herman Melville: The Author of *Pierre*," *Yale Review* 59 (Winter 1970): 197–214; and Amy Puett Emmers, "Melville's Closet Skeleton: A New Letter about the Illegitimacy Incident in *Pierre*," *Studies in the American Renaissance* 1 (1977): 339–43.

16. *Melville Log*, ed. Leyda, 1:412.

17. Ibid., p. 435.

18. Ibid., pp. 449–50.

19. Ibid., pp. 451–52.

20. See ibid., pp. 452, 457, 461, 464.

21. James R. Mellow, *Nathaniel Hawthorne In His Times* (Boston: Houghton Mifflin, 1980), p. 417.

22. Leyda speculates that Melville may have burned his attempts at the "Agatha" story along with other unpublished manuscripts when the family moved from Arrowhead to the town of Pittsfield, Massachusetts, in 1862. See *Melville Log*, 1:xiii.

23. George Washington Peck, review of *Pierre, American Whig Review*, November 1852, excerpted in *Melville Log*, ed. Leyda, 1:463.

24. Review of *Pierre, Literary World*, August 21, 1852, excerpted in ibid., pp. 457–58.

25. Review of *Pierre, Boston Post*, July 1852; Peck, review of *Pierre*; review of *Pierre, Literary World*; all excerpted in ibid., pp. 456, 455, 463, 464, 458, 463.

26. Newton Arvin has found and admired similar stylistic inventiveness in *Moby-Dick*. See *Herman Melville: A Critical Biography* (New York: Viking, 1957), pp. 162–65. Warner Berthoff, however, finds Melville's vocabulary in *Pierre* "grotesquely inventive" and "freakish." See *The Example of Melville* (1962; rpt. New York: Norton, 1972), p. 51.

27. Peck, review of *Pierre*; review of *Pierre, Godey's Lady's Book*, October 1852; excerpted in *Melville Log*, ed. Leyda, 1:463, 462.

Index